LEARNING AND
TEACHING IN HIGHER EDUCATION

Second edition

Learning and Teaching in Higher Education

THE REFLECTIVE PROFESSIONAL

Second edition

Greg Light, Roy Cox and Susanna Calkins

Los Angeles | London | New Delhi
Singapore | Washington DC

First Edition published 2001
Reprinted 2003, 2004, 2005, 2006, 2008
Second Edition published 2009

Reprinted 2010

SAGE Publications Ltd
1 Oliver's Yard
55 City Road
London EC1Y 1SP

SAGE Publications Inc.
2455 Teller Road
Thousand Oaks, California 91320

SAGE Publications India Pvt Ltd
B 1/I 1 Mohan Cooperative Industrial Area
Mathura Road, Post Bag 7
New Delhi 110 044

SAGE Publications Asia-Pacific Pte Ltd
33 Pekin Street #02-01
Far East Square
Singapore 048763

Library of Congress Control Number: 2008939459

British Library Cataloguing in Publication Data

A catalogue record for this book is available from the British Library

ISBN 978-1-84860-007-2
ISBN 978-1-84860-008-9 (pbk)

Library of Congress catalogue record available

Typeset by C&M Digitals (P) Ltd, Chennai, India
Printed and bound in Great Britain by CPI Antony Rowe, Chippenham, Wiltshire

contents

authors' details

Greg Light is the Director of the Searle Center for Teaching Excellence and an associate professor in the School of Education and Social Policy at Northwestern University in Chicago. In 2002 he designed and developed the Searle Fellow programme for the improvement of teaching at Northwestern University. Prior to coming to Northwestern, he was a lecturer at the Institute of Education, University of London, where he was a member of the Centre for Higher Education Studies (CHES). In 1998 he established the Professional Accreditation of Teaching in Higher Education programme at the Institute of Education, of which he was the Director. He has given talks and workshops in teaching and learning on three continents. Recent publications have focused on student learning, faculty conceptions of teaching and academic practice and the relationship between research and teaching in higher education.

With a background in psychology and philosophy **Roy Cox** possessed a wide experience of research and practice in learning and teaching in higher education. He helped establish one of the first centres for learning and teaching in higher education in the world at the University of London, where he was a Senior Lecturer with the Institute of Education. In his last years he conducted educational research and evaluation for the Cambridge-Massachusetts Institute of Technology. His many publications drew on his educational research in a range of disciplines and his teaching in higher education in over 30 countries.

Susanna Calkins, an Associate Director for Faculty Development at the Searle Center for Teaching Excellence, has been teaching history at university level for over ten years. She has given multiple talks and workshops on teaching and learning and, since 2006, has been directing the Searle Fellows programme at Northwestern University. Her recent publications have focused on faculty conceptions of teaching, learning and mentoring; student learning in the history classroom; and a critical examination of technology in teaching.

preface to the first edition

This book is, above all, a book about learning. It is primarily for 'faculty' engaged in learning and in facilitating student learning in higher education, including professors, lecturers, teachers, researchers, teaching assistants and all those who are in one way or another supporting learning. It draws upon over three decades of research, scholarship and teaching experience – at the Institute of Education (University of London) – providing programmes for enhancing learning through improving the quality of teaching. Indeed, the joint authorship of this book reflects a fifteen year collaboration of research, scholarship and teaching about learning and teaching in higher education which has immeasurably enriched our own learning.

The authors do not for a moment pretend there is a 'solution' to the many challenges confronting learning and teaching in higher education. If anything, the book extends the range and scope of the challenge. It does, however, propose a comprehensive way of approaching this challenge, a way embodied in the book's subtitle: *The Reflective Professional*.

Learning and Teaching in Higher Education: The Reflective Professional addresses the practice of learning and teaching within a rapidly changing higher education sector challenged by escalations in the number and diversity of students, tougher demands for professional accountability, increasing calls for educational relevance, thinning resources and the exacting demands of a global education market. In this respect, the book brings together key issues of theory and practice to develop an over-all professional 'language' of teaching situated within communities of academic practice. This 'language' provides teachers with a conceptual 'vocabulary' and 'grammar' for understanding and improving practice, enables them to critically reflect upon their teaching in a range of key 'genres' of practice, and proposes a strategy for conducting and producing evidence for continuous professional development in learning and teaching. It is not intended to be prescriptive but, rather, to provide a structure for developing teaching and learning strategies appropriate to the distinctive subjects and conditions of the individual university teacher and his or her academic community.

The book is divided into four sections: an introduction and three parts. Chapter 1 introduces the context of the book and the challenges which teaching in higher education faces. It is concerned with the theoretical issues surrounding the changing nature of higher education, the changing role of the teacher within higher education, and the development of the teacher as both professional and reflective practitioner. In response to the challenge, we propose the concept of the 'reflective professional' and sketch a model for a professional 'language' of practice with three interrelated components: a critical conceptual framework, relevant and appropriate genres, and a general strategy for professional realization.

In Part 1 of the book, we examine the themes of the first component of this language. It is chiefly concerned with situating this 'language' within three conceptual locations. Chapter 2 addresses the first of these – a general theoretical framework of human communication and knowledge. The second location is taken up in Chapter 3 and explores a model of the reflective professional within academic practice, suggesting that the three roles of student, teacher and researcher converge in one model centred on learning. Chapter 4 focuses on the character of learning in higher education. It develops a critical matrix of learning, providing teachers with a conceptual tool for designing, developing and implementing their teaching across the various 'genres' of their teaching practice.

Part 2 of the book is concerned with different 'genres' of teaching practice. While it recognizes that teaching is a holistic practice not comfortably divided into different sections, it nevertheless accepts that teaching in higher education has come to recognize certain distinctive core 'genres' of teaching, which may be usefully addressed separately. Chapters 5–11 focus on these 'genres'. They are, respectively, designing, lecturing, facilitating, supervising, innovating, assessing and evaluating. Each of these chapters addresses key practical teaching issues and activities of the 'genre', relating them to relevant theory and recent research. Part 3 is concerned with the professional development of the 'language' in practice. In this respect, Chapter 12 draws upon the discussion to propose and describe a general strategy of 'professional realization': a strategy for engaging with and mastering the critical 'language' of the reflective professional.

Greg Light
Roy Cox

preface to the second edition

The new edition of this book is dedicated to the memory of our friend and colleague, Roy Cox. It was Roy who urged us to take the opportunity of writing a second edition when it arose. Unfortunately, Roy died in his home in London on 23 December 2007 before it was complete. He was, however, very much engaged with the planning of this edition, including our decision to incorporate as a fellow author of this book, Susanna Calkins, whom Roy had met on a number of trips to Chicago. Roy's life was devoted to the study of learning and teaching – particularly the nature and construction of meaning and the practices of good teaching as a way of assisting students to achieve such learning across the disciplines and practices of higher and professional education. Despite his death, this edition is very much his as well as ours. Through him, the work presented here is linked back to the seminal work which he and his colleagues conducted almost 40 years ago in London, a lineage of which we are very proud.

While the essential character and approach of this book have been retained, this new edition has been substantially updated with references to recent research, literature and teaching practices. When the book was first published, the millennium had just happened. Now, after almost a decade, we have seen startling changes in the use of technology in higher education and the increasing globalization of learning and teaching. Having been situated in both London and Chicago during this time, the authors were also conscious of the international tensions differentiating the study and practice of learning and teaching – particularly between the UK and the US. This new edition consciously draws upon the diverse body of international literature and describes key areas of agreement. We can, of course, only touch the surface of the broad range of research being produced in what is increasingly looking like the creation of a global learning and teaching framework.

Greg Light
Susanna Calkins
Chicago, 2008

acknowledgements

The authors of this book gratefully acknowledge the widespread encouragement and important contributions of many, many colleagues, friends and family members through two editions of this book. We would like to record our appreciation to all the members and graduate students of the Centre for Higher Education Studies at the Institute of Education, University of London, as well as faculty and staff at Northwestern University, particularly at the Searle Center for Teaching Excellence. They have provided an ongoing, stimulating and critically acute intellectual climate for debating and developing the essential ideas and issues presented in the book. Particular thanks, in this respect, go to Ronald Barnett, Gareth Williams and Michael Young, as well as to Neeraja Aravamudan, Ken Bain, Ron Brautigam, Denise Drane, Steve Fisher, Melissa Luna, Marina Micari, Su Swarat, Pilar Pazos, Larry Pinto, and Bernhard Streitwieser, for their conversation, insights and continuing support. A very special thanks must go to David Guile and Angela Hobsbaum who read the original manuscript and offered insightful and practical comments throughout its development, bringing their experience and expertise as researchers and teachers to bear on our project. We would like to give a special thanks to Katie Metzler, our editor, who has guided us through this second edition with patience, good humour and thoughtfulness.

We would also like to acknowledge an immense debt of thanks to the faculty and teachers from both the UK and the USA who have participated in the professional and faculty development programmes on which we have taught over the past 10 years. Their generous reflections, comments and willingness to engage openly with the ideas of this book have made it immeasurably richer.

Finally, we are also grateful for the support we received for this project from our families in both the first and second editions of the work, especially Margaret Light, Angela Hobsbaum and Matthew Kelley.

All the above have been our teachers.

introduction

THE CHALLENGE OF PROFESSIONALISM

This introduction situates the development of teaching and learning practice within the social and economic forces shaping higher education. We describe how these forces have produced a new challenge, based on a discourse of excellence imported from industry and shaped by persistent calls for accountability. This discourse has dramatically increased the demands and transformed the nature of academic work, especially the specification of broader and higher-order student learning outcomes. We conclude by proposing a new professional framework and language – to be elaborated over the rest of the book – for addressing the challenge.

THE ACADEMIC STORM

A post-millennium storm is sweeping higher education. It is a storm fed by increasing calls for accountability and excellence, fuelled by globalization, and accelerated by the forces of commercial exchange. For academics, working in higher education today often feels like a pervasive onslaught that must be constantly weathered. The demands on their time and the complexity of those demands are changing and escalating almost exponentially. Academics have been overwhelmed with a rapid expansion in both the number and diversity of students, without a corresponding boost in staff or resources. The burden in terms of faculty–student ratios, teaching time, advisory provision, assessment responsibilities, evaluation and feedback has swelled enormously. Pressures to increase research and scholarship activities have mushroomed as they have taken unprecedented priority in university preoccupations, while research funds have become more fiercely contested, more difficult to attain and often the realm of already powerful departments. New academic practices and consultancy activities have grown, often demanding more time and attention in the competition for new income streams. At the same time, the relationship of these activities in terms of academic career progress and status has become murkier, with many academic activities (although expected and required) not counting at all. At the same time, mounting criticism of the quality and efficiency of the twin pillars of academic practice – research and teaching – has increased the proportion of time spent on what has now become the third pillar of practice: academic administration and service.

Like all storms, this academic storm is the result of changes in powerful and prevailing systems. It is the result of changing relationships among higher education, knowledge (its primary material) and society. Historically, higher education has been an institution in society, privileged and governed by an almost linear relationship through which academics defined and produced knowledge, which was then imparted and infused within society through its graduates and the dissemination of its research (Barnett, 2003; Thelin, 2004). This relationship characterized the university's separation and freedom, and gave rise to its description as an 'ivory tower' in a 'real' world. The one-way nature of this relationship may be exemplified by the phrase 'academic freedom', a concept central to the fabric of academic life, but rarely accompanied by its customary social counterpart, responsibility. 'Academic freedom', as Donald Kennedy, the past president of Stanford University, notes: 'is a widely shared value; academic duty, which ought to count for as much, is mysterious' (1997: 2). This mystery, he suggests, is due to a dissonance in the way in which society and higher education see their relationship. It is a dissonance, moreover, which has recently seen an escalation of public criticism and policy concern over the issue of the accountability of higher education (Geiger, 2005).

This concern for accountability represents the wider change in the complex relationship between higher education and society. Higher education no longer simply resides in society; it is of society, increasingly subject to society's prevailing ideologies, ways of viewing the world, its transitions and upheavals. Higher education no longer simply shapes society through its knowledge contributions; it is rather shaped by society through the knowledge specification – both in terms of students and research – which the latter contracts with higher education to deliver (Light, 2000).

Current social and economic transitions, particularly those associated with the concepts of globalization, the shift to a knowledge-based economy and lifelong learning, characterize this specification. Given the nature of these social changes – converging on knowledge and the lifelong education of the workforce – higher education has become a key recipient of society's focus and demands, fixed firmly within society's gaze. Society has also concluded that the traditional structures of higher education are not adequate to deliver effectively the requirements of the specification. Higher education, society insists, must transform itself, and remake itself in the new social mould.

THE DISCOURSE OF EXCELLENCE

The new social mould expected of higher education has been wrought and shaped by a 'discourse of excellence' (Readings, 1996). This discourse, imported from industry, focuses on 'excellent' delivery and 'excellent' performance, and presumes a new way of thinking and talking about higher education. Within a relatively short space of time, the idea of excellence has come to dominate higher education (Bok, 2003; Ramsden, 1992/2003). This is no accident. Universities trumpet the term in their mission statements, in their websites and in their public relations materials. Indeed, very few university mission statements risk omitting the term. Its very universality makes its absence more telling than its presence. Not pursuing excellence is tantamount to an admission of failure. In respect of the values and ideals of higher education, excellence has been criticized as having 'no content' and as marking 'the fact that there is no longer any idea of the University' (Readings, 1996: 39) – and mission statements as being 'ubiquitous, vacuous and inter-changeable' (Coffield and Williamson, 1997: 1). Indeed, a university may exude 'excellence' but, as Harry Lewis, a former dean of Harvard College, has noted, still lack a soul (Lewis, 2006).

On the other hand, the idea of excellence does function extremely well as the torch-bearer of the structural revolution that has embraced higher education as a whole. Because excellence is less concerned with *what* than *how*, higher education can be conceived anew. Excellence measures how the university performs its social role, by measuring its inputs and outputs; it does not measure the role itself. The notion of excellence, thus, is a means for making the university accountable, using externally agreed marks of itself within the knowledge specification that society contracts with higher education to provide. A new bargain is thus struck, between society and the university, which is based on the elusive quality of excellence (Kirp, 2003). This specification defines excellence in terms of performance indicators of both the efficiency with which higher education delivers the product and the quality of product. It is less encumbered by issues of cultural significance or educational value, as by issues of social and economic effectiveness and efficiency. Drawn up under a social and economic agenda characterized by such issues as globalization, a knowledge-based economy and lifelong learning, the specification is replete with notions of competitiveness in terms of number, expansion and retention of student numbers, expansion of knowledge base, competitive advantage, efficiency gains, employee productivity and so on. It is a conception of accountability in which 'the quite proper demand that universities be *accountable* gets translated into the reductionist idea that everything is simply a matter of *accounting*' (Harvey, 1998: 115). This is clearly light years from how the university understands academic duty, however mysterious it might be.

The insistent call for excellence has serious repercussions for the day-to-day affairs of academic practice. Indeed, a profound change in the very language framing higher education exemplifies the challenge of professionalism facing the academy today. The successful colonization by terms such as excellence, competition and efficiency has been accompanied by an attendant 'industrialization of the language' (Coffield and Williamson, 1997: 1). Higher education is business. It is big business, international business, part of the burgeoning global service sector. This commercial language, drawn from the corporate world, has infiltrated most, if not all, of the features of higher education, sitting uncomfortably alongside older terms it augments or even replaces. Higher education now speaks of 'customers', 'sales', 'branding' and 'products', jostling with banks and travel agents, films and restaurants, hairdressers and accountants to retail its wares, consciously competing for a limited sum of expendable income with a wide range of other services and products (Kirp, 2003). The essence of that product is knowledge, a commodity bought or consumed by customers to suit their needs, and valued as an investment in time and money. Indeed, the current generation of college students, often referred to as the 'millennials', along with their parents, increasingly view themselves as consumers (Howe and Strauss, 2003; DeBard, 2004).

In making its pitch, higher education focuses on the specialized skills it possesses in the generation and dissemination of that knowledge: research and teaching. Within this language, research and teaching are not distinguished so much by their activity as by the nature of their customers and the description of the financial relationship with those customers, be that through block grants, research contracts or student fees. For example, the allocation of university funding based on the research assessment exercise

(RAE, n.d.) scores – a measure used in the UK to assess the quality of research in institutions of higher education – says as much about how the UK government perceives the status of the constituencies it serves, as it does about productivity and performance within the university sector. In the USA, the National Science Foundation (NSF) report on *Rising above the Gathering Storm* is couched in similar terms of economic performance and competition (COSEPUP, 2007). This academic product is increasingly marketed and delivered in accordance with the perceived needs and trends of the market. The whole operation is managed by line managers (course leaders, heads of departments, deans, etc.) who are responsible to senior management teams and chief executives for meeting 'targets' who, in turn, are looking for both increases in efficiency gains and product quality.

Within the discourse of excellence, efficiency gains and, to a large degree, product quality, are accompanied and driven by a culture of competition. Higher education institutions not only compete generally for expendable income within the national economy; within their own knowledge sphere they are competing ever more aggressively with other national and regional universities and colleges for research, students, consultancy and status. With the globalization of the economy, competition has extended into a race to develop foreign markets, while simultaneously defending home markets. As if this competition were not enough, universities have seen escalating direct competition for their products from non-academic sources, including 'commercial laboratories, government research centres, think tanks and consultancies' (Robertson, 1997: 91). In addition, institutions of higher education are nationally measured, scored and rewarded for their competitive success (Meredith, 2004). In the UK, for example, college and university rankings, such as *The Times University League Table*, provide measurements of quality and excellence across a range of institutional criteria, including research and teaching. In the USA, national scores of university excellence have been published for decades, led by the popular *US News and World Report College Rankings*, despite criticism of the measures behind such rankings (Ehrenberg, 2000; Holub, 2002). More recently, scores of excellence have gone international with separated rankings of the top universities in the world assembled and published by both *The Times Higher Education Supplement* in the UK and Shanghai-Jiaotong University in China.

The impact of excellence, in the guise of both increasing efficiency and competition and ever more intrusive measurements of quality, is extensive and pervades all aspects of an individual academic's work. Efficiency and competition have meant that the activities of faculty and academic staff have been scrutinized more minutely for efficiency gains and tied more directly to their personal role in income generation. Concerns about having fixed staff in areas of declining customer base, whether this be due to changing market trends or the result of poor competitive operations, have led to management looking to use more flexible arrangements and patterns of academic staff or faculty deployment. This has resulted in a vast increase in part-time and short-term contracts and more non-tenured faculty in the USA (Ehrenberg and Zhang, 2004), and includes the outsourcing of faculty to agencies with all the insecurities that such policies engender. Pressures have subsequently increased on staff to become flexible, both in terms of the kinds of duties and the range of subject areas in which they are engaged. The ability to teach, for example, in subject areas progressively more distant to one's areas of subject expertise and to engage in work developing new income streams – such as consultancy – for which one has little or no training, is becoming more common.

There is also a growing focus on the development of abilities more akin to the modern entrepreneur than the traditional academic. These include the talent for marketing oneself, one's teaching, one's research and one's institution. They encompass a diverse range of skills from media presentation to brochure and leaflet design, from product development (research, scholarship, courses) to product design (more accessible and customer-friendly modular programmes) and product packaging (online courses delivered to the home). In more extreme cases, it may even require academics to become direct sales people: universities have sometimes acted like call centres, providing faculty members and their students with lists of potential students whom they were required to 'cold call' to inform them of the advantages of their various 'products': courses and programmes.

Where the impact of competition and efficiency on individual academics leads, the impact of intrusive systems of quality assessment and assurance follows. The recent intense focus on academic accountability in terms of quality has had significant repercussions on the nature of the academic's changing role. For many academics, research and scholarship activity is increasingly perceived and conceived within the scaffolding of numbers: numbers of published articles, numbers of citations, quantity of research funding and, in the USA, Graduate Record Examination (GRE) scores of admitted graduate students and so on. There is, moreover, a gallows silhouette to this scaffolding – 'publish or perish' – as academics are reminded that their probation, employment contracts, tenure and promotional prospects are directly linked to their ability to scramble and clamber within it, the dark image of a noose ever present and threatening. While productivity may have increased, it has not done so without significant repercussions on the process and nature of research and scholarship. This includes, for example, uncomfortable trends towards more hurried work published before it is ready, towards work which is more practical or applied, less theoretical or pure, more trivial work and/or work which is increasingly felt to be isolated and irrelevant. An explosion of journals accompanies these trends, with ever more specialized articles read by fewer and fewer readers. In addition, academics spend more time developing, writing and submitting research proposals that may be rejected as funds are more hotly contested.

Growing expectations for accountability in teaching have further pressured academic time. The USA has seen an increased focus on the assessment of student learning outcomes during institutional accreditation (HLC, 2007; CHEA, 2008), while in the UK the institutional audits by the Quality Assurance Agency have institutionalized society's interest and oversight of academic standards (QAA, 2008), although political and market forces are putting increasing, if yet to be fully determined, pressures on both systems of accountability (Aldermann and Brown, 2005). Quality assurance, quality assessment, quality audit, quality enhancement and quality transformation (Middlehurst, 1997) have not only introduced a new, often confusing vocabulary, they have also added a multitude of more formal and systematic administrative practices to the academic workload. New and changing institutional quality assurance and assessment systems, for example, require academic staff to spend additional time complying with and contributing to institutional policies, strategies and paperwork, increasing considerably as external audit and assessment exercises approach. In addition, academics' relationships with their students have been characterized by increased paperwork, as well as by more formal and comprehensive systems of monitoring student assessment, evaluations, support, completion rates, post-undergraduate destinations, etc., coupled with developing strategies to learn and improve from such monitoring. Finally, academics are increasingly expected to engage in a wide and diverse set of personal development activities, ranging from occasional lunchtime brown-bag discussions with colleagues on issues of mutual relevance and importance, to ongoing, long-term professional development programmes. Such activities are frequently accompanied by formal systems of appraisal, peer observation and, particularly for new staff, mandatory programmes in teacher training.

In the UK, the Dearing Committee report (NCIHE, 1997) recommended that all 'institutions of higher education begin immediately to develop or seek access to programmes for teacher training of their staff, if they do not have them, and that all institutions seek national accreditation of such programmes' (1997: Recommendation 13). While not yet mandatory, such accreditation has become widespread in the UK (HEA, 2007), and increasingly so in the USA. In the latter many faculty have voluntarily undergone accreditation and review (Lubinescu et al., 2001), often with the help of institutional self-study assessment tools such as those offered by the Higher Learning Commission (HLC, 2007). Nevertheless, although some faculty have found ways to work collaboratively within their institutions to alleviate the work (Morse and Santiago, 2000; Sorcinelli, 2006) for many academics, faculty development and accreditation of teaching is yet another substantial time commitment without a substantial increase in resources.

Working in a culture of 'excellence' – with its industrial vocabulary manifested in the twin guises of competition/efficiency and quality/accountability – has undeniably presented a substantial test for academic life. This test has been exemplified by changes in the nature of academic roles and the pressures associated with these changes. As we will discuss in the next section, 'excellence' challenges academics to think about their role in relation to both knowledge and the student. The disposition of this challenge both announces the new call for academic professionalism in teaching and learning and supports the nature of its response.

THE CHALLENGE OF EXCELLENCE

The challenge of excellence presents higher education with opportunities for substantive, meaningful and positive change. The shift towards professionalism in teaching and learning is a natural manifestation of the discourse of excellence. In terms of the social and economic accountability of higher education to society, it is long overdue. While the challenge – immersed as it is in an accounting mode – is deeply suspect, it provides a necessary jolt to critical thought and reflection. This does not mean, however, that the challenge of excellence should be passively accepted or, for that matter, that academics should rage blindly like modern King Lears within their towers, as the storm strips off the last remnants of ivory veneer. It is vitally important that academics take up this challenge and think. What, for example, does this new focus on excellence mean for how academics relate to their students? To student learning? To their own learning? What is the impact on the edifice of knowledge which surrounds these relationships?

As we have seen, in a knowledge-based economy, knowledge is the product of modern society and subject to its market structures: it is traded as is any other commodity or service. It is increasingly traded on global communication and information systems that, by virtue of their growing impact, have themselves become a serious component of the knowledge market. In this model, universities no longer sustain the monopoly they once enjoyed. They are simply one of many social and corporate organizations developing, managing, disseminating and competing with knowledge. Indeed, they are often in partnership with corporate organizations that by virtue of financial muscle demand and are given the control of knowledge (Chomsky, 1998; Press and Washburn, 2000). The academic relationship with knowledge is increasingly dominated by competitive economic structures which any dominant and powerful product ('knowledge is power') engenders.

Within such a framework, the nature of knowledge and our perception of what it entails inevitably change. Traditional elitist distinctions between 'high' or 'elite' knowledge and 'mass' or 'popular' knowledge, for example, begin to dissolve (Usher et al., 1997). Produced, moreover, within new sites with different priorities and a wider set of organizational and technical goals, knowledge has mutated and increasingly taken on an active voice. Active forms of knowledge that can be employed to increase economic competitiveness and personal effectiveness are increasingly displacing the passive knowledge of truth, contemplation and personal awareness. Gibbons et al. (1994) have described this change in terms of a move from disciplinary-based knowledge situated in an academic context (in which experts construct knowledge), towards trans-disciplinary knowledge located in a context of application (in which students construct knowledge for themselves). Echoing this distinction, Barnett (2003) describes the university as a site of rival versions of what it is to know the world, embodied in the distinction between academic and operational competence. Academic competence is, for example, described as having a focus on *knowing that* and stressing propositions evaluated by criteria of truth. Operational competence, in contrast, focuses on *knowing how* and stressing outcomes evaluated by criteria focused on their economic impact. The pressures in the direction of operational competence are, he suggests, changing our very epistemological existence (Barnett, 2003).

The challenge of excellence not only interrogates our traditional ways of conceiving and using knowledge but also contests the academic relationship to the student. In particular, academics feel pressured to recognize a professional responsibility to students in terms of the quality of their knowledge and learning. While providing knowledge has always been a role of the academy, within the terms of the knowledge specification presented to higher education, however, students have themselves now become more firmly regarded as product for whom the university is accountable to society (Kirp, 2003). In the language of excellence, and the ironic paradoxes that such language raises, students have become consumers of higher education's product, in order to become productive within our society. As such, it is precisely the nature of student-as-product which has recently become the focus of social and economic concern. Collectively, the student-product needs to be larger in number and more diverse. Individually, students need to have developed a range of key transferable and higher-order thinking skills, including meta-learning, the ability to learn from learning.

Over the last few decades, the student body which higher education serves has radically changed from an 'elite' to a 'mass' system (Trow, 2001; Thelin, 2004), with student participation rates in the UK, for example, more than trebling and the number of institutions called universities more than doubling. Accompanying this enormous rise in student numbers has been an increase in the diversity of students, including growth in the participation of women, mature students, ethnic and minority students, students from less privileged classes and overseas students (DeBard, 2004). Underlying both the increase in numbers and in diversity has been the focus on widening access, again primarily 'to contribute to improved economic competitiveness and to local economic success' (Robertson, 1997: 88).

At the same time, the entrance en masse of the millennials – students born between 1982 and 2002 – into higher education has raised new concerns about consumer demands and the perceived educational values and expectations of those students and their parents (Howe and Strauss, 2003). Millennial students tend to have lived more sheltered and protected lives and, as such, to be more rule-abiding and conventional, and more likely to expect authorities to intervene when problems arise. They look for structure and answers, and expect the terms of their learning to be clearly defined. Although team-oriented they also feel pressured to perform individually to succeed. Moreover, they are more technologically literate than any generation that has preceded them, and expect to be able to connect virtually with others at any time. Finally, they are more likely to be socially aware of diversity and the importance of social and civic engagement, and expect a college to provide them with a sense of purpose (Howe and Strauss, 2003; DeBard, 2004; Shapiro, 2005).

This socioeconomic imperative is also manifested in the individual features specified by society. A recent report generated by the Association of American Colleges and Universities (AAC&U), and put out by the LEAP

National Leadership Council, has pointed out that the usual metrics as enrolment, persistence and degree attainment, while important, are insufficient in determining if students 'are actually achieving the kind of learning they need for a complex and volatile world' (NLC LEAP, 2007). The learning described in the report focuses on critical inquiry, engaging students in 'real world' problems, fostering civic, intercultural and ethical learning, and helping students find ways to apply learning and knowledge to new problems. Higher education should be providing society with educated individuals who have developed a range of higher-level transferable skills, along with the more general ability and willingness to 'learn to learn' (also called meta-learning or lifelong learning). Transferable skills – which include communication, teamwork, leadership, ethics, problem-solving and information technology, etc. – support the economic requirement of flexibility and adaptability which graduates expect to use in their future employment and careers, as well as in their life practices and activities. Meta-learning characterizes individual lifelong learning: the graduate's ability to continue to learn new knowledge, skills and practices. Rather than having a core subject curriculum, this points to a set of 'core characteristics, qualities and kinds of outcomes for all who enter and re-enter higher education' (Duke, 1997: 67).

Five terms thus epitomize the nature of the challenge of professionalism to teaching and learning in higher education:

- The increasing numbers of students in our classrooms.
- The increasing diversity of background, experience, and needs and expectations which our students present.
- The emerging curriculum of transferability, which includes acquiring new global competencies.
- The insistent pervasiveness of technology, and expectations for its use in academic practice, including electronic learning opportunities for distance learners.
- The conceptual shift in our thinking about our practice from teaching to learning, from delivering knowledge to developing and fostering independence of learning in which students develop the ability to discover and reconstruct knowledge (and their lives) for themselves.

These terms, very roughly, outline the shape of the professional challenge. In response to this challenge, a new professional paradigm realizing learning and teaching expertise in higher education has emerged, contesting two earlier paradigms of teaching development (see Figure I.1) (Light, 2000).

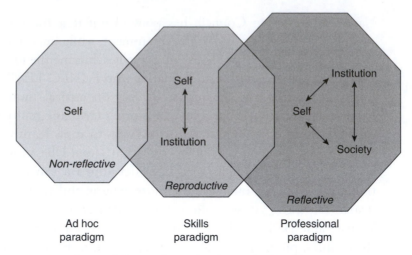

Figure I.1 *Paradigms of the academic development of teaching*

The first paradigm, which we refer to as the *ad hoc* paradigm, is located primarily within the individual teacher, and essentially asserts that a good teacher is born, not made. Associated with 'elite' systems of student participation and prevalent until the late 1960s and early 1970s (although still prevalent in much of higher education), its underlying assumption is that teaching is something one picks up and grasps informally and individually. It is non-reflective in the broader sense. The teacher is left to her own devices and draws upon past experience of being taught, trial and error, help from sympathetic colleagues when available, and her own natural affinities for teaching. The second paradigm – expanding more or less in tandem with the growth of student numbers from the 1970s onwards – we call the *skills* paradigm. Its basic assumption is that the development of teaching is an add-on process and rests in the accumulation and reproduction of performance and communication skills, competencies and tips. These skills are generic and provided by trainers and consultants who often have no formal experience of the discipline in which the teachers are working or even of higher education teaching. The provision of training has generally been located within the institution's support services, and separated from its core academic activities.

Ironically, the very teaching and learning challenge which excellence has articulated has often failed to address the substance and complexity of the challenge itself. While demanding higher education to go beyond the *ad hoc* first-paradigm solutions to the challenge, it has confined its own general response to the narrowly prescribed *skills*-centred approaches of the second paradigm. 'Excellence' has often elicited approaches for developing expertise in teaching and learning, which address the new state of complexity by imposing a reductionist (and 'accounting') framework to simplify it. Curiously, the discourse of excellence engages the uncertain by assuming a known context with clearly understood attributes (Barnett, 2003). The result is an approach that specifies increasingly narrow outcomes and competencies of expertise, establishes behavioural standards for them and insists on compliance with these standards irrespective of the professional, disciplinary and institutional context.

The third paradigm – the *professional* – is the focus of this book. It is a relatively recent development and is only beginning to overlap with and compete with the first two paradigms. Like most professions, the location of the professional paradigm goes beyond the practitioner's self and institution to embrace wider issues raised by society. As Bennett (1998) suggests, professional status derives from the value that society places on higher education, the inclusion of specialized knowledge and the reliance on higher-order abilities critically to acquire, apply, reflect on and elaborate that knowledge. As such it is essentially a reflective paradigm. It is not detached from the core academic and professional activities of the academy, but integrated within it and subject to the same critical requirements and standards with respect to knowledge, theory, values and practice. In the next section we shall begin to examine a third-paradigm approach that we believe more adequately addresses the challenge of excellence; indeed which challenges excellence to a qualitatively higher-order excellence.

THE REFLECTIVE PROFESSIONAL

The different responses elicited by the challenge of professionalism in learning and teaching may be illustrated by an important distinction between the call *for* professionalism and the call *to* professionalism. The former is primarily a call from the discourse of excellence for accountability, an external call for standardized professional organization, practice and evaluation procedures. It reflects the overall desire for increased efficiency and competitiveness within an accounting framework of quality. The latter, on the other hand, is a call to defend academic values and practices from the worst excesses of externally imposed frameworks of excellence, but also to acknowledge the challenge, to take possession of and transform it. The call to professionalism is a call towards a new way of thinking about learning and teaching which neither falls back on traditional laissez-faire academic versions of the benign amateur (Ramsden, 1992/2003) nor succumbs to newer versions of behavioural competence. It is a call to change, but it is also a call to ongoing reflection and change, to an ongoing transformation centred in the learning situation and reflecting the changing nature of that situation as characterized in the four features described above. It is a call to professionalism.

This call requires a model of practice that must account not only for the events and situations that arise in practice but also for the changing social context of that practice. Here, the model of practice most commonly advocated in opposition to the narrow competence model – the reflective practitioner (Schon, 1983, 1987) – is not sufficient. Reflective practice has been successful in articulating a conception of professional practice that goes beyond the application of previously mastered competencies which are then rather mechanistically applied to events. Stressing the conception of *reflecting-in-action*, this model describes the practitioner's ability to employ professional knowledge during practice in such a manner as to devise, choose and apply appropriate responses to unexpected and complex events and situations. Nevertheless, the model of reflective practice is primarily located in and bounded by those events and situations.

Extending the concept of the reflective practitioner to the reflective professional embraces not only the locus of practice but also the sphere of the professional. It encompasses what Barnett (2003) refers to as *professing-in-action*, which includes an understanding of the wider professional and academic context. If the former reflects on practice, the latter critically reflects on multiple and diverse discourses, on practice within the broader contexts and critical frameworks of his or her professional situation, however situated, constituted or clustered: teaching–research–administration; discipline–department–institution; ethical–social–economic–political; and local–national–international. These provide a changing set of multiple discourses in which the reflective professional works. Both the competence model and the reflective practitioner model describe two very different ways of responding to the multitude of situations and events describing practice, but they both essentially assume a relatively static environment in which these situations and events take place. As Barnett suggests:

> The key challenge of modern professionalism is just this, of trying to make sense of disparate discourses in one's professional actions. It may be that, on occasions, the discourses collide such that one cannot act under them coherently ... The challenge, then, that faces the modern professional is the management of incoherence. (1997b: 141)

Working as a reflective professional means managing the incoherence brought about by changing:

- academic roles;
- knowledge bases;
- ways of knowing;
- the nature of the student body;
- student needs;
- departmental requirements;
- institutional demands;
- external agency demands; and
- professional accreditation demands.

Being a reflective professional rests in the ability to situate oneself and one's practice critically within an environment of substantial uncertainty and change, and, to manage that change, academic faculty need to make sense of, and work within, these widespread changes. But, as Barnett (2000) suggests, this is precisely the problem. Living as we do in age of supercomplexity, we lack a cohesive conceptual framework for making the world intelligible (Barnett, 2000: 75). We must find a new conceptual framework to ride out these changes, by finding an 'appropriate language linked to theoretical ideas' (Entwistle, 1998: 1). The language we develop must be critical and open and, as Kuhn (1970) suggested in his now classic work on paradigm shifts in academia, must allow for concrete problem-solutions that can be devised, implemented, evaluated, negotiated, modified and/or set aside in an ongoing cycle of critical performance. Such a language must be suitably open and elastic to accommodate diverse personal circumstances within rapidly shifting curriculum expansion and development, over a wide range of disciplines (and their escalating disciplinary and interdisciplinary contours), and set within a diverse cluster of higher education departments and institutions.

THE NOVICE TEACHER

Developing this language and conceptual framework may be a particularly important challenge for novice teachers. Whether they are new faculty, post-docs, adjunct or part-time lecturers, postgraduate students or from the professional fields, new teachers are seeking to understand and negotiate their new roles and identities at university. While they will bring a wide range of background, skills and experience to their new positions, they may know very little about what teaching in higher education entails beyond knowledge of their own content area. Their prior opportunities to engage in teaching may have been very limited. As postgraduate or graduate students, they may have served as teaching assistants, supporting a faculty member. Those in the professional schools, such as journalists, doctors, engineers and artists, will have been immersed in what they do, but may not have done much teaching except in a very *ad hoc* way.

At the same time, novice teachers are beset by the same pressures that plague other teachers in higher education: poor teacher–student ratios, declining resources and competing demands of research, teaching, service, administration and, for those in the professional fields, clinical expectations as well. As perceptions of teaching quality are increasingly linked to personnel decisions and job security (hiring, retention, promotion, tenure, salary increases, etc.), teachers may feel increasingly pressured about their performance in the classroom (Oppenheimer, 2008). Wrestling to meet these competing demands, new teachers may look informally to senior colleagues for feedback and advice, solace and comfort, information and wisdom (Mullen and Forbes, 2000). Yet even such experienced teachers may not have all the answers. Indeed, many are likely to be struggling themselves to meet and balance their numerous professional obligations. The professional language and conceptual frameworks described in this book can provide a useful structure for helping new teachers negotiate their new academic identities, especially as it helps them integrate their own learning and domain expertise with the demands of student learning and teaching.

CONCLUSIONS

In this Introduction we have addressed the challenges which teaching in higher education faces, describing the theoretical issues surrounding the changing nature of higher education, the changing role of the teacher within higher education, and the development of the teacher as both professional and reflective practitioner. In response to the challenge, we have proposed the concept of the reflective professional. We aim, in the rest of this book, to describe the nature of a professional language of academic development and how it might be used in practice. There are three inter-related components to the language: a critical conceptual framework, relevant and appropriate genres, and a general performance strategy (see Figure I.2).

In Part 1, we explore the first component of this language in three conceptual locations: 1) a general theoretical framework of language and knowledge; 2) a model of the reflective professional within academic practice; and 3) a critical matrix of learning in higher education. In Chapter 1, we consider the first two of these, looking at the relationship of language and

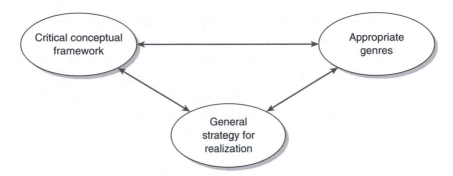

Figure I.2 *The language of learning and teaching*

knowledge to academic practice. We argue that the academic relationships between knowledge, student, teacher and researcher converge in one model focused on learning. In Chapter 2, we examine the character of learning in higher education. Specifically, we develop a critical matrix of learning, providing teachers with a conceptual tool for designing, developing and implementing their teaching across the various genres of teaching practice outlined in the second part of the book.

In Part 2, we consider the different genres of teaching practice. Although we recognize that teaching is a holistic practice not comfortably divided into different sections, we accept that teaching in higher education has come to recognize certain distinctive core genres of teaching, which may be addressed separately. Thus, the genres of teaching respectively addressed in Chapters 3–9 include: Designing, Lecturing, Facilitating, Supervising, Innovating, Assessing and Evaluating. Within each chapter, we address key practical teaching issues and activities related to that genre, connecting it to relevant theory and recent research. While these genres focus on a variety of learning and teaching activities in which academics engage, they are not presented as an exhaustive list, nor are they intended as closed systems within themselves. They may be separated and combined in a wide array of sub-genres.

Finally, in Part 3, we address the third component, which focuses on the development and improvement of the learning and teaching. In Chapter 10, we propose and describe a general strategy of professional realization: a strategy for engaging and mastering the critical language of the reflective professional. The essence of this component is 1) to locate the development of teaching and learning within the concrete disciplinary and departmental situation; and 2) to link this development with the ongoing improvement of practice.

Final questions: These three components are not intended as a prescriptive generic programme but, rather, to provide a structure for designing a wide range of individual teaching and learning strategies. The model of practice proposed here does not ask academics to submit to a barrage of techniques, tips and prescribed practices but, rather, to engage in a critical way of thinking about their own practice. This involves asking critical questions about their wider disciplinary and professional roles and responsibilities in higher education: how important is teaching to my discipline and/or profession? What professional responsibilities do I have for student learning? How, or in what ways, am I accountable for my teaching? What standards of excellence do I hold myself and my colleagues to with respect to my students and profession? What responsibility do I have for my growth as a teacher? What are the critical challenges of learning in my discipline – for both my students and myself? At the very least, the model of practice proposed here is intended to be mildly subversive and liberating, providing space for the development of critical being in the world (Barnett, 2003). This, we contend, is the essence of the reflective professional.

NOTE

[1] There are different terms for 'academics'. In the US, academics who teach in a higher education setting are referred to as 'faculty', 'instructor', or 'professor', while in the UK the terms 'staff' or 'lecturer' are more common. We have used the terms interchangeably throughout the book.

PART 1

THE ACADEMIC AS REFLECTIVE PROFESSIONAL

chapter 1

THE REFLECTIVE PROFESSIONAL IN ACADEMIC PRACTICE

In this chapter we describe the first of two conceptual frameworks that support the idea of the reflective professional in academic practice. We argue that the three core worlds of 'student', 'teacher' and 'researcher', and the academic encounters between them, are deeply and theoretically inter-related. We contrast traditional assumptions – reflecting models of teaching and research practice pulling these worlds apart – with more recent models, drawing on dialogic views of language and constructivist theories of knowledge that integrate them under a common point of convergence in learning. Finally, we suggest that academic values and principles rest in common models of practice.

INTRODUCTION

In the Introduction we raised the issue of developing a professional language of practice for negotiating the changing context of teaching in higher education. Such a language and its mastery, we suggested, are at the heart of the idea of the reflective professional. Over this chapter and the next we shall examine the conceptual frameworks supporting this professional language of practice. They are:

- a theory of the reflective professional within academic practice; and
- a critical matrix of learning in higher education.

With these two frameworks we set out a theoretical narrative, sustaining the idea of the reflective professional and the associated language of practice. It is not our intention to construct an uncompromising structure in granite but, rather, to disclose the broader theoretical frameworks which practitioners might profitably engage with in their own unique situations.

These frameworks provide a way for understanding the vital role that the academic context plays in the practices of research, teaching and learning at the heart of higher education. In turn, how they are practised reflects underlying theories of knowledge and communication which are shaped by the nature and scope of academic roles and audiences. Being a reflective professional means having the capacity to negotiate and reconcile these different academic worlds – critically and creatively to remake conceptual frameworks which are inherently contestable, uncertain and ambiguous. This also means recognizing the importance of developing a critical capacity to help students negotiate the contestable and ambiguous frameworks they will encounter in their own professional and academic worlds.

In this chapter we describe the first framework informing the language and practice of the reflective professional. We examine contrasting models of teaching and research reflected in the tacit theories employed in their practice and understanding. We compare traditional assumptions, describing models that pull the worlds of practice apart, with models that draw them together under a common point of convergence in learning. Finally, we suggest that academic values and principles rest in common models of practice. We begin, however, by briefly describing two critically important features of this framework: the social-constructivist nature of knowledge and the dialogic quality of language which characterize academic relationships.

THE REFLECTIVE PROFESSIONAL: KNOWLEDGE AND LANGUAGE

Knowledge and social constructivism

The theoretical framework developed in this chapter is constructivist in nature. Constructivism, broadly speaking, refers to the view that knowledge is constructed by individuals through the use of language and other symbolic and cultural systems (Bruner, 1996). While constructivism takes many forms – indeed, Phillips (1995/2000, 2007) has suggested that it has become 'something akin to a secular religion' with many rival sects holding different theoretical positions – theorists generally agree on its most basic tenets (Kivinen and Ristelä, 2003). These tenets essentially consist of the view that, despite being born with cognitive potential, humans do not arrive with either pre-installed empirical knowledge or methodological rules. Neither do

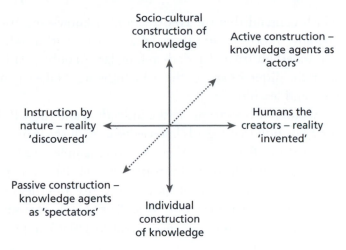

Figure 1.1 *Constructivism: three dimensions*
Source: Adapted from Phillips, 2000

we acquire knowledge ready formed or pre-packaged by directly perceiving it. On the whole, knowledge – and our criteria and methods for knowing it and the disciplines to which this knowledge contributes – is constructed. There is, however, significant variation between the many theoretical positions described as constructivism and/or social constructivism.

Phillips describes the variation along three dimensions (see Figure 1.1), which provides a useful map for locating the framework discussed in this chapter. The main horizontal dimension describes the classic disputed 'reality: discovered or invented' (see, for example, Penrose, 1989; Rorty, 1989). At one end, knowledge is independent of human agency: nature serves as a kind of 'instructor', its store of knowledge discovered and absorbed or copied somewhat passively. At the other end of this dimension, knowledge (and reality) is essentially made or invented by creative and active knowers. At some point towards the 'discovered' end of this dimension, a theoretical position is no longer constructivist but takes a strong realist position in which knowledge is in effect imposed from without. There is no effective space for human agency in the formation of knowledge. At the other extreme of this dimension, the theoretical sites take stances describing radical relativist positions. Knowledge is relative to the knower or knowers. It is essentially the result of individual or group invention.

Our position rests between these two extremes, conceiving knowing neither as discovery nor invention but as social narrative. Social narrative, or social constructivism, is addressed by the vertical dimension of Figure 1.1. The vertical dimension of the map describes the tension between theories which contend that the construction of knowledge arises within internal cognitive processes and those which argue that knowledge is socially and culturally constructed and, therefore, largely public. This tension is distinct from the different approaches which theorists take when looking at knowledge and learning.

An approach focusing on the individual and the self does not mean taking a position that regards knowledge as exclusively or even primarily inner or cognitive. Piaget and Vygotsky, for example, are both concerned with how individuals learn and construct knowledge, and approach the subject from an individual psychological perspective, but they differ significantly in their views of what that comprises. Piaget (1950) stresses the biological and cognitive mechanisms, whereas Vygotsky (1986) emphasizes the social factors in learning.

The third dimension focuses on the degree to which the human construction of knowledge, whether it is social and public or inner and private, is an active or passive process. Although there are close parallels here with the first dimension, the tensions inherent in this dimension do not map narrowly on to the first. 'Spectator' here is not simply the passive receiver of knowledge from nature and 'actor' is not merely the active constructor of personal knowledge. These terms describe a relationship with knowledge which highlights the active involvement, or lack of it, which human agents have in the process of learning. Again, these agents may be individuals or social communities. Our theoretical framework is broadly located on this map close to the middle of the first dimension but leaning robustly along the other two dimensions towards the 'social' and 'active' poles respectively. Knowing is a social process by which individual experience and meaning are constructed within a system of shared socio-cultural meanings or narratives. As such this book takes a social-constructivist approach to the description of knowledge and human learning.

Language and dialogue

If social constructivism describes the nature of knowledge, dialogue describes the nature of language in which knowledge is shared and developed. Indeed, dialogue is a necessary condition of language and the construction of meaning. The key ideas here may be briefly illustrated by contrasting the views of key theorists of language. The noted linguist Saussure (1966: 9) distinguished language as system (*langue*) from its use (*parole*) and notes that in the latter 'we cannot discover its unity'. The latter, as Holquist (1990: 45–6) notes, is 'quickly consigned (by Saussure) to an unanalyzable chaos of idiosyncrasy', and abandoned as an area of study. Bakhtin (1986: 70), however, claimed that such abstractions ignore the active process of the speaker and the role of the other in the actual use of language in favour of vague formal terms ('signs') 'interpreted as segments of language'.

Bakhtin argues that linguistic confusion and imprecision 'result from ignoring the real unit of speech communication: the utterance. For speech can exist in reality only in the form of concrete utterances of individual speaking people' (1986: 71). He distinguishes between utterance as a concrete unit of speech communication (inclusive of speaker and situation) and sentence as an abstracted unit in a language system. Bakhtin describes utterance as 'determined by a change of speaking subjects'. Any utterance, he writes, 'is preceded by the utterances of others and its end is followed by the responsive utterances of others' (1986: 71). Speaking (and writing) is by its very nature a response, existing in a stream of related responses and counter-responses distinguished and bounded by a change of speaker, not by full stops and paragraphs. Utterance is defined by dialogue: *otherness* is presupposed by the speaker as the other to whom the utterance is responding and the other from whom the utterance elicits a response. Language is an intersubjective phenomenon (Rommetveit and Blakar, 1979). It is not possible as a private, individual, subjective activity – see Wittgenstein's famous (1968) argument against the concept of a private language – nor is it an independent symbolic system. At its core language is essentially dialogue. Dialogue characterizes all forms of human communication and, as we shall see, is therefore critical to the active construction and exchange of knowledge, or the learning, which exemplifies the academic world. The failure to achieve learning in the academic world, moreover, is often grounded in the failure to realize meaningful dialogue and fully permit the active construction of knowledge.

WORLDS APART

The academic world – immersed in its disciplinary and institutional histories, social narratives, discourses and procedures, its ways of thinking and working, of congregating and communicating, of distributing power, authority and status (Becher and Trowler, 2001) – characterizes the student–teacher encounter before a word is even exchanged. It substantially shapes the teacher's professional experiences and tacitly confronts the student's first tentative encounters with higher education. For the student, the academic world is typically new and strange, its languages and practices frequently unfamiliar and mysterious, even exotic and bizarre. The student's encounter with higher education is not simply an intellectual grappling with new ideas, concepts and frameworks, but also a personal and emotional engagement with the situation. If the academic context is more familiar for the teacher, its features more explicit and transparent, the teaching encounter with students is immersed in a host of uneven relationships and concerns, including the status of teaching in higher education.

Often unknown to students, teaching has become the poor relation to research and scholarship. The relative status of teaching to research is exacerbated by the financial rewards and status that accompany the latter even as, ironically, concerns on both sides of the Atlantic can be heard to improve the status of the former (US Department of Education, 2006; HEA, 2007). At the heart of the struggle is an all too pervasive understanding that teaching is something an academic does, whereas research and scholarship are what make an academic special. Where many students approach learning in higher education, hesitant and uncertain, cautiously embracing new cultures and ways of thinking, an increasing number of teachers (including many with a natural love of teaching) approach the teacher–student encounter with ambivalence and an underlying sense of dissatisfaction.

There is, then, in the general teaching and learning situation an imperfect encounter of three worlds of experience – student, teacher and researcher – which, ironically, are defined by one another in substantial ways and yet separated by underlying tensions. The teacher, for example, is a teacher in so far as he or she has students. Students, however, do not fully share a world with their teacher, and there is, by definition, a disparity in the knowledge and expertise each possesses. The teacher, moreover, has the authority to teach the particular subject of a discipline in higher education by virtue of his or her work as a researcher or scholar, and yet teaching is typically viewed as detached from and even undermining research. Teaching detracts from the time and effort available to put into research and often contributes to a reduction in the status of the academic, as if being good at teaching precludes one's ability to be a good researcher (Boyer, 1990; Colbeck; 1998, Wolverton, 1998). Teaching so conceptualized has built into it the seeds of its own undoing: it undermines the research and scholarship that provide the authority to teach in higher education. Teaching contests and diminishes itself by definition. Evidence of this may be seen, for example, at the doctoral level, where the less research and scholarship an academic does undermines their authority to both attract and supervise postgraduates. The correspondence and tensions between the three worlds describing teaching in higher education

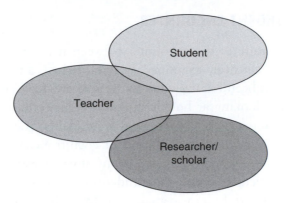

Figure 1.2 *The worlds of teaching*

(see Figure 1.2) characterize the ways in which dialogue and learning occur or do not occur within the myriad situations of these three worlds.

The quality of the meaning and learning achieved in these situations and associated practices is dependent on the extent and quality of the correspondence. How much of the potential correspondence do we permit in practice? How much do we exclude? In a narrowly construed correspondence, we construct situations that reduce the potential for the construction of meaning, irrespective of the quantity of meanings used. In such situations, dialogue can descend into a mechanical and linear process. The listener is effectively detached from the speaker, not because there is nothing to say but, rather, because the social situation militates against it. Dialogue becomes monologue. Meanings are merely transmitted across the situation rather than mutually constructed within it. Deeper meaning is not achieved. The potential for dialogue and the realization of genuine engagement within such fragmented situations and encounters is minimal.

The challenge for professionals in higher education (and it is not limited to those engaged directly in teaching and learning) is to find ways of critically engaging (reflecting and acting) and integrating the academic worlds in which they practise. In the next section we will consider these issues by exploring two relationships between the three worlds highlighted in Figure 1.2: the teacher–student encounter and the teacher–researcher encounter. There is no overlap or relationship shown for the researcher–student encounter since the academic's role as teacher will mediate this relationship for the vast majority of students. For a small minority – mainly research students – this encounter may be unmediated in a relationship that we shall suggest transforms the way in which we conceptualize research and teaching.

TEACHER–STUDENT ENCOUNTER

The nature of the encounter between teacher and student has been the most extensively examined and researched, although until recently even this has been relatively limited. There are, for example, a wide number of studies looking at how teachers in higher education understand or conceive of their practice *vis-à-vis* their students. Such conceptions are not the result of innate personal traits or cognitive characteristics but are, rather, 'theories' (often undisclosed or intuitive beliefs) in accordance with which the particular 'world' – the student–teacher encounter – is interpreted and experienced. In a meta-analysis of 13 studies of teachers' views of teaching in higher education, Kember (1997) identified five general conceptions of teaching in higher education that fall under two broad orientations: teacher-centred/content-oriented and student-centred/learning-oriented. These conceptions range from teachers who view teaching as essentially imparting information to those who conceive it as facilitating conceptual change in their students.

Prosser and Trigwell's (1999) phenomenographic study describes a somewhat parallel typography of six faculty conceptions of teaching. The first two conceptions of teaching describe teaching as a transmission of concepts. The second pair of conceptions describe teaching as helping students acquire the concepts of a course. A final pair of conceptions focused on teaching as facilitating conceptual development or conceptual change. In a two-year study of the teaching conceptions of American faculty two of the authors of this book found comparable conceptions of teaching reflecting Prosser and Trigwell's categories: teacher-focused, student-focused, learning-focused (Calkins and Light, 2008; Light and Calkins, 2008) (see Table 1.1).

Teacher-focused conceptions

In the first conception, the teacher regards the practice of teaching as one in which he or she, as an expert, imparts or transmits information to a passively receptive or compliant student. Teaching mainly rests in the content of the curriculum and quality of the knowledge that the teacher has and controls. In this content-oriented conception, good teaching consists of having sound academic knowledge, which is well structured and clearly delivered or transmitted. Student learning is not a central concern of the teacher. Students are expected to accept the knowledge and content which are passed to them and the learning achieved is up to the individual student (Calkins and Light, 2008).

Table 1.1   *Conceptions of teaching in higher education*

Categories of conceptions of teaching	Aspects of conception			
	Student learning	Student relationship to course content	Teaching	Focus of good teaching
Transmission Teacher-focused	Student learning is not the teacher's concern	Passive-compliant acceptance	Transmission, soliloquy-monologue	Quantity, quality, structure and transmission of content
Acquisition Student-focused	Student learning as acquisition of course concepts and skills is teacher's concern	Compliant-active acquisition	Explanation, demonstration, active-monologue towards dialogue	Strategies and tips that help students acquire the course concepts and content
Engagement Learning-focused	Student learning as conceptual development and understanding is teacher's concern	Active-reflective construction	Facilitation, intersubjective–active-dialogue	Developing ways to help students improve and change their conceptual understanding

Sources: Adapted from Calkins and Light, 2008; Light and Calkins, 2008

While the teaching practice is essentially a monologue – a one-way communication from teacher to student – the separation of teaching from learning furnishes this conception with the quality of a soliloquy. Teaching is basically a display of content by the teacher overheard by the student. Indeed, in the most extreme version of this conception, the teacher believes that, if they have delivered the course content, teaching has occurred even if no student shows up to that class. A teacher holding this conception fails to recognize both the dialogic quality of communication and the social-contructivist nature of learning, by failing to recognize the extent and complexity of the premises shared by teacher and students.

Student-focused conceptions

The second conception focuses on the student as someone who will acquire the skills, knowledge/content and strategies for learning that the teacher as expert already possesses. A teacher holding this conception will retain some features of the teacher-focused model – that meaning and knowledge are the preserve of the teacher for 'transfer' to student – but they will also recognize that teaching needs to go beyond transmission to play a more active role in helping students acquire the content of that transmission. The teacher regards the student as being a more active, if still somewhat compliant, participant in a shared situation in which the teacher provides the knowledge and skills to be acquired on the course, but also is concerned that the students do, in fact, obtain this knowledge and skills. The situation is not simply a void across which content and knowledge are transmitted but, rather, a more integrated environment focused on student reception of the knowledge as well. The teacher still defines and frames the knowledge, but through explanation and demonstration rather than transmission, and the student is encouraged to achieve it for themselves (Calkins and Light, 2008).

Good teaching in this conception goes beyond a concern for the quality of the content and how clearly it is structured and delivered to include an interest in developing teaching tips and strategies for connecting the course content to students and satisfying their expectations about obtaining this content (Akerlind, 2005). While the underlying assumption of teachers holding this conception retains, in part, views of teaching as monologue – teaching causes learning – the focus on student acquisition of knowledge recognizes the importance of entering into a kind of dialogue with students and their minds. In focusing on learning as accumulation of concepts as provided, this conception does not, however, recognize the essential social-contructivist nature of knowledge.

Learning-focused conceptions

The third conception focuses on the learner, and on promoting conceptual change. Teaching is not simply regarded as aiding students' accumulation of knowledge presented to them, but rather the process of facilitating a student's construction of knowledge for herself. The teacher will help the student develop and change his own conceptions of the subject and in many ways himself as a person. The development and changes in student conceptual understanding go beyond regarding learning as active compliance in the acquisition of the course concepts to a recognition of learning as an active and reflective construction of those concepts. In this respect, knowledge is understood as socially constructed by the student, and the exchange of that knowledge is, at heart, an intersubjective dialogue of shared meanings between teacher and student.

Good teaching consists of developing ways to help students' improve and change their conceptual understanding. And, in developing those practices, it recognizes that meaning and knowledge are outcomes constructed by students in an active dialogue within the socially rich situation of the course and programme. Knowing and communicating are virtually the same and are grounded here within a situation in which the overlap between the meanings of the student's world and those of the teacher's world are extended and shared as fully as possible. Teachers recognize that they are engaging people in an authentic dialogue the quality for which – in terms of the student constructions of knowledge – they have a shared responsibility.

Indeed, many teachers holding this conception of teaching recognize a further responsibility which takes them beyond facilitating the construction of knowledge to acknowledging their key role in assisting and supporting the student to develop (or 'reconstruct' themselves) as persons. There is a practical recognition that it is not merely knowledge that is constructed in social dialogue, but also a kind of critical being (Barnett, 1997b).

It should be pointed out that the variation between these three categories of conception focuses around how faculty understand student learning and their own relationship to that learning. They need to be differentiated from models of classifying teaching which distinguish between teaching-centred and student-centred based on differences in the kind of classroom methods and activities they employ. Thus teachers who lecture are described as teacher-centred and teachers who employ small-group, active learning techniques are described as student-centred. Such models often distinguish teacher-focused teaching from student-centred teaching simply in terms of the teaching process. These models are unable adequately to explain those teachers whose lectures are magnificent examples of engaging students in conceptual change or teachers whose small-group activities turn out to be a series of unstimulating monologues.

The suggestion, moreover, that student-centred approaches are not concerned with content/knowledge is misleading as knowledge is critical to all conceptions of teaching. The issue, as noted above, is how teaching contributes to the ways in which students engage with knowledge – i.e. to the quality of their learning. Indeed, it is the continuity of knowledge which underpins the hierarchical relationship between conceptions; the more sophisticated conceptions adding to or subsuming the less sophisticated conceptions (Prosser and Trigwell, 1999; Biggs, 2003). Where the first category of conception focuses on knowledge as the teacher's to transmit, the second accepts the importance of the teacher knowledge but extends it to include a focus on the student acquiring this knowledge and permits a role for dialogue in this acquisition. Finally, the third subsumes both the importance of the teacher and student's knowledge in a fully dialogic relationship, but extends it to include the concern for the quality of learning in terms of how the student constructs or reconstructs the concepts and knowledge shared on the course.

TEACHER–RESEARCHER ENCOUNTER

Since the birth of the idea of the modern research university – with Humboldt and the German Idealists (Thelin, 2004) – teaching and research have defined the nature of higher education and the university. For the vast majority of academics, the teaching–research/scholarship relationship is the principal feature defining their own academic practice. Even those academics whose practices (and institutions) lie primarily at one or other end of this relational axis will feel the pull of the other end in their academic lives. They will have other roles and an increasing number of roles (as noted in the Introduction), but for the most part faculty will understand these roles in relationship to this central axis of practice.

In this respect, teaching and research are inseparable (Barnett and Hallam, 1999), a unity in which the former, as we saw, derives its authority from the latter. As such this unity is often perceived and conceived by academics as deeply uneven. Research, which confers authority and status, takes precedence. Consequently, it is research, not teaching, which provides the key to their identity as an academic professional. It impels faculty to 'feel primary obligations less towards students ... and more towards protecting and advancing private interests viewed in terms of discipline' (Bennett, 1998: 47).

This situation has been supported by the growth of national and international academic infrastructures almost exclusively focused on research interests. It is research, firmly imbedded in its disciplines, that provides the expertise, the professional qualifications, the membership associations, the scholarly journals, the national meetings and so on. The very idea of academic professionalism – particularly as it has developed and been understood in this century – has diminished the teacher–researcher overlap and the potential of that encounter. It is that overlap and the nature of the shared meanings that characterize it that our framework impels us to reconsider. It requires a new model or way of thinking about research and teaching. The primary issue here, then, is not so much how we bring the teaching–research axis into balance but, rather, how we conceptualize the relationship. Indeed our very use of the words 'axis' and 'balance' can be misleading as it suggests a uneven relationship between research and teaching in which positive changes in one bring about negative changes in the other. Figure 1.3 depicts these two ways of conceptualizing the research–teaching relationship.

Diagram A in Figure 1.3 depicts the teaching–research relationship in terms of two detached practices at either end of a scale. One practice is

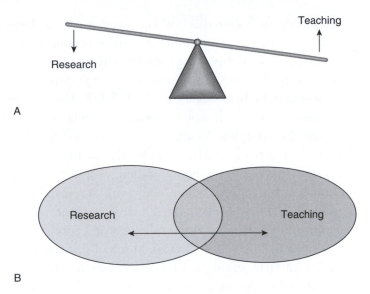

Figure 1.3 *Conceptualizing research and teaching: A) linear model; B) dialogic model*

achieved (often in terms of time and status) at the expense of the other practice: the incompatibility thesis (Barnett and Hallam, 1999). Professionalism in
this model has traditionally tilted towards research, often with negative effects
for teaching. Thus, for many academics, one of the essential measures of a
more advanced level of professionalism is the distance from teaching responsibilities (particularly at undergraduate level) and from students. Indeed, time
spent on teaching – doing it, conceptualizing it, developing it and so on – has
frequently been regarded as distinctly unprofessional. It is a model, moreover,
in which the compensations for professionalism – promotion, status, influence and the accompanying financial rewards – have encouraged 'imbalance'.

The development and promotion of teaching and learning in higher education have generally been conceptualized and articulated within the terms
of this linear model. It speaks, for example, in terms of achieving a 'balance'
between teaching and research (Kennedy, 1997) and of raising the status
and importance of teaching separately from the issue of research (DfES,
2003). This approach – conceptualizing a new professionalism which, for all
intents and purposes, is separate from the existing conceptions of academic
professionalism – may present a challenge to the supremacy of research, but
it fails to challenge the existing model. Indeed, the very challenge to research
bolsters the model as one in which the two main protagonists are fundamentally detached from one another, competing for time, status and reward.

Ironically, success in this new endeavour runs the danger of achieving an alienated academic professionalism encompassing two incompatible components. Signs of this are apparent within the central element of this 'teaching' professionalism: professional programmes for the accreditation of teaching in higher education (HEA, 2007). Here, for example, the ongoing 'generic versus discipline' teaching skills debate discloses the gap between the discipline location of research and the perceived a-discipline location of generic teaching skills (in teaching centres or educational departments). Similarly, many academics and faculty perceive such programmes as unrelated to their 'real' work as researchers.

This model has also generated a large number of studies, primarily correlation studies, looking at the relationship between teaching and research (Jenkins et al., 2003; Brew, 2006). Much of this research is predicated on a widespread view among academics that such a link exists. The inherent conflict within this model would effectively disappear if it could be established that there was a strong, conclusive correlation between research excellence and effective teaching. Indeed, the few studies that suggest a correlation are used as arguments within the prevailing model to suggest that a renewed emphasis on teaching is unnecessary and, thereby, to maintain the dominant position of research. That such a correlation is not, as Brew and Boud (1995: 265) point out, interpreted the other way around – 'that being good at teaching makes for better research' – is telling and symptomatic of a political need for a link.

In the end, the issue is rather artificial. Despite this desire for the inherent conflict within the model to be so resolved, these studies are inconclusive overall. They show a negative correlation as often as a positive one and meta-analyses of over 58 of these studies suggest that the correlation is essentially zero – being a good researcher does not imply being a good teacher and vice versa (Marsh and Hattie, 2002). The dialogic model of understanding research and teaching (depicted in diagram B) proposes a compatibility thesis, describing the relationship in terms of the overlap between teaching and research. Rather than constructing this essential relationship in terms of an inherent conflict (see Box 1.1), it attempts to reconceptualize it in terms of what the two areas of practice share in common. It looks to further the potential for constructive engagement by developing and extending the shared meanings rather than locking the two practices within a series of incompatible and competing set of meanings. Diagram B suggests mutual ways in which research practice might share its meanings with teaching (right arrow) and ways in which teaching might share meanings with research (left arrow).

Box 1.1 *Research and teaching as disconnected practices*

For Tasha, an early career lecturer in economics, teaching and research are disconnected practices at the undergraduate level. As she explains: 'I don't necessarily feel that there is a strong inherent link between teaching and research. Certainly, teaching the material has made it easier for me to think about my own writing in clear ways. But I feel the two are really quite separate tasks.' She believes that the topics she teaches in her undergraduate macroeconomics survey course, for example, are so broad that they are only in the most general way connected to her own research on Chinese international trade relations. At the same time, she considers her research to be so specialized and precise that it would be well beyond the scope of her course to bring it into her work, and very likely outside the students' immediate grasp. Only on occasion, when she is reviewing the textbook or prepping her lecture, does the teaching material remind her about interesting questions or background in her own research. The only real connection she sees between the learning that she engages in as a professional economist and the learning engaged in by her students is that they need to communicate their written ideas clearly. Only if she were teaching an advanced undergraduate or postgraduate course on Chinese economics would she be able to see clear connections between the two and, even then, the connection is primarily in terms of similar content.

Instead of regarding these academic practices as separate, often rival practices of the discovery and construction of knowledge through research, or the transmission of knowledge through teaching, this model asserts that they are compatible, analogous practices. Ultimately, research and teaching are simply names for practices in higher education, practices whose goals are essentially the same: the advancement of learning and knowledge. As Light (2008) suggests:

> *while the former may lead to 'cutting edge' advances in scientific theory, medical treatments, historical understanding, artistic achievement at a national or international level, and the latter to 'cutting edge' advances in individual mastery and construction of personal knowledge of critical concepts in science, economics, philosophy or film studies at the undergraduate level, the structure of the learning and the nature of knowledge is the same – albeit at substantively different levels of achievement.*

While the term 'cutting edge' here is pervasive in academic research parlance, it is rarely used in connection with student learning. And yet it has essentially the same meaning, the construction and discovery of ideas and knowledge which are new, exciting and meaningful for oneself and one's peer groups. While the research peer group is national and international in scope and new often means the construction of knowledge and skills never before encountered, *ever*, and the student peer group is local, the learning and knowledge can, nevertheless, be new, exciting and meaningful for the student and his peer group. Indeed, teachers holding the third learning-focused conceptions above seem to understand the importance of facilitating 'cutting edge' learning opportunities for their students.

The incompatible relationship between research and teaching – frequently, even habitually, regarded as competitors, time and status pitting them against one another – translates into a battle of competing goals: the learning of academics against the learning of their students. The model is built upon a 'rivalry of learning' replete with important issues regarding the power (and associated ethical considerations) which academics exercise in how the rivalry plays out. There are two ways for unravelling this contradiction, for constructing a more compatible model. One way focuses on developing and describing more compatibility between the practices. A second focuses on the similarity of the goals.

With respect to the first, Boyer (1990) suggests extending the idea of 'scholarship' to teaching. Indeed, he writes of the idea of scholarship – 'engaging in original research ... but also stepping back from one's investigation, looking for connections, building bridges between theory and practice, and communicating one's knowledge effectively' (1990: 16) – as embracing all academic practice. It is noteworthy that he writes of such a 'scholarship of teaching' that it does not lie simply in transmitting knowledge but also in investigating, transforming and extending it. Such processes take place, moreover, both in active dialogue with one's students and in active dialogue with oneself and one's colleagues in the whole context of the design and preparation of teaching for students. As such the 'scholarship of teaching' assumes learning-focused conceptions of teaching. It is primarily distinguished from research (the 'scholarship of discovery') in terms of the audience it addresses and the methods it employs. It presupposes a conceptual framework of 'dialogue' and shares with research what Clark calls 'a culture of inquiry' (1997: 252). This approach for unravelling the paradox has been extremely influential, generating substantial research, literature and discussion in both the UK and USA (Hutchings and Shulman, 1999; Kreber, 2002; Trigwell and Shale, 2004; Brew, 2006).

While the scholarship of teaching and learning (SOTL), as described above, engages teachers in focusing on the quality of their students' learning and encourages learning-focused conceptions of teaching, the focus is primarily on how some faculty might focus their scholarship on teaching as opposed to other traditional research scholarships such as the scholarship of discovery or the scholarship of application (Boyer, 1990). It does not provide an adequate model for the integration of research into teaching in the work of potentially all faculty (Light, 2008). Recognizing the similarity in the goals of both teaching and research provides a richer way of integrating research and teaching. Its most radical formulation is to recognize that teachers with learning-focused conceptions (and associated practices) are essentially building research capacity in their students and as such contributing to the academy's overall research mission.

Building research capacity resides in the ability to facilitate the capacity to 'think critically, to identify and develop interesting problems and questions, to problem solve, to engage and collaborate with peers, to critically and creatively analyze and evaluate evidence, to synthesize ideas, to generate results, to draw conclusions, to produce reports or tangible texts and artefacts for assessment and review' (Light, 2008). In contrast to SOTL, where scholarship resides in the teacher's study and publishing of their teaching, scholarship and research reside in the learning capacities and outcomes of the students.

If the character of research elucidates more precisely those qualities of inquiry and discovery at the heart of excellent teaching, the practice of teaching similarly discloses more clearly the critical issues of learning at the heart of research. Research is a process of learning. It is equally concerned with 'questioning one's own pre-existing knowledge and understanding in light of new ideas and new evidence' (Brew, 1999: 297). It constructs its meanings within culturally and academically established situations with their own particular approaches, methods, 'languages' and criteria of success. In this sense academics are in effect master learners in their field, and this expertise in learning is what they can bring to teaching (Bain, 2004; Light, 2008). Both research – facilitating one's own and one's colleagues' learning – and teaching – facilitating one's own and one's students' learning – operate with different methods, in different contexts with different constraints and criteria of achievement. At their core, however, they share the same essential structure and meanings. They are not fundamentally distinct activities but are integral parts of the same academic enterprise (see Box 1.2).

Box 1.2 *Teaching and research as connected practices*

Quentin, an anthropology professor, asks his students to think of themselves as investigators, as they probe material and ask themselves critical questions. He designs even the most basic assignments so that students must use the tools of a professional in the field, so that they learn different observation techniques, report writing and interpretation. In their coursework – both in and out of class – students must grapple with more sophisticated concepts concerning the ethics, values and responsibilities that an anthropologist has to consider, even though he does not expect them all to be professional anthropologists. It does not matter to him that the content of the class is not always connected to his research directly; he still regularly shares his preliminary data and published findings with his students so they can understand how he has investigated similar problems in the field.

There is evidence, moreover, that many academics do, indeed, integrate such a model within their own understanding of their academic work. In a study of faculty conceptions of learning across their academic practices, Light and Calkins (2006, 2007) reported contrasting conceptions within two general categories of understanding: unconnected and connected. Faculty in the former category reported experiences in which the relationship between research and teaching was regarded as non-existent or as related only in terms of an overlap between the content of their research field and the course they were teaching. These faculty regarded their own learning as qualitatively different from that of their undergraduate students, student learning consisting of the passive acceptance of concepts presented to them, while their own learning was characterized as a constructive process of asking questions, addressing problems, making connections with personal experience and drawing on existing knowledge. There were, however, faculty in the connected categories who reported substantial relationships between research and teaching, not merely in terms of the content but particularly in terms of the learning required in the field. Student learning was modelled on their own learning as researchers and, as above, was described as a constructive process of conceptual change through engaging with meaningful questions and problems.

In these connected encounters – typically spare at the undergraduate level – meaningful correspondence between researcher and student is established. The enriched social meanings of learner (researcher) and learner (student) are shared and enhanced (see Figure 1.4). Together they generate the dialogical conditions for an overall integration of the 'worlds' of academic practice. As such, they provide the essential conceptual location upon which the concept of reflective professionalism developed in this book is based. The 'professionalization' of learning and teaching in higher education is not limited to learning and teaching. It requires critical reflection on the whole of academic practice, including research and scholarship. It is a challenge that is both substantially in advance of current practice (Brew, 1999) and at the heart of a broad proposal for reinventing undergraduate education as essentially a research endeavour (Boyer, 1998; Light, 2008).

PRINCIPLES OF ACADEMIC DIALOGUE

In the above discussion of the key encounters of academic work, the dialogic nature of language and the social-contructivist nature of knowledge were highlighted as critical features of meaningful understandings of teaching, research and student learning. In this section we describe the academic principles and

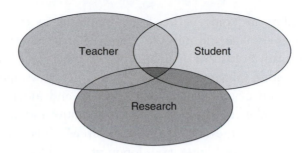

Figure 1.4   *The worlds of teaching revisited as research*

values that characterize these practices, stressing the importance of these same dialogic and constructivist features. These values and principles comprise commitments to:

- *scholarship and research*: in teaching as well as to one's own discipline;
- *collegiality and consideration*: with and for all members of the learning community including students, teachers, researchers, those supporting teaching, and so on;
- *equity and opportunity*: to encouraging participation in higher education and to equality of educational and learning opportunities;
- *difference and empowerment*: to respecting, developing, and empowering individual students within their common and different learning situations; and
- *reflection and improvement*: to continued critical reflection and evaluation of practice and its innovative and creative improvement.

The values underlying these commitments are, however, much easier to acknowledge than to achieve. Superficially, at least, they draw upon the finest principles and interests of academic tradition and are almost impossible to reject. In practice they require as substantial and significant a transformation of understanding and 'being' as those advocated for teaching and research. We may usefully consider these principles in terms of two models of 'being' an academic (or of 'academic being'): the 'autonomous' and the 'relational' (Bennett, 1998, 2003). These models condition the relationship between self, others and community in higher education. They also closely correspond to the conceptual distinctions described with respect to teaching and research.

The first model, 'insistent individualism', is lodged in the idea of self as individual and detached. It 'emphasises separation, individual autonomy, privacy, fragmentation and self-sufficiency' (Bennett, 1998: 12). Such a person specializes in 'academic freedom', arguing at its extreme that the scholar's merit is absolute and intrinsic, essentially inaccessible to external evaluation, particularly from other disciplines or even other specialist areas or sub-specialist areas within the same discipline. This model draws upon both the academy's celebration of uniqueness, distinctiveness and independence of mind, and upon its inherent suspicion of the collaborative and the co-operative. It fosters a conception of research and scholarship which is individually designed, executed and aimed, first and foremost, at 'making a name for oneself'. Academic rewards reinforce it: better to author than co-author, better to be first author than second author; better to be distinctive than find commonality. Even students (particularly research students) – through the promotion of student 'followings' and 'cults' suitable to the academic's interests and needs – are regarded and valued in terms of their contribution to this individual mission.

At the heart of this model is the notion of 'unilateral power' (Loomer, 1976), the power individually to control and shape others while at the same time resisting being controlled or shaped by others. It is a power defined by contest, by 'winning' over others who 'lose', by academic pecking orders and freedom from academic responsibilities which do not contribute to individual academic status, power and reputation. Its primary arena is disciplinary in character, an arena of battles waged over specialized intellectual 'corners' and niches requiring insistent and uncompromising defence.

Ironically, the emphasis of this model on individuality, separateness and self-sufficiency is conditioned by social relationships and social constructions of meaning and importance. Indeed, the battle is about meaning, about what we construe as meaningful and important in the community, about what is knowledge. Academic individualism recognizes that knowledge and discovery are not the private accomplishment of the individual in isolation but are, rather, achieved in social situations (Bennett, 2003). Its character is defined less by the idea of a private, separate individual than by the quality and practice of social relationships within the academic community. Insistent individualism does not describe an individual (versus a social) model so much as a 'corrupted' social model, one in which the conception and practice of social relationship has been degraded towards 'monologue' rather than socially constructed in genuine 'dialogue'. Its singular character discloses a fundamental 'impoverishment' which – in so far as academic self-identity emerges through such relationships – also describes the individual's academic self.

The alternative 'relational' model of academic self, Bennett (2003) contends, is deeply imbedded in earlier academic traditions defined by a common sense of community and shared purposes. These are traditions receding under increasing specialization, market pressures, the growth and diversity of faculty and their conditions of employment. It is a model that does not regard others in academia as merely the means through which to pursue private ends, as competitors for resources, advancement and reputation. It constructs, rather, a genuine dialogue by extending value to others as colleagues, recognizing that self, other and community are also locations of human worth. It requires the recognition of the essential importance and worth of others in the whole academic enterprise. Against 'unilateral power', this model rests in the idea of 'relational power', and 'the notion that the capacity to absorb an influence is as truly a mark of power as the strength involved in exerting an influence' (Loomer, 1976: 17). In this respect, relational power inheres in the dialogical idea of 'active responsive understanding'.

This focus on the 'other' is not merely an intellectual acknowledgement of the social nature of practice but also, importantly, a concern for others. It is a concern that discloses academic practice as an inherently ethical as well as intellectual enterprise. The principles of academic dialogue are better regarded as virtues than rules, virtues with intellectual significance: 'not mere expressions of feeling, but guides to behavior that correlate importantly with learning and the increase of knowledge' (Bennett, 1998: 35). Bennett goes on to describe these virtues in terms of the concepts of 'hospitality' and 'thoughtfulness', and later 'spirituality' (Bennett, 2003), although we will focus on the first two.

'Hospitality' retains its widespread sense of being open and welcoming to the other, and of listening and accepting, but in a disciplined and rigorous way. It neither suspends critical judgement in the face of inadequate evidence nor enters dialogue with judgements already irrevocably formed. It does not include, therefore, complicity with indulgent, conspiratorial or even simply easygoing practices, but rather of being open to the full potential of the other's experience and thought irrespective of difference, status and privilege. It embraces a willingness to engage with the strange, the different and the uncertain; to evaluate it sincerely and honestly; to enlist and empower this other in the pursuit of learning and knowledge.

'Thoughtfulness' also embodies its commonly understood qualities of being intellectually 'reflective' and 'critical' and of being ethically 'sensitive' and 'considerate'. In both it draws upon the virtues of fidelity and courage: intellectual fidelity to the spirit and rigour of the inquiry and ethical fidelity to the needs and concerns of the others, be they students or colleagues. It similarly recognizes the importance of courage in sustaining

41

responsible and rigorous exchange and discourse. It neither yields intellectual or ethically to an abuse of power by others, nor succumbs to the practice of such abuse of power towards others. Courage requires the recognition and acceptance of one's vulnerability and responsibility to the mutually shared freedoms of the other.

This relational model provides the conceptual framework supporting the practices and behaviour described by the inter-related principles of academic dialogue mentioned above. A commitment to *scholarship and research*, for instance, goes beyond a concern for informing one's teaching through ongoing study and learning in one's own disciplinary fields. It recognizes the importance of ongoing scholarship and the research of one's students and of one's own teaching practices, conducted with students and colleagues. It is a commitment essentially to integrate the whole of academic practice within the larger context of continuous learning. Such a commitment by definition embraces the other principles. It recognizes, for example, the dialogic location of academic practice and the ensuing requirement that principles of *collegiality and consideration* govern relations with the whole spectrum of staff, students and all external persons with which one's academic projects are engaged. Such a principle entails an understanding of how we create and express ourselves in academic exchange, of what enhances exchange and of what undermines it:

> *undisciplined rhetoric is destructive. Polarizing rhetoric, careless and self-indulgent discourse, being candid only when personally convenient, and dwelling in unchecked negative complaining, corrode the very foundation of a community. The collegium disappears when members are too abrasive, when aggressiveness dominates exchange, when learners are abused, or when concepts insisted upon are isolating and obscuring rather than inclusive and illuminating. A constant threat to any collegium is individual insecurity and jealousy – diminishing community and generating isolation and insulation.* (Bennett, 1998: 29)

This, it should be emphasized, does not mean conformity, 'group-think' or superficial consensus which would merely substitute group 'monologue' for individual 'monologue'. The model stresses, rather, a genuinely open, critical and constructive dialogue that draws upon all its constitutive voices. It sustains both the principles of equity and opportunity and of difference and empowerment, asserting an active dialogue, which respects and values the difference (as well as the commonality) disclosed by 'others' in the dialogic situation. It provides opportunities and encouragement to participate in the appropriate academic discourses and learning situations. It appreciates the obstacles to participation that diverse groups may face for reasons such as gender, race/ethnicity, class, age, etc., and it actively works to overcome such obstacles.

It is a model insisting, moreover, that learning and teaching within an integrated conception of academic practice is actively maintained and continually refreshed to ensure both its vigour and to prevent its collapse into a model of insistent individualism. Robust intellectually and ethically informed academic dialogue is characterized by principles of continuous *reflection and improvement* conducted collaboratively with colleagues and students. The relational model of 'being an academic' within a genuine dialogical situation insists, almost by definition, upon reflection on practice and social exchange. It is reflection with purpose: critically to improve academic practice – enhancing and extending learning and knowledge – with and for the 'other(s)' implicit in the socially shared situation.

CONCLUSIONS

This chapter has described the *dialogic* or *relational* character of academic practice that lies at the heart of our concept of the *reflective professional*. We have argued that the three central worlds of *student*, *teacher* and *researcher* are deeply and theoretically inter-related. They not only share significant overlaps in their various social and academic roles but also share the essential structures of their associated conceptual frames of understanding. Each is characterized by opposing conceptual frameworks – relational versus individual or dialogic versus monologic – with substantial implications for academic practice. Furthermore, in the dialogic model these worlds converge in the crucial concept of learning – the third location of our conceptual framework. A detailed discussion of the nature of learning and the constitutive role that it plays in our understanding of the reflective professional will be the subject of the next chapter. Finally, it should be emphasized that this chapter was informed and characterized by an acutely ethical component which is inextricably embedded in the dialogic framework and conceptually entrenched in the idea of the 'other' which defines academic 'being' and practice. It provides the foundation upon which principles of academic dialogue – commonly accepted and cherished by academic tradition – are established.

Final questions: Concerted efforts to ensure that an integrated understanding of academic learning and the values of academic dialogue genuinely and pervasively characterize academic practice are the most significant factors in bringing about real change in practice. They, therefore, probably represent its toughest challenge and raise critical questions for academic practice. Are the facets of academic work essentially rival or complementary practices? How is expert learning understood in the context of research and scholarship, or in the clinical and professional domains? How is student learning different? Need it be different? What lessons might I take from an understanding of my own learning to that of my students' learning? Are the principles of academic dialogue between colleagues similar to those exhibited with students?

chapter 2

A CRITICAL MATRIX OF LEARNING AND TEACHING

This chapter focuses on learning, the central theme arising from the previous chapters. We present a wide range of relevant research and literature on learning pertinent to higher and professional education, and organize this research through two complementary frameworks. The first framework discusses the research on learning in terms of five learning gaps that students and teachers often face in the education of college and university students. The second framework proposes a critical matrix for constructing learning environments to transverse these learning gaps. This matrix integrates the intellectual, personal, social and practical dimensions of learning with key modes for structuring the learning environments: giving support, developing independence and encouraging interdependence.

THE ACADEMIC WEAVE

The previous chapter explored the first of two critical conceptual frameworks describing the language and practice of the teaching in higher education: a theory of the reflective professional within academic practice. This chapter will develop the second framework: a critical matrix of learning in higher education. In this framework, we address the key issue towards which our discussions so far have been moving – learning. Learning emerged in the first chapter as a central feature of the knowledge specification that society contracts with higher education to deliver. There, it mainly focused on student learning and the challenges presented to teachers in higher education. Learning was not considered in terms of learning particular disciplines or areas of knowledge, but with issues of meta-learning (learning to learn) and transferable learning (and the development of transferable skills) within an increasingly changing, uncertain and contestable world. Learning, in this broad sense we argued, challenges the teacher to become a reflective professional.

In Chapter 1, we explored the dialogical and social contructivist character of learning. We considered this understanding of learning in the academic context in terms of two models of academic practice. These two models – *individual/monologue* and *relational/dialogue* – were consistent across the main academic roles of research and teaching. The monologic model, however, contributed to the fragmentation of academic roles, while the dialogic model offered the opportunity for the mutual regeneration of research and teaching through an understanding of learning as central to academic being. Not simply the outcome of one practice (teaching) and of marginal interest to another (research), learning provides the defining feature of both practices and is central to a comprehensive model of academic practice more generally and the reflective professional in particular.

In this chapter, we examine the nature of learning in detail, particularly as it relates to higher education, articulating the conceptual framework set out in this part of the book. Learning, as it relates to students, is not merely a set of concepts or principles that teachers in higher education should be aware of and reflect upon in their own professional practice, but rather frames the whole academic enterprise. Academics are not simply expected to help students meet the demands of their formal studies and the challenges in their lives beyond these studies, but also to meet the demand for ongoing learning themselves. In this sense, learning is situated, part of the ongoing social situation, fundamental to 'life itself' (Jarvis, 1992: 10). As such, it is the very weave of academic and professional being. For students to engage meaningfully in learning, they need to engage legitimately in that weave, admittedly as peripheral participants to begin with but, nevertheless, the learning experience needs to be legitimate, authentically emulating the expert academic and professional learning which is central to the community of practice (Lave and Wenger, 2000a; Wenger et al., 2002) into which they are entering.

Acknowledging learning as the social weave of academic and professional existence provides a useful starting point from which to address the sheer complexity and paradoxes (Jarvis, 1992) of learning. This weave of learning encompasses a range of intellectual, personal, social, cultural, ethical, political, practical obligations, interests and concerns which students will need to both address and balance in their lives. These go far beyond the learning demands of specific discipline knowledge or of general transferable skills. Barnett uses Habermas's term 'life-world' to describe 'the total world experience of human-beings' (1994: 178) which higher education must address. He contrasts it with teaching that limits its practice to the intellectual 'academic competence' of the discipline-world or to the practical 'operational competence' of the work-world.

Teaching needs to address and engage the wider multiple discourses of the 'life-world'. These may include, for example, an ability to respond meaningfully to and critique one's own responses to political debates, health issues, cultural matters, social and family relationships, works of art, diverse social groupings and ways of thinking, voluntary and charitable services, the media, leisure activities and even religious experience. It requires an ability to critique these from multiple frames and perspectives in open, democratic and socially just ways. It even demands the ability to critique one's grounds for critique. Learning so conceived is not a process of individual knowledge construction within a socially and culturally stable situation, but is unstable and uncertain precisely because, paradoxically, it is constructed within both an increasing globally connected world and an increasingly fragmented and changing world.

Faced with the complexity of the 'life-world' alongside its apparent limitless potential for change, describing the nature of this 'learning weave' is difficult, let alone developing strategies for facilitating, assisting, supporting, fostering and nourishing it. While it may be commonplace to assume that teachers organize learning, this is not the case. Teachers cannot manage the sum of their students' learning, for indeed, learning is not entirely (or even mostly) in the power of the teacher. To suggest otherwise would be naive. Teachers cannot substantially change the character and nature of individual abilities and styles of learning, predispositions towards different intelligences (Gardner, 1993), individual circumstances and histories *vis-à-vis* different educational issues or diverse social and cultural backgrounds. Nevertheless, despite the limits of their influence on 'presage' characteristics (Dunkin and Biddle, 1974) which students bring to the encounter, or the enormity of the teaching challenge, teachers cannot abdicate their responsibility for facilitating substantial learning. Teachers have a huge role and moral obligation in student learning.

Student learning has become a ripe area for research in recent years, developing a productive consensus in many areas. In the following discussion, we shall frame our choices within two general structures. The first is considered within a schema of *learning gaps* (Cox, 1992) which characterize the present and future professional lives of our students. It is used for developing knowledge and understanding of the key issues across a wide range of research and scholarship relevant to student learning. The second presents a *critical matrix of learning*. It describes different ways of framing and shaping learning environments and the central features – knowledge, learner, assessment and community – which constitute them (Bransford et al., 2000). The matrix provides teachers with a conceptual tool for designing, developing and implementing their teaching across the various 'genres' of their teaching practice. Both provide useful conceptual charts for navigating the challenges of understanding and facilitating student learning.

LEARNING GAPS

As we saw in Chapter 1, teachers often see learning as an outcome in terms of a state of knowledge, which students achieve as detached selves, rather than as an outcome in terms of a process of constructing, which they achieve within a given social situation. While teachers may know what they would like their students to achieve, they frequently have a very limited idea of why students are failing to achieve. This situation, moreover, is picked up and acutely felt by students who have no idea of what the nature of the problem is. In such situations, the teacher's response may be limited to rather unhelpful comments about, for example, the student's exam results or coursework not being up to standard, or suggestions that the student is not working hard enough. A deeper understanding of why learning is not achieved is missing: it remains hidden in a kind of 'shadow' land. Here we explore some of the relevant research and literature in terms of how learning might occur. We do so within a framework of five learning 'gaps'. Briefly, these gaps fall between:

• recall and understanding;
• understanding and ability;
• ability and wanting to;
• wanting to and actually doing; and
• actually doing and ongoing change.

These gaps lie within a continuum of different areas of learning – each encompassing the previous ones – laying out the extent of the professional challenge (see Figure 2.1).

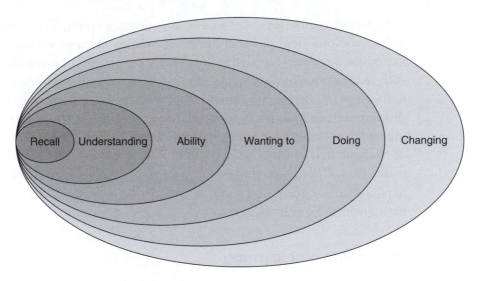

Figure 2.1 *Learning gaps*

At the most basic level, there is a *gap* between the ability of learners to recall or recognize information and being able to understand it. Even if understanding is achieved, however, there can then be a gap between that and being able to or having the abilities/skills actually to put that understanding into practice (practical understanding). In subjects like medicine and dentistry, it has long been clear that students may often be able to write reasonable examination answers and yet be incompetent when faced with real patients. Sometimes efficient learning situations can be devised which result in students with knowledge, understanding and the ability to use that understanding, and yet they end up not actually wanting to use it. The very efficiency of some systems may indeed contribute to turning students away from a real commitment to their subject or their work.

An even bigger gap, one that can be quite disturbing for teachers as well as students, occurs when the student understands, is able to put that understanding into practice, even wants to do so, but still does not actually do so. Of course, there are many excuses, such as timetabling or pressure of work, but there is often a great deal more to it than this.

A final gap – dealing with multiple competing perspectives – emerges with understanding, ability, wanting to and actual doing coupled with a failure to change as the situation of our practice mutates and changes. Many of these gaps have more to do with conceptions of self and the anxieties and threats which students (and teachers) perceive about them, rather than ignorance or a lack of competence.

In exploring these gaps, we focus on key areas of learning. The organization we propose provides a holistic, integrated schema for approaching learning-in-practice, yet is not intended as an all-embracing model of learning. Indeed, such models often 'get in the way of developing an understanding of the differing strategies necessary to enable diverse adults to learn different things in different settings in different ways' (Hanson, 1993: 107). We explore competing traditions, examining their distinctive contributions for the development of teaching. Individually, they allow us to look at the pertinent features of particular gaps. Collectively, they establish a rich conceptual framework of learning that teachers might find useful in critically reflecting upon and improving their professional practice.

Motivation and learning

To a large extent, motivation characterizes the learning gaps. Traditionally, motivation has been viewed within two dimensions, intrinsic (a person acts out of spontaneous interest or an inherent satisfaction in seeking out novelty or challenges) and extrinsic (a person acts to attain a separate outcome) (Ryan and Deci, 2000). For Ryan and Deci (2000), distinguishing between intrinsic and extrinsic cannot fully encapsulate what moves people to act (or not). Indeed, they suggest that much of what people do is not intrinsically motivated at all. Human beings require autonomy and self-determination – a sense of choice and control over their own actions and environment – in order to grow and develop. People may be moved to act by a variety of factors, but only when the process is internally controlled and authentic (self-authored or 'real') will individuals be excited, interested and confident. We see this in persistence, creativity, enhanced performance, heightened self-esteem and wellbeing, which may be lacking when people feel more externally controlled (Ryan and Deci, 2000).

On one end of the motivational continuum, an individual may not act at all, or act without intent. This occurs when the person sees no value in an activity, lacks confidence or has no expectation of the desired outcome. The activity is seen as completely beyond the individual's perceived locus of control. Similarly, if an individual performs a behaviour to satisfy an external request, such behaviour may be viewed as controlled or alien ('University regulations say that I need to attend class'). An individual might 'take in' a regulation, but not accept it; the behaviour is performed to avoid failure (guilt or anxiety) or to prove one's worth (pride) ('If I fail this course, my parents will not pay my tuition' or 'I have to do better than Denise and Marina').

Moving along the continuum, an individual may perform a behaviour because he or she consciously values or owns it as personally important ('It's important that I receive top marks in university, because I've always identified myself as a top student'). Finally, although an individual may not be moved to act completely out of an innate sense of satisfaction, a person can come very close when regulations and behaviours are congruent with one's values and needs, and assimilated to one's self ('I really enjoying learning biology; this will help me one day when I am a doctor'). This is very close to intrinsic motivation, but is still considered extrinsic because the action is done to attain separate outcomes, rather than for an inherent pleasure that is completely internally controlled. Essentially, motivation is enhanced when individuals feel a strong sense of control by being offered choices and autonomy. Ultimately, the decision to act depends on the degree to which a person 'internalizes' a value or regulation, and the extent to which he or she 'integrates' the value or regulation (makes it their own) (Ryan and Deci, 2000). Thus, motivation plays out differently in each of the gaps discussed below.

1. THE GAP BETWEEN RECALL AND UNDERSTANDING

The gap between the knowledge that a student can recall and her real understanding of that knowledge can be substantial. Essentially it is concerned with the distinction between seeing learning as simply the ability to remember and reproduce facts and ideas, or as the ability to understand and reconstruct those facts and ideas in terms of one's own experience. Researchers using a phenomenographic approach for analysing learning have focused on issues central to this gap. Phenomenography is a qualitative research programme that is concerned 'with what is culturally learned and with what are individually developed ways of relating ourselves to the world around us' (Marton, 1988a: 181). Phenomenographers 'do not make statements about the world as such, but about people's conceptions of the world' (Marton, 1988b: 145). The key contribution of this perspective – that learning occurs with 'a change in conception' (Dahlgren, 2005: 34) – is that 'what' we experience and understand of our social reality is inseparable from 'how' we experience and understand it (Marton et al., 2005).

Approaches to learning

While personality differences play some role in student approaches to studying and learning (Biggs et al., 2007), research has shown that students' approaches to learning are linked to their perceptions of their academic

Table 2.1   *Approaches to learning*

Deep approach

Transforming
Intention – to understand ideas for yourself:
- Relating ideas to previous knowledge and experience
- Looking for patterns and underlying principles
- Checking evidence and relating it to conclusions
- Examining logic and argument cautiously and critically
- Becoming actively interested in the course content

Surface approach

Reproducing
Intention – to cope with the course requirements:
- Studying without reflecting on either purpose or strategy
- Treating the course as unrelated bits of knowledge
- Memorizing facts and procedures routinely
- Finding difficulty in making sense of the new ideas presented
- Feeling undue pressure and worry about work

Strategic approach

Organizing
Intention – to achieve the highest possible grades:
- Putting a consistent effort into studying
- Finding the right conditions and materials for studying
- Managing time and effort effectively
- Being alert to assessment requirements and criteria
- Gearing work to the perceived preference of lecturers

Source: Adapted from Entwistle, 2005: 19

environment, particularly to the perceived quality of the course, in terms of the content, context and demands of the learning task (Richardson, 2005). Phenomenographic research on student learning has suggested that there are three qualitatively distinct approaches to learning: deep, surface and strategic (Entwistle, 2005) (see Table 2.1).

Students who take a *deep* approach to learning intend to understand the subject in a way that is personally meaningful, engaging their own experience and previous knowledge in an interactive (dialogical) process with the relevant content, logic and existing evidence of the subject. Learning is essentially a transformative experience in which the students make or construct personal meaning out of the shared meanings available. Their intention is to understand ideas for themselves by constructing their own meaning. On the other hand, students who adopt a *surface* learning approach intend to *use* or *reproduce* the available meanings in an instrumental way to deal with course requirements. The students will use the meanings, but perceive them as alien and externally imposed. As such, they are often simply approached through memorization or by reproducing the course material; there is no sustained personal engagement with the student's own experience and their previous knowledge. Learning is a reproductive experience and students who take a surface approach often struggle with new material and may feel pressured in their work.

The *strategic* approach to learning is sometimes seen as adopting elements of both the surface and deep approaches. *Strategic*-focused students are mainly concerned with achieving the highest possible grades, and tend to be alert and responsive to the cues they pick up about the nature of the tasks and demands made upon them. They will seek to determine and meet the instructor's learning outcome preferences. Learning is essentially an organizing experience in which effort and time are strategically managed to achieve the best grades. Even students who are inclined to take a deep approach to their learning will at times find it is more strategic to employ a surface approach if, for example, the assessment methods suggest that memorization of facts will meet the requirements more effectively (Entwistle, 2005).

Study orientations

The categories of approach to learning correlate significantly with similar dimensions disclosed in a range of other research on student learning (Entwistle, 2005). They have, for example, been linked to three general *orientations* to study: *meaning, reproducing* and *strategic* (Ramsden, 1992/2003). Pask (1976) has also reported similar distinctions in learning, contrasting 'comprehension learning' which uses analogies to build up meaningful descriptions of topics by emphasizing the outline of ideas and interconnections, with 'operation learning' which relies on a step-by-step, logical approach often emphasizing the reproduction of factual details. Biggs (2003) distinguishes between *intrinsic* (meaning-oriented) and *extrinsic* (outcome-oriented) motivations in student learning. Students are intrinsically motivated to learn when the task or activity intrigues them, and motivated extrinsically when they perform a task to achieve a specific outcome. He also identifies an *achievement* motivation where students learn in order to compete against other students.

Conceptions of learning

Students will also hold a *conception* of learning that may be different from their approach to learning and studying. The idea of 'conception of learning' grew out of the original research on approaches to learning. A conception of

Table 2.2 *Conceptions of learning*

1. A quantitative increase in knowledge	
2. Memorizing	*Reproducing*
3. Acquisition of facts and methods, etc.	
4. The abstraction of meaning	
5. An interpretative process aimed at understanding	*Transforming*
6. Developing as a person	

Source: Marton et al., 1993

learning, however, refers to the general perceptions or preconceived ideas of learning from past experiences that students bring to the learning context (Marton and Saljo, 2005). Conceptions of learning describe students' (and teachers') broad experience or understanding of what learning consists of. An individual can also have a conception of a discipline or subject, such as history or mathematics (Entwistle, 2005), or a conception of a particular practice such as essay writing (Hounsell, 2005) or creative writing (Light, 1995). Even more narrowly, a conception can describe how students understand a particular topic or idea in a syllabus. We focus here on the wider application of this concept as a key descriptor of more general ideas and understandings of learning. Table 2.2 presents six learning conceptions divided into two general categories: *reproducing* and *transforming*.

The contrast between reproducing and transforming conceptions corresponds closely to the above distinctions in both approaches to learning and learning orientations described above: a correspondence demonstrated by Van Rossum and Schenk (1984). It is very difficult to encourage the development of deep approaches to learning in a particular learning situation with students who hold a general reproducing conception of learning. These conceptions may also be seen as constituting a developmental continuum. Students may enter higher education with initial reproducing conceptions, but are expected to leave with more developed 'transforming' conceptions. Their more general learning will largely rest in such change. The research describing conception has essentially been characterized by a cognitive perspective. The sixth conception, developing as a person (which was added later), indicates features of conception that go beyond the cognitive to encompass more personal characteristics, although these are not fully developed.

Entwistle and Entwistle (1992) suggest that understanding is best viewed 'not as a cognitive process, but as an experience' characterized by feelings of satisfaction, confidence and significance. In their study of conceptions of learning, they describe a hierarchy of the forms of understanding described by students. At the least sophisticated level, the student is 'limited to grasping material presented directly by a lecturer or through required reading' (Entwistle and Entwistle, 1992: 13) and is basically concerned with remembering facts or procedures. In contrast, at the most sophisticated level, the student independently and actively develops his or her own structures and extends the breadth of material across topic, course and discipline.

This research on learning approaches, orientations and conceptions enables us to reflect on how our pedagogical strategies, and the teaching and learning environment we establish, might aid or hinder students' negotiation of the gap from recall to a more genuine understanding. Students' choices of assessment, what they choose to study and how they choose to study, as well as their workload and the overall quality of teaching, all play an important role in the development of learning (Ramsden, 2005). Bridging this first gap is a valuable starting point, but it is not enough.

2. THE GAP BETWEEN UNDERSTANDING AND HAVING THE ABILITY/SKILLS TO PRACTISE EFFECTIVELY

We might expect, from the above discussion, that a student who takes a deep or transforming approach to learning – with its emphasis upon meaning making and the relationship to personal experience – will be more likely to possess the abilities to perform than a student taking a surface or reproducing approach. Research, however, has not generally made a great deal of this relationship, tending to focus on the purely intellectual arena with less importance given to practice.

Experiential learning

The work of Kolb (1984) and others who stress the critical importance of experience in learning helps explain the gap between understanding and having the ability and skills to practise. In his now classic work, *Experiential Learning* (1984), Kolb develops a comprehensive theory of learning that stresses the fundamental role of experience in learning: '*Learning is the process whereby knowledge is created through the transformation of experience*' (Kolb, 1984: 38, emphasis in original). Echoing the idea of learning as a 'transformation' in the previous section, experiential learning focuses on a transformation that is both active by definition and explicitly grounded in the concrete social environment in which experience occurs.

Building on Dewey (1938), Kolb describes experience as a transaction between an individual and what, at the time, constitutes his environment. It is a 'fluid interpenetrating relationship such that once they (person and environment) become related, both are essentially changed' (Kolb, 1984: 36).

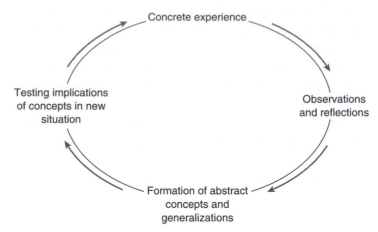

Figure 2.2 *Experiential learning cycle*
Source: Kolb, 1984: 21

Drawing on the organizational development work of Lewin (1951), Kolb further argues that learning is 'best facilitated in an environment where there is a dialectic tension and conflict between immediate, concrete experience and analytic detachment' (1984: 36). He has concisely illustrated his theoretical discussion in the widely used cycle of experiential learning (see Figure 2.2). In this four-stage cycle, immediate concrete experience provides the basis for observation and reflection. These observations are, in turn, assimilated into abstract concepts and generalizations ('theories') from which implications for action can be read and developed. These implications may be regarded as 'hypotheses' that then serve as guides for action, for testing in new concrete situations and, thereby, for generating new concrete experiences.

The experiential learning cycle incorporates a feedback process directed towards active experimentation and the abilities/skills that that requires. In higher education, such abilities will differ according to different curricula but may include such things as:

- writing essays and reports;
- giving presentations;
- engaging in discussion;
- leading discussion;
- working on a task as part of a team;
- performing experiments;
- solving a group problem;

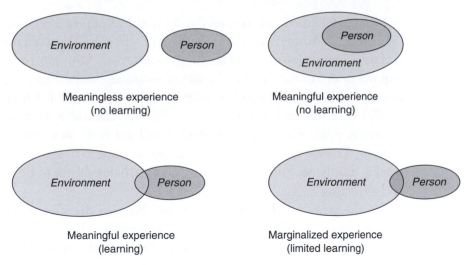

Figure 2.3 *Learning: response to experience*

- engaging in research;
- carrying out clinical duties;
- undertaking projects;
- assessing peers; and
- evaluating teaching and learning environments.

At its most effective, this learning cycle ensures critical and reflective, goal-directed action and evaluation of the consequences of that action. Although the Kolb cycle has been criticized for not fully capturing the complexity of the process (Jarvis et al., 1998: 48) and for leaving out important aspects of experience such as emotions and feelings (Boud, 1995), its main contribution, for our purposes, is the intrinsic space it provides within active learning for the development of the skills and abilities inherent in the generation of new and meaningful experience.

Experience and meaning

An important feature of the effectiveness of an experiential learning cycle is getting the balance right between experience, reflection, theory and the action they lead towards. While one must be careful about reducing what is essentially a holistic cycle to its constituent parts, it does provide a way of looking at problems that may be blocking the achievement of learning. Not all experience, for example, is 'meaningful' or results in learning. Figure 2.3 illustrates a series of relationships between experience and learning.

Meaningful experience requires that an initial set of premises or meanings – knowledge, skills, attitudes, values, beliefs, etc. – be shared between the student and their specific learning and teaching environment. Learning, paradoxically, requires a 'disjuncture' in the sharing of meanings: 'disjuncture, or discontinuity, between biography and experience of the wider world is a fundamental condition of human learning' (Jarvis, 1987: 80). If there is a full overlap of meanings, while it may be meaningful, it will not result in new meanings or learning. There is nothing new to the learner, nothing to be learnt. Indeed, the overlap may be so complete, repetitive and unchangeable as to be oppressive and alienating.

On the other hand, a full 'disjuncture' between the student's life-world and the situation will render the experience meaningless. There is nothing for the learner to make a connection with. Importantly, life-world experience can be marginalized by the learning environment so as to undermine the possibility of meaningful connections. While there is an overlap of relevant meanings between the student and the environment, the prevailing authority and discourses within the environment are perceived as not accepting or permitting the student's experience – for a range of social reasons including issues of class, gender, age, ethnicity, etc. (Light, 1996) – and will thereby limit the student's learning.

Stereotype threat

In recent years, more attention has been paid to 'stereotype threat' – the idea that learning environments that raise prevailing social stereotypes around academic ability can trigger significant hurdles to learning in even the most intellectually able students whose experience of ethnicity, race, gender or class is linked to those stereotypes (Steele, 1997). Members of stereotyped groups may feel extra pressure or anxiety about performing if they believe that their performance will confirm a negative reputation, such as women's ability to perform quantitative work or African-Americans' ability to achieve a high score on standardized tests (Steele, 1997; Aronson et al., 1999). As Rodney Ellis, an African-American state senator from Texas, once remarked: 'For some reason I didn't score well on tests. Maybe I was just nervous. There's a lot of pressure on you, knowing that if you fail, you fail your race' (1997, cited in Aronson et al., 1999: 29). In the short term, the individual's academic performance may be injured, but faced over the long term, stereotype threat may invoke a sustained defence 'against the chronic exposure to ability impugning stereotypes and the low performance that it can provoke – a disengagement or "disidentification" from the threatened domain, a dropping of the domain as a basis of self-esteem' (Aronson et al., 1999: 35).

While stereotype threat is often associated with members of minority or under-represented groups, Aronson and his associates (1999) further found that members of any social group can be affected negatively by stereotypes, enough to impair their academic abilities, even if that person is not regularly subjected to stereotyped assumptions. For example, researchers suggested to high-achieving white males that a group of achieving Asian males might outperform them on a standardized maths exam. The results showed a sharp decline in intellectual performance 'much like the members of groups for whom stereotypes regarding their intellectual abilities *do* exist and *are* widely known and cognitively available. Clearly, then, chronic feelings of stigmatization were not a necessary factor in their underperformance' (Aronson et al., 1999: 40). But they did have to care about their personal identity in terms of performing well, in order to be bothered by the underlying assumption of the stereotype that they lacked a valued ability.

Reflection and experience

Like the social meanings embedded in the personal experience students bring to the learning situation, reflection on that experience is also a more complex relationship than is often thought. Responses to experience may result in non-reflective as well as reflective forms of learning (Jarvis, 1987). Non-reflective learning includes reproductive practices such as memorization, imitation and the development of rote skills. Reflective learning includes contemplation, experimental learning and the development of reflective skills. Boud and Walker (1998) point out that 'acts of reflection can become ritualized', particularly when they are encouraged, even imposed through prescribed activities within the learning situation.

Reflection, like experience, is context dependent, sensitive to the social and political environment in which it occurs. Reflective learning may also occur during action or actual experience. Schon (1983) distinguishes 'reflection-on-action' – which the Kolb cycle suggests – from 'reflection-in-action' occurring simultaneously with an activity or practice. Argyris and Schon (1978) also differentiate between two theories of action employed in practice: 'espoused-theory' used to explain actions and 'theory-in-use' that actually governs practices and actions. An existing but incompatible theory-in-use may inhibit learning new 'theory'. Although a student may appear to have a new understanding, their actual skills and abilities are not being developed, as they are still embedded in already fixed theories.

Table 2.3   *Learning environments*

1. *Affectively complex*	2. *Perceptually complex*
• Focus on here-and-now experiences, legitimization of expression of feeling and emotions • Situations structured to allow ambiguity • High degree of personalization	• Opportunities to view subject matter from different perspectives • Time to reflect and roles (e.g. listener, observer) which allow reflection • Complexity of multiplicity of observational frameworks
3. *Symbolically complex*	4. *Behaviourally complex*
• Emphasis on recall of concepts • Thinking or acting governed by rules of logic and inference • Situations structured to maximize certainty • Authorities respected as caretakers of knowledge	• Responsibility for setting own learning goals • Opportunities for real risk taking • Environmental responses contingent upon self-initiated action

Learning environments

The literature associated with the gap between recall and understanding revealed the key role that the pedagogical formation of the learning situation plays in relation to student learning. The experiential learning literature linked to the gap, here, between understanding and ability focuses our attention on the role of the learning situation in construing experience, and the students' opportunities for developing abilities and skills to put their understandings into practice. Working through its implications leads to a more complex and differentiated view of learning environments.

Kolb, for example, analysed four different types of environment (see Table 2.3), which illuminate the affectively complex, the perceptually complex, the symbolically complex and the behaviourally complex. It is worth noting that the 'symbolically complex' environment (in Table 2.3) maps closely to the 'teacher-oriented' transmission teaching conceptions described in the last chapter. The other three, however, begin to map the learning environment more closely to different aspects of the 'learning-oriented' teaching conceptions. While this experiential learning perspective may aid us in the alignment of teaching and learning environments more conducive to promoting skills and the ability to put understanding into practice, designing learning environments to meet the wide range of learning needs and wants of students is still problematic. Indeed, this may be particularly the case with today's millennial students who, as research suggests, may enter college as high achievers, and yet in their pressure to perform may paradoxically lack basic problem-solving and decision-making skills and abilities (Howe and Strauss, 2003).

Learning environments that focus specifically on providing students with the experience of learning in the context of real-life problems have become more common at institutions of higher education, since they first emerged in the late 1960s. Such environments are designed around problem-based learning, project-based learning, inquiry-based learning and inquiry-guided learning activities. They may differ in implementation and structure. For example, in problem-based learning, an entire course or curriculum may be designed around a problem (Boud and Feletti, 1997/2001), while in inquiry-based learning, the problem may be the focus of one lecture or one assignment (Lee, 2004). They do, however, employ similar approaches, requiring students to tackle one substantial, open-ended or 'ill-structured' question or problem, or a set of related questions and problems. Students often work in groups or teams to address the problem, although individual self-directed learning is also expected.

3. THE GAP BETWEEN HAVING THE SKILLS/ABILITIES AND ACTUALLY WANTING TO USE THEM

It may be that courses and degrees which are effective in increasing knowledge, encouraging understanding and the acquisition of appropriate skills and abilities will also, almost as a corollary, be effective at developing a willingness, even an aspiration, to go on learning or working in a particular field. Yet many courses encourage the feeling that, after the certificates and the degrees have been awarded, the books will be shut for good. And while the accumulation of qualifications and letters after the name might have its own emotional satisfaction, in the present social and economic climate, the experience of learning needs to be a willing part of lifelong professional development. Certainly the immense satisfaction that so often arises in understanding and deriving meaning from almost any aspect of life – from the jigsaw puzzle to the most complex questions of nature – is a crucial part of *wanting to*. This is particularly true of meaning which one is able to integrate with one's own experience and put into practice. Nevertheless, for a variety of reasons this may not be sufficient. Wanting to and a corresponding commitment to act may falter.

Drawing on his long work with students at Harvard, Perry (1970, 1998) became very concerned with this question of commitment. He found that very often there is a distinctive developmental process related to students' changing conceptions of learning, teaching and knowledge, which is at the same time part of a more personal development involving emotional issues of personal commitment. He identified a complex developmental process illustrating how the progress of students through higher education is punctuated by a number of important positions and transitions which often have a profound influence on their learning. His widely reported 'scheme of intellectual and ethical development' – depicted here in a simplified version (see Table 2.4) – describes nine positions in student development (Perry, 1998).

The first three positions in Table 2.4 move through a dualistic perspective in which the student regards knowledge and learning as something external and objective, right or wrong. This sort of epistemological perspective is extremely difficult to give up if it is held with any conviction, a conviction that quite often goes back to early childhood and may be strongly invested with emotion. Teachers and the learning environment may have been vested with many of the qualities of parental or childhood authority figures. The difficult transition from the security of dualism into the insecurity of relativism is not simply a matter of absorbing new ideas or information, but is very much a restructuring at an emotional as well as a cognitive level, and may be accompanied by extreme anxiety. If, on the other hand, the student remains defensive about uncertainty, they may become certain with a comparable conviction that anything goes and that there are no valid reasons for anything!

The move into the final three positions can again be accompanied by anxieties where the student recognizes learning as making and balancing commitments within relativism, within ever changing situations. When students make this move, however, commitments may be an extremely important source for wanting to do things. Longer-term and deeper commitments will arise out of seeing that commitments need revising because of deeper understanding and new experiences. Wanting to do things becomes part of a new, evolving structure and one which will hold interesting challenges and new perspectives in the future (Perry, 1998).

Perry's model has been critiqued and developed by scholars concerned that his scheme of intellectual and ethical development did not adequately encompass the decision-making frameworks and worldviews of others beyond the mostly male Harvard students interviewed in his original study. Most notably, Belenky and associates (1986/1997) considered the epistemological development of women. They grouped 'women's ways of knowing' into five major epistemological categories:

- *Silence* (women experience themselves as 'mindless and voiceless and subject to the whims of external authority').
- *Received knowledge* (women view themselves as receiving, or reproducing knowledge, from external authorities, but unable to create their own knowledge).

Table 2.4 *Intellectual and ethical development*

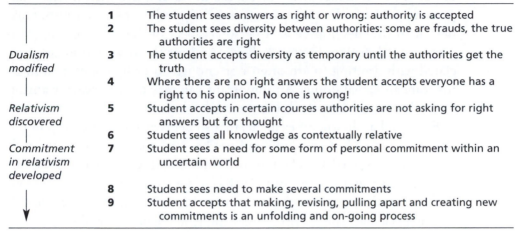

	1	The student sees answers as right or wrong: authority is accepted
	2	The student sees diversity between authorities: some are frauds, the true authorities are right
Dualism modified	**3**	The student accepts diversity as temporary until the authorities get the truth
	4	Where there are no right answers the student accepts everyone has a right to his opinion. No one is wrong!
Relativism discovered	**5**	Student accepts in certain courses authorities are not asking for right answers but for thought
	6	Student sees all knowledge as contextually relative
Commitment in relativism developed	**7**	Student sees a need for some form of personal commitment within an uncertain world
	8	Student sees need to make several commitments
	9	Student accepts that making, revising, pulling apart and creating new commitments is an unfolding and on-going process

Source: Perry, 1998

- *Subjective knowledge* (women view truth and knowledge as 'personal, private, and subjectively known and intuited').
- *Procedural knowledge* (women are 'invested in learning and applying objective procedures for obtaining and communicating knowledge').
- *Constructed knowledge* (women perceive all knowledge as contextual, consider themselves to be creators of knowledge and 'value both subjective and objective strategies for knowing') (Belenky et al., 1997: 15).

Intellectually effective and efficient teaching practices are frequently not sufficient to encourage students to put their understandings into practice. They must at the same time understand and construct the social and emotional context for wanting to make commitments. Paradoxically, much successful teaching does not consist of finding ways for constructing knowledge, but of ways for deconstructing some of the fiercely dualist and even purely relativist positions to which students cling. Such positions constrain them from wanting to make commitments and to put into practice their developing understandings and skills.

4. THE GAP BETWEEN HAVING THE ABILITIES, WANTING TO USE THEM AND ACTUALLY DOING SO

From the previous section, we can see that the teaching environment supporting the development of wanting to involves much more that simply providing knowledge and skills. A genuine wanting-to requires a significant degree of change in many of the ways students perceive and understand knowledge and, indeed, the world in which their intellectual, personal and social commitments must be made. There is a resonance here with the 'developing as a person' aspect of the transforming conceptions of learning discussed above. And yet the deeper changes associated with wanting to are often not enough to bring about action, to instigate an actual doing. An important gap may exist between wanting to do things and actually doing them.

Research has shown, for example, that students avoid seeking help in the classroom out of both practical and psychosocial concerns. As Ryan et al. (2001) have suggested, the physical environment and culture of the classroom are important. A large vacuous classroom, for example, may not be conducive to student questions but, even more significantly, the classroom culture (implicit and explicit norms, rules and requirements) may also inhibit or discourage a student from seeking help. Students may also believe that there is no point in asking for help if they hold a negative opinion of the instructor's expertise or knowledge, or if they believe it will take too long to get the assistance they need (Ryan et al., 2001).

Even if a classroom environment is conducive to questions, students may still avoid seeking help out of a strong, possibly misplaced, desire for autonomy ('I can do it myself') or because they are reluctant to display a perceived weakness or lack of competence. Students may, for example, believe their peers or professor will view them as 'dumb' if they ask for help, especially if they view themselves as low achievers or less competent than their peers. Similarly, students who perceive themselves as less socially competent than their peers will also find it more challenging to seek help (Ryan and Pintrich, 1997; Ryan et al., 2001). Finally, student perceptions of instructor support (Karabenick and Sharma, 1994) play an important role in help-seeking behaviour, as do achievement and performance goals established by the instructor and the social/interpersonal climate of the classroom (Ryan et al., 2001).

There are, of course, very real practical reasons why people do not do things, but quite often these things can be a smokescreen for something else: deep concerns and threats which are felt, for example, in the face of taking on some new role. The problem, here, is often related to issues of self and self-identity. In order to act on new knowledge and skills, it may be that developing a new perspective is not sufficient. A student needs to develop a new self. This requires a deeper transformation of self.

Adult learning

Knowles (1978) originally coined the term 'andragogy' to describe a model of learning that he felt was distinctive of adults. He contrasted it with

Table 2.5 *Model of adult learning*

1. The learner's need to know	Why, what, how
2. The concept of the learner	Being self-directing
	Responsible for own learning
3. Prior experience of the learner	Being a rich resource for themselves and each other
	Mental models
4. Readiness to learn	Life-related
	Developmental task
	When they experience a need to know or do something in order to perform more effectively (can be encouraged)
5. Orientation to learning	Task or problem-centred
6. Motivation to learn	Internal, intrinsic
	Self-esteem
	Confidence
	Self-actualization
	Personal payoff

Source: Adapted from Knowles et al., 2005

'pedagogy' which he felt was more concerned with the learning of children. Updated in 2005, the main features of the *andragogical* model (see Table 2.5) focus on the concept of self as being responsible for one's own life, of being self-directed, a concept Knowles initially argued was characteristic of adults (as opposed to children). It attributes to adults a rich social and cultural reservoir of meaningful experience, a readiness to learn characterized by a real need to know and do; a life-centred, problem-centred and task-centred orientation to learning; and intrinsic, personal and emotional motivators such as confidence and self-esteem.

While andragogy was originally sharply contrasted with pedagogy, the two are better conceived as a continuum. The social context of the learning situation favours or hinders particular experience in such a way that some 'pedagogic' assumptions are more appropriate for adults and some andragogical assumptions more appropriate for children. Adult refers to a social age, rather than a biological age (Knowles et al., 2005). The marginalization of relevant experience might, for example, contribute to reducing the student's experience and moving him or her towards the 'pedagogical' end of the continuum. This is especially significant for higher education, because of the large number of younger students who are often poised – socially and biologically – between the two ends of the continuum. They can be particularly vulnerable to courses which, however unintentionally, 'demote' them, in the face of the superior knowledge, expertise and confidence of the teachers.

Andragogy does not, then, define a unique theory of learning with respect to 'adultness', but it does raise important issues for teaching practice (Merriam, 1993). This is especially so regarding the development of a 'self-directed' learning self, as opposed to a 'teacher-directed' learning self. To surmount this gap, quality of experience, volume of experience and even transformation of experience in the construction of knowledge are not sufficient. It is the role they play in the transformation of the person towards a critically self-directed and emancipated self that matters. To put into practice their understandings, actually to 'do', may require a critical reconstruction of self within the broader social, cultural and political situation. It must recognize the freedoms (Boud, 1989) that such a reconstruction requires (freedom in learning) and generates (freedom through learning). It encompasses 'conscientization' (Freire, 2000) or perspective 'transformation' (Mezirow, 1983). Mezirow describes an 'emancipatory process of becoming critically aware of how and why the structure of psycho-cultural assumptions has come to constrain the way we see ourselves and our relationships, reconstituting this structure to permit a more inclusive and discriminating integration of experience and acting upon these new understandings' (1983: 4).

The failure of doing, of actual concrete action, is often an issue of whether the student has constructed a learning self which is truly self-directing within the social overlap of his or her experience and the experiences of the learning situation. As we noted above, the experiential overlap is critically important and undermined by courses that ignore or marginalize student experience. The structure of the learning situation itself is also important, particularly the opportunities it affords the student to take responsibility and control of their learning and also of the methods, procedures and activities which structure the learning environment. Encouraging self-direction means not only sharing the social and cultural premises or meanings of the learning environment but also sharing control of the teaching and learning activities. This constitutes the nucleus of self-direction in learning: 'At the heart of self-directness is the adult's assumption of control over setting goals and generating personally meaningful evaluative criteria. One cannot be a self-directed learner if one is applying techniques of independent study within a context of goals determined by an external authority' (Brookfield, 1986: 19). Self-directed learning occurs when teaching and learning become the same thing, neither leading nor trailing one another. For Rogers this is closely associated with meta-learning:

> the goal of education, if we are to survive, is the facilitation of change and learning. The only man who is educated is the man who has learned how to learn; the man who has learned how to adapt and change; the man who

has realised that no knowledge is secure, that only the process of seeking knowledge gives a basis for security (1969: 103).

The construction of such learning environments is, again, not easy, particularly for young students in the first years of their undergraduate studies. It may also be inappropriate to the learning situation and counterproductive to learning. But the development of self-directed students – students who have not only developed a deeper understanding of their subject and the abilities and skills to put it into practice, but also want to and actually do put them into practice – is one of the key challenges facing teachers in higher education.

It is not sufficient to encourage students to cross a limited number of these gaps. Teaching must provide the opportunity for all to be positively addressed. The tacit message at the centre of many learning environments is that if you follow the prescribed programme and methods and work hard you will be successful. But at what cost? Success may simply result in the construction of conformist and dependent selves and self-identities, identities that play an extremely important role in preventing us from doing what we want to do.

5. THE GAP BETWEEN ACTUALLY USING THE SKILLS/ABILITIES AND CHANGING

It appears odd to refer to this as a gap in which one position is change. As the above comment from Rogers illustrates, change has been a crucial theme in all the learning issues that we have been addressing in this chapter. What is meant here, however, is something more complex. If helping students to cross the other learning gaps has been a key process of change, crossing this gap is also a process of change, but it is a process to a position of *changing*, to a situation in which change is an ever-present and defining feature. This gap is concerned with the integration of continuous change as an intrinsic aspect of learning and practice, of being in the life-world, of supercomplexity. Students leaving college today will find the world they enter 'to be one of ever-widening uncertainty, challenge and conflict, bearing on the three domains of knowledge, action and self. Criteria of truth, the will to act and the sense of one's identity will be relentlessly tested and will be subject to continuing change' (Barnett and Hallam, 1999: 149).

Yet, even this articulation is not fully sufficient to describe the 'supercomplex' condition for which we are preparing our students and ourselves.

The issue is not simply facilitating the capacity for change *over* time – and the reconstruction of knowledge, action and self which this entails – but also facilitating the capacity for change *within* simultaneous time. It requires the ability to operate with and switch between different synchronous perspectives and frames of thinking and action. Students need to develop the ability to make a series of ongoing commitments and challenges, as well as the ability to shift between them, to cope with change within the 'synchronous' demands of multiple perspectives. This condition of 'changing' requires capabilities for:

- the construction of multiple identities and selves which can be sustained simultaneously;
- the practice of these multiple frames of knowledge-action-self to critique one another;
- the management of this multiplicity and synchronicity of thought, action and being within the appropriate present and future situation; and
- the continuous integration, critique and development of this synchronous multiplicity in future learning.

The challenge is to construct a 'curriculum of the future' (Young, 1998) which is not simply for the future but of the future.

Being of the future, this curriculum must reflect in its vision, design and implementation the 'uncertainty, unpredictability, contestability and challengeability' (Barnett, 2000: 159) which the future, increasingly and more pervasively, injects into the present. It is this escalating overlap of the future with the present that defines the nature of the 'supercomplex' condition. Our teaching and pedagogical structures need to reflect this condition in our own understanding, the students' understanding and the shared learning environment. Barnett describes such a new conception of higher education as having three key objectives: to create epistemological and ontological disturbance in the minds/beings of students; to enable students to live at ease with this perplexing and unsettling environment; and to enable them to make their own positive contributions to this supercomplex world (2000: 160).

The overall challenge for teaching and learning, which this fifth gap discloses, is to prepare our graduates for conditions mirroring the teacher's own professional conditions. It is no less an important teaching challenge for being shared with our students. It means that ownership of the learning environment that we design and construct should not only be shared with our students but with ourselves as well. As teachers with learning responsibilities (research, scholarship, professional practice, etc.) within a range of disciplinary and institutional structures and traditions this design must go further than the traditional teaching situation. It must, as we saw in Chapter 1, incorporate other academic practices and will include the ability to reframe one's teaching and learning within the multiple frames of research and service. Our own professional development as academics is, thus, implicit in our own teaching.

THE LEARNING SITUATION: STRUCTURES OF MEANING

The boundaries between many of the different theoretical perspectives on learning discussed in the above schema of learning gaps are not intended to be precise or definitive. Overlaps and vital inter-relationships abound. Many of the issues relating to the achievement of learning in one 'gap' are of central importance in others as well. Despite their different approaches, these theoretical perspectives provide a useful basis for reflection on the complex issues characterizing the achievement of student learning – issues which teaching can successfully address. As Laurillard suggests:

> Students will not suddenly switch to being the model of holistic, deep and epistemologically sophisticated learners ... Teaching must create a learning environment ... at every level of description of the learning situation: i.e. conceptual structure, actions, feedback and goal must relate to each other so that integration can work. (1993: 93)

In this section, we develop a model of the structure of meaning characterizing the teaching/learning context. It is intended as a conceptual 'tool' to assist practitioners to address the above learning 'gaps' while exploring their own teaching responsibilities and practices.

The above discussion touched on a wide range of pertinent issues and themes, but the central concepts throughout were 'meaning' and 'context': meaning constructed within the social context in which the learning encounter occurs. The key to traversing each gap is an active construction and integration of meaning in the social situation. Learning is not concerned with decoding and recalling information but rather with the process of social and practical understanding. It is an active and meaningful construction of facts, ideas, concepts, theories and experiences in order to work and manage successfully in a changing world of multiple and synchronous demands. It goes beyond the intellectual to encompass the personal, practical and social dimensions of students' learning life. For all intents and purposes these dimensions refer to how students think, feel, act and interact in the world (Bain, 2004).

The multidimensional nature of learning is a product of the social context, its character, development and practice. It is also substantially shaped by the nature of the learning environment offered to the student. Even recognizing that the meaningful integration of learner, knowledge, assessment and community is central to successful learning environments (Bransford et al., 2000), the ways or modes of structuring those meanings are equally important. The modes of this learning environment – the methods and procedures by which the 'learning situation' exercises and realizes its meanings – have a significant role in assisting (or hindering) the student through the gaps described above. Such modes have sometimes been regarded as categories of strategy. Gibbs and Jenkins (1992) refer, for example, to 'control' and 'independence' strategies which teachers may take. These strategies or modes are closely related to the learning contexts from which they arise and which they help to create. Biggs (2003) refers to such contexts as climates and distinguishes between 'X and Y climates'. Teachers forming 'X' climates assume students 'need to be told what to do and what to study', whereas teachers operating in 'Y' climates 'assume students do their best work when given freedom and space to use their own judgements'. Teachers will generally operate with combinations of the two but individual teaching philosophies or conceptions may incline us towards one more than the other.

For the purposes of this discussion, we refer to three general modal contexts which structure learning environments: support, independence and interpersonal. In contexts described by support, *the principal modes of meaning* (e.g. course content, course objectives, teaching strategies, assessment methods, evaluation, etc.) and their implementation are primarily provided by and dependent on the teacher. The modes of meaning in independence contexts, on the other hand, are primarily given to the individual student to specify and perform independently. Finally, the interpersonal context and associated modes of structuring meaning are specified, developed and distributed among the students and with the teacher. Because these contexts inform the different kinds of meaning prevalent in the learning situation differently, we can relate them to the four dimensions of learning and meaning noted above – intellectual, personal, social and practical (see Figure 2.4).

It is not the intention of Figure 2.4 to suggest that certain contexts align more closely to specific dimensions but, rather, 1) that these contexts relate

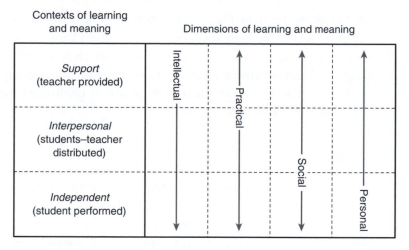

Figure 2.4 *Learning environments: a critical matrix*

to and subsume all four dimensions; and 2) that they are not mutually exclusive but may be usefully integrated within a given learning environment. In thinking about how to address the issues raised in the 'gap' schema, teachers might wish to think about the modal context(s) of meaning they will be using and the most appropriate dimension(s) to focus on, given the learning issues they want to address. There is an extensive range of options and possibilities and those that are the most appropriate will depend upon an array of variables. These will consist of the nature of the discipline, student numbers, student composition, academic background, degree level, and will include a variety of academic, institutional and even national constraints. There is no prescribed 'right way'. Experience generally suggests that a balanced approach is the most effective. 'Balanced', of course, means different things to different professionals in different contexts.

None of the many theories considered here actually advocates a strong controlling environment. Such an environment might encourage a debilitating form of intellectual and personal dependency that would make crossing the individual 'gaps' difficult, and probably impossible. On the other hand, at certain points in the learning process, carefully controlled and managed environments may also be extremely supportive and encouraging. Indeed, the development of self-directed learning depends upon an element of risk-taking. An emotional context that is perceived as independent, cold and aloof may be personally threatening and one in which risks and the development of positive qualities of intellectual independence are avoided. While students might need support in discovering and locating the intellectual material and practical experiences from which they will learn – and are to that degree dependent on teachers and the learning context – they do not need to be told how they should learn from those experiences. In certain situations, considered confusions, contradictions and discrepancies have also been effectively used to encourage students to examine their own assumptions and to make them more aware of habituated ways of perceiving, thinking, feeling and behaving.

CONCLUSIONS

This chapter has drawn upon a wide and diverse range of research on students and adult learning to explore both the potential learning gaps that challenge students in higher and professional education and to draw out the implications for the learning environments which teachers can construct to facilitate student learning. The critical matrix (Figure 2.4) provides a general structure for mapping existing learning environments and for creating new ones. The shape and balance between the various elements of the matrix which teachers will want to achieve in the environments they construct will vary enormously. At this stage, it is intended as an instrument for exploring and reflecting upon the general issues and problems about learning raised in this chapter. It will be extensively referred to in the next part of the book, providing teachers with a range of different ways for thinking about and achieving their teaching – specifically relating the elements of the matrix to the different aspects or genres of teaching practice.

Final questions: in so far as the learning matrix addresses the area between developing a professional language and the specific, concrete use of that language, it suggests a range of questions which teachers might like to consider as they approach the design and implementation of teaching. What can I do to promote learner-focused teaching in my courses? What does learning consist of in my course? Can I improve it? What dimensions of learning (intellectual, social, practical, personal) will be included? What kind of learning gaps might need to be addressed? What learning contexts are most appropriate to the learning environment I want to create? Reflections and ideas with respect to these kinds of questions can provide a substantive platform for engaging in the genres of teaching described in Part 2 of this book.

PART 2

GENRES OF TEACHING IN HIGHER EDUCATION

chapter 3

DESIGNING: COURSE AND CURRICULUM DESIGN

A curriculum is more than its knowledge components; much more. Interpreted broadly and correctly, curriculum embraces the students' engagement with the offerings put before them ... The ordering and presentation of those knowledge elements in a curriculum reflect a sense on the part of the educator as to what counts as a genuine act of knowing. (Barnett, 1994: 45–6)

This chapter examines the genre of course design, addressing questions of course aims and objectives, content/material, course length and teaching staff in relation to the critical matrix presented in the previous chapter and the distinctive genres of teaching practice. We look at the development of an overall course plan or blueprint which integrates the areas of teaching covered in Part 2: designing, lecturing, facilitating, supervising, innovating, assessing, evaluating. We discuss the different, often contrasting, approaches and styles that may be taken to course design. The chapter also looks at the impact of the various contexts in which design is situated (curriculum, departmental, institutional), addressing issues such as modularity, faculty–student ratios, subject/discipline, etc.

INTRODUCTION

Course and curriculum design is changing. As we observed in Chapter 2, higher education faces increasing social and economic pressures to generate a wider range of knowledge, skills and attitudes for coping with the demands of our 'supercomplex age'. The current pace of technological and social change is compelling teachers to think in terms of educating students not for today's problems but for those of tomorrow. We demand greater flexibility and imagination in educating for the future and want our students to develop learning skills and the ability to transfer what is learnt to new and more complex situations. In the process, our very concepts of learning – and teaching – are also changing. Learning is itself regarded as a process of change; change not only in relation to intellectual re-conceptualization but also, as we emphasized in the previous chapter, transformations in personal, social and practical domains.

In the previous chapter, we conceptualized the need to engage in a diverse range of experiences by proposing a learning matrix. In this chapter, we explore how the critical dimensions raised in that matrix can be incorporated into course design. Indeed, course design is, in many ways, the core 'genre' of the language of learning and teaching, the 'genre' every teacher has to master. It raises the most fundamental issues of learning and teaching, drawing together its diverse elements into a comprehensive and coherent whole, informed by a substantial body of knowledge and conceptual understanding of learning. It fully embraces the work of the reflective professional.

Three developing areas of research are integral for exploring course design. The first area of research explores how students learn. As we saw in the previous chapter, research on learning has increased substantially in the last 30 or so years and has had a substantial impact on learning and teaching in higher education more generally. The second area focuses on the variation in students' disposition towards learning environments. Gardner's work on multiple intelligences, for example, has extended the more general concept of 'intelligence' beyond its rather narrow focus on the intellectual dimension – the linguistic, spatial and logical/mathematical aspects of our thinking – to include other 'intelligences', including the interpersonal, intrapersonal, musical, visual, bodily/kinaesthetic and, most recently, existential, concerned with wider issues of being and purpose, and naturalist, concerned with classifying (Gardner, 1993, 1999). Building on the work of Bruner and Piaget, Fleming (1995) created VARK, an instrument designed to help learners develop awareness of their particular learning preferences (visual, aural, read/write and kinaesthetic).

The third area concerns developments in innovation theory and is also concerned with understanding processes of organizational change. Most of this work has been focused on change in business and industry (Anderson and King, 1995), but has increasingly been applied to higher education

Table 3.1 *The learning matrix in relation to learning theory, learning preferences and innovation theory*

Matrix dimensions	Learning theory	Learning preferences	Innovation theory
Intellectual	Deep/transforming Relational Relativist/committed Task/problem-centred Reflection-on-action	Verbal/linguistic Mathematical/logical Visual/spatial Naturalist	Gain/loss Empirical/rational strategy Openness to new ideas External changes
Emotional/personal	Personal change Active Personal experience (valued) Reflection-in-action Adult self-directed Learning in response to readiness/need Committed viewpoint Self-actualization Identity Confidence	Interpersonal Intrapersonal Bodily/kinaesthetic Musical Visual/spatial Existential	Ownership Unfreezing Deskilling Normative strategy Environment Trust
Social	Sharing verbalizing Alternative perspectives	Interpersonal Intrapersonal Bodily/kinaesthetic Musical	Unfreezing Linkage Normative strategy Leadership Power Environment (informal)
Practical	Active Practice Emotional context for remembering	Linguistic (practice) Mathematical/logical (practice) Visual/spatial Interpersonal Intrapersonal	Gain/loss Ownership

(Van de Ven and Poole, 2005) and the development of teaching as a process of change in particular (Kolb et al., 1994), and in larger curricular reform (Colbeck, 2002). Table 3.1 presents the relationship between the key ideas in these three areas with respect to the four dimensions of the learning matrix.

Understanding courses in terms of these three areas will not merely assist us to improve course design but will also contribute to our understanding of the essential principles of teaching and our ability to improve more traditionally delivered courses. Later in this chapter, we will explore in some detail the role of the three theoretical areas in terms of the four central dimensions of the learning matrix – the intellectual, the personal, the social and the practical. In addition, achieving balance in these four will be set within the broader matrix contexts of providing support, encouraging independence and developing the interpersonal. To begin with, however, we will examine the central concerns of course design, drawing on the fundamental issues and principles raised in the earlier chapters. These include the following:

- The requirement for a curriculum of transferability and the development of the student's higher level meta-learning abilities (Introduction). They are in tune with the important new emphases on developing wider professional skills and with demands of supercomplexity.
- The construction of an environment/community in which communication, learning and knowledge are understood and practised as dialogue with students and not monologue (Chapter 1). They make it more difficult to acquiesce in the transmission model while providing strong incentives to move towards the engagement model of teaching.
- The potential extension of the social context from ones solely focused on the learning of students to one which encompasses the mutual learning experience of the teacher as well (Chapter 2).
- The integration of research/theory and practice and an understanding of the nature of the potential 'gaps' of learning which they describe (Chapter 2).
- The importance of creating learning environments that facilitate intrinsic or higher levels of student motivation in terms of what students value personally in their lives: learning environments that foster real student engagement (Chapter 2).
- The full range of dimensions – intellectual, personal, social and practical – and contexts – support, independence and interpersonal – of the learning matrix (Chapter 2).

As the above comments suggest, the key to understanding course design is how the teacher regards the learner in the environment that they are designing. Who is the learner, what are they bringing to the course, what kinds of change are we intending to facilitate and assist them with? What aspects of the learner should course design take into consideration?

Students as whole people

Teachers must consider students as people rather than simply as intellects. As important as it is to recognize that students are bringing intellectual frameworks and ideas to the course which will need to be probed and addressed, it is also critical to recognize that they are people in a myriad of other ways. This needs to be a feature of any course design that is seriously concerned with the needs of students within the complexity of today's professional life.

Recently, a whole new area surrounding the concept of 'holistic student development' has emerged (Kuh, 1994; Baxter Magolda, 2000), the central premise being that student development has many features, the intellectual being only one small component.

Change

There is no point in teaching a course if an instructor cannot bring about a significant change in knowledge in terms of approach, conception, attitudes and behaviour. This is an important requirement of traditional undergraduate teaching, but where the 'transmission' model predominates, the focus is frequently on remedial work and the assimilation and accumulation of basic knowledge and skills.

It is difficult for significant change to occur if the process is simply regarded as one of assimilation. Deeper change often means going through a process of ambiguity and uncertainty. Critically probing the view that teaching is essentially about putting across our knowledge in a clear and interesting way, nuclear physicist Edward Teller (1991) noted, for example, that 'Confusion is not a bad thing: it's the first step towards understanding'. Paradoxically, however, we need to recognize that meaningful change takes time and critical judgement. As British novelist Ben Okri reminds us, 'Understanding often leads to ignorance, especially when it comes too soon' (1995).

Meta-learning

More traditional approaches often attend to transferable skills as isolated skills, to be 'bolted on' so to speak. Under such circumstances, their prospects for being developed long term and becoming an important feature of professional life are diminished. Problem-solving, learning to learn, interpersonal and social skills, interdependence and communication skills, and the intelligent use of resources are essential features of a course that focuses on change, and these need to replace the formal tokenism which can be the way they appear within non-integrated skills courses.

Community

The creation of a learning community is important. Certain courses may have more scope to develop this, although it is often not given substantial emphasis and the pressures of overloaded curricula often make it difficult to provide the necessary space for its development. The emphasis on group work and learning from colleagues which, as we have seen, is a feature of workshops/short courses, is an important lesson for traditional courses. While many are already successful in developing such communities, others are frequently little more than a collection of individuals who learn little from their peers and contribute less.

Self-evaluation

Finally, evaluation is often practised as a bureaucratic imposition, adding little to the quality of learning or, ironically, even to course improvement, and opportunities for self-evaluation are generally overlooked. The integration of serious educational reflection with social interaction and the development of learning skills is crucial, but is not always successfully extended to many undergraduate courses. Time for reflection, diaries, commentaries and group follow-up meetings can both enhance student learning and provide opportunities for students to develop reflective practices over the long term.

COURSE AND CURRICULUM DESIGN

The overall design of a course can essentially be summed up by the answers to four key teaching questions:

- What learning outcomes do you want your students to achieve (intellectual, social, practical and personal) as a result of taking your course?
- How will your course help your students achieve these learning outcomes?
- How will you know if the students on your course have achieved these learning outcomes?
- How will you know if and how your teaching has contributed to your students' learning outcomes?

In this section, we explore some of the key issues at the heart of these questions by considering the central design choices that teachers need to make in designing their courses, including course alignment, course objectives, course content and course structure. We will primarily focus on the first question and its key concept of 'learning outcomes' which is at the heart of these design choices. Implications for design features as teaching and assessment methods at the heart of the other three questions will be noted here, but later chapters will provide full discussions on each of them.

Course alignment

The focus on 'student learning outcomes' in each of the four teaching questions raises the issue of how well the elements of a course design are aligned. The requirement set out by these questions is that the teacher's objectives for the course in terms of the students' learning need to be fully aligned with the teaching activities and assessments employed to facilitate and measure that learning. While it seems a rather obvious requirement, course design which has traditionally focused on the content of the course, and not on the learning arising from students' engagement with the content, has often resulted in students receiving mixed messages as to what is expected of them. Teachers' remarks to their students that they would like the students to become critical thinkers, for example, are undermined by teaching activities and assessment methods that basically require that students memorize and reproduce knowledge.

Alignment further raises the issue of the quality of the learning that is being sought from the students. It is not sufficient for a course simply to be aligned. It also needs to be aligned around meaningful learning outcomes. Even an aligned course may be aligned in a reproductive way – that is, students may simply reproduce the information and meanings transmitted from the teacher and class on the course assessments. The learning experiences (activities and assessment) are aligned with low-level, surface learning outcomes. This is reproductive alignment. In constructive alignment (Biggs, 2003), on the other hand, the learning experiences (teaching activities and assessment methods) are aligned with high-level, deeper learning outcomes in which students construct their own deeper meanings from the course content through their encounter with connected teaching and assessment methods (see Figure 3.1).

Course objectives

Learning objectives, aims and outcomes

'Objectives' have long been a key aspect of course design, and in recent years have been the focus of renewed emphasis from national agencies such as the Quality Assurance Agency in the UK and in higher education generally. In the USA, for example, the focus of accrediting bodies on 'learning outcomes' has raised a similar emphasis on objectives from which learning outcomes are often derived. Learning objectives can be distinguished from both course aims/goals and learning outcomes. While there is still some debate about these terms, course aims refer to what the teacher

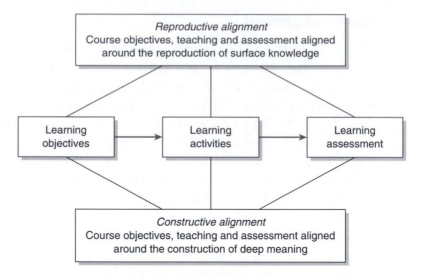

Figure 3.1 *Course alignment*

is generally trying to achieve in his or her course. Learning objectives are more specific and refer to what the students are expected to learn. Learning outcomes are more behavioural, describing what students are actually able to do in observable terms having successfully completed the course:

- **Course goals/aims** are best thought of as general statements of educational intent.
- **Learning objectives** are more *specific* and *concrete statements* of what *students are expected to learn* (Ramsden, 1992/2003).
- **Learning outcomes** are specific outcomes with specific observable/measurable statements of the learning students achieve.

The following example from an 'Introduction to psychology' course helps clarify these terms in practice:

- *Course goal*: students will learn fundamental principles and key concepts in psychology.
- *Learning objective*: students will develop an analytical understanding of empirical research related to human cognition.
- *Learning outcome*: students are able to critique the methodology in a published experiment and design a follow-up study.

Objectives have often been used interchangeably with 'learning outcomes', suggesting a rather linear and causal relationship which needs to be critically addressed. Rigidly constructed objectives described – even prescribed – in detail and linked to learning outcomes offer little space for student involvement in the development of their own learning. They need to be carefully considered and explored with course teams, previous students and, if possible, scope provided for negotiation within the course. The issue may be compounded if the teacher takes over a course with previously defined aims, objectives or outcomes, which is increasingly the case for new faculty. The lack of such a critical exploration may encourage a superficial understanding of what the course is about. It is worth noting, however, that the construction of learning objectives and outcomes provides a way of developing that unique pedagogical aspect of a course which lies between the course as a simple unit of institutional credit and the syllabus as the unit of content. This aspect of the course and the solutions to the four questions above which characterize it define the nature of students' encounter with knowledge and what counts as an 'act of knowing'. Indeed, Pring uses the term 'curriculum' to refer to it:

> Course ... refers to a set of arrangement procedures and college syllabus which meet the relevant criteria (standards) ... The curriculum refers to the learning experiences (planned for the most part by the teacher) through which that course is put into practice ... Teaching and leaning styles are part of the curriculum. Curriculum is a richer concept than that of syllabus or course ... The same syllabus can be taught in different courses, the same course taught by different teachers – in each case producing different curricula. (1995: 81)

Sources of objectives

The development of course objectives is conditioned, to a large degree, by the overall educational and/or ideological perspective of the course, including the institution and disciplinary context in which that course is situated. Warren Piper's (1976) 'three plus one' taxonomy of the sources of general educational objectives is still meaningful today (see Figure 3.2). The first three are the cultural, which regards education essentially as a process of passing the richness of our culture on to the next generation; the functional, which views education as a way of creating an educated workforce to ensure national development and global competitiveness; and the social service perspective, focused on providing opportunity for citizens. The fourth is the course itself, which has more local facilitative objectives to ensure students are learning successfully and happily on that course.

These sources of educational objectives are not necessarily mutually exclusive but, as Toohey (1999) suggests with respect to a similar categorization,

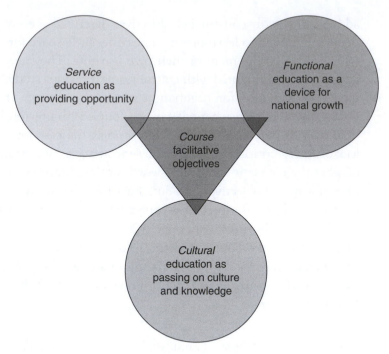

Figure 3.2 *Sources of educational objectives*
Source: Adapted from Warren Piper, 1976: 115

they need to be carefully considered. They will often draw upon different epistemological understandings of what knowledge is, what content should be included, how they are best assessed and so on. The current concern in the UK for the development of transferable or key skills, for example, has been very much informed by the functional view, but this does not mean that objectives which consider such skills cannot draw upon service or cultural perspectives and the engaged facilitative approaches which we have stressed in the previous parts of the chapter.

Approaches to objectives: rational v. reflective

The decision on where to situate course objectives will, to a large degree, be related to their stance to two different approaches to the use of objectives: the rational and the reflective. The more formal objectives are closely associated with behaviourism and the associated rational view suggested earlier that courses are designed to provide uniform outcomes in a linear and causal way. Precise and strict definitions of what the course is trying to do are important and they should be measured by formal standardized procedures to determine how far these prescribed outcomes have been achieved.

Figure 3.3 *Approaches to objectives*

Diversity, while not eliminated, is nevertheless reduced and standardization is a high priority.

In the second, more expressive or reflective approach to objectives, courses are not designed to produce uniform products but, rather, to provide a rich environment of learning experiences to which students will respond in different ways. These include valuable experiences, including developing creativity, flexibility, open-mindedness, and complex understanding (Eisner, 1994). The teacher is not subject to a prescribed rational system but will reflect on the objectives in terms of the ongoing changes of the course and make professional judgments-in-action. Although this approach will provide more diversity and independence of student response, it does not entail, as some would fear, that standards are jeopardized. It simply provides a means for more fully engaging students in the various aspects of their learning environment, offering some degree of choice in what and how they study and, even, where appropriate, in how they are assessed.

While these two approaches are diametrically contrasted here, they should not be regarded as exclusive. They are best understood and practised as occupying the two ends of a continuum (see Figure 3.3). Different courses within different disciplines will be working with different constraints and need to make professional choices as to where on the continuum they wish to locate their course and programme. Within the constraints of formal professionally accredited courses based on formal specifications of objectives there is still considerable scope for increasing opportunities for choice and independence through different ways of learning and the use of additional, more diverse outcomes.

Similarly, even within very radical project-oriented courses encouraging creativity and flexibility and living with the consequences of that creativity, structures and standards are important. Ironically perhaps, the recent emphasis on 'prescribing' outcomes for transferable skills – encouraging independent meta-learning – calls for a substantial review of highly structured courses offering little scope for independent work in which students become technically proficient but lack flexibility and creativity.

Categories of objectives

The discussion has tended to focus on 'horizontal' aspects of objectives, comparisons between different sources, approaches and so forth. Objectives also have what might be called a 'vertical' dimension: differences of complexity and standard. The most often cited taxonomy of higher education objectives in this vein is that of Bloom (1956), which has recently been revised (Anderson et al., 2000). While Bloom distinguishes between kinds of objectives – relating to knowledge, attitudes and skills – his key contribution here concerns his six-level classification of objectives by complexity. Biggs (2003) – through his 'Structure of the Observed Learning Outcome' taxonomy (SOLO) – has also usefully classified objectives by complexity and level. While both taxonomies take a different approach, there are close parallels between them. Table 3.2 compares both, presenting associated verbs that identify what students are being asked to do with respect to each level.

Once again, teachers will wish to consider carefully at what level they are pitching and aligning their course and/or individual teaching sessions. Courses that often purport to be emphasizing the higher levels of these taxonomies, nevertheless, deliver material and construct assessments aimed at and eliciting significantly lower levels of attainment. Assessment systems, in particular, indicate to students at what level they should be aiming their learning and are, therefore, a useful way of encouraging students to take these levels seriously (Chapter 8).

Course content

Criteria for devising a syllabus

Exploring course objectives will inevitably involve choices concerning course content. In some cases the content will suggest specific objectives, in others objectives may indicate appropriate content. It is a close, at times almost dialectical, relationship which will vary substantially between disciplines and topics. Specifying content will always be necessary in course design, but teachers need to avoid simply thinking about content in terms of lists of topics to be covered. Emphasis also needs to be focused on the tasks the student should be able to perform which may form an essential part of their education. Table 3.3 provides an overview of the criteria that might be considered when deciding the content of a course.

Content overload

It is worth concluding these remarks on course content with a brief note on the issue of content overload, which is, perhaps, the most

Table 3.2 Cognitive objectives and associated verbs

	Quantitative phase →				Qualitative phase →
Biggs' SOLO	*Pre-Structural*	*Uni-structural*	*Multi-structural*	*Relational*	*Extended abstract*
Associated verbs	Misses the point	Identify; do simple procedures	Enumerate, describe, list, combine, do algorithms	Compare/contrast, explain, analyse, relate, apply	Theorize, generalize, reflect, hypothesize
Bloom's revised taxonomy		*Remembering* — Recalling information	*Understanding* — Explaining ideas or concepts	*Applying* — Using information in another familiar situation; *Analysing* — Breaking information into parts to explore relationships	*Evaluating* — Justifying a decision or course of action; *Creating* — Generating new ideas, products or ways of viewing things
Associated verbs		Recognizing, listing, describing, retrieving, naming, finding	Interpreting, summarizing, paraphrasing, classifying, explaining	Implementing, carrying out, using, executing; Comparing, organizing, deconstructing, interrogating, finding	Checking, hypothesizing, critiquing, experimenting, judging; Designing, constructing, planning, producing, inventing

Simple ————————→ Complex

Sources: Anderson et al., 2000; Biggs et al., 2007

Table 3.3 *Criteria for choosing course content*

Criteria	
Philosophical	Enhances intellectual development of students – not an end in itself Raises moral, ethical and social considerations Goes beyond technical matters Contributes to a deep and critical perspective of knowledge
Professional	Addresses the appropriate theoretical and practical experience of accreditation/ registration Addresses professional principles, values and ethics Avoids overload; distinguishes 'mastery' from 'acquaintance' content
Learning	Avoids excessive fragmentation Provides opportunities to develop higher-level intellectual skills in reasoning, problem-solving, critical thinking and creativity Addresses the development of appropriate attitudes and values Draws on accessible and/or suitable alternative materials
Resource	Is linked to relevant and available teaching resources (library, computer equipment, labs, people, patients, environments, etc.)
Student	Reflects needs and interests of the student group Is matched to the intellectual and maturity level of students Addresses the diverse life experiences, backgrounds of the students
Teacher	Is appropriate to the teacher's level of knowledge and understanding Is interesting, engaging and ethically acceptable to the teacher

Source: Adapted from Newble and Cannon, 1989

significant problem confronting course design in higher education. It is at the centre of transmission approaches to teaching (see Chapter 1) which judge teaching by content transmitted, quality of teaching by content chosen and challenge to the student by the quantity and volume of content transmitted. Courses where student contact (transmission) time is high, and content overload is a pervasive feature, are associated with surface learning outcomes and a propensity for teachers to focus their teaching on knowledge reproduction, basic comprehension and application at the expense of the higher levels of analysis, synthesis and evaluation.

Ironically, such a focus – and the typical method of delivering it, lectures – is not even an effective way of ensuring basic comprehension and knowledge recall (Bligh, 2000b). Students rarely 'know' more than a third of the content at the completion of a course and substantially less six months or a year later. Emphasis on such low-level objectives also contributes – as a department of mechanical engineering reported (Cox, 1987) – to substantial issues of demotivation. An overloaded course is experienced as mere conformist grind instead of an opportunity for a challenging exploration of key issues within the subject and the development of a sense of occupational identity that is often an important issue in attracting students to the subject. One possible solution to overload is to distinguish 'mastery' content from 'acquaintance' content. What is essential to master in order to achieve the course objectives? Making those choices and reducing course content is, however, much easier said than done. There is much truth in the saying that changing a course is rather like moving a cemetery, there are many emotional attachments, even after expiry.

Course structure

A host of factors help determine the structure of a course, such as course length, modularity, sequencing and available resources, including technology.

Course length

There is no ideal course 'length'. The length of a course is typically related to bureaucratic guidelines and regulations, themselves constrained by trends and changes in wider academic and professional requirements. Length is also crucially related to its objectives and content and, as such, is ultimately dependent on learning. The volume of content, which a teacher covers over the length of a course, may not be related to the speed with which students can cope. In this respect, reducing the length of the course and/or class time, while extending external opportunities for study and learning through study groups, peer groups, problem/task-based activities, the use of the new technology and so on, may extend the educational 'duration' of the course without increasing its 'length'. Such opportunities should not generally be seen as times to introduce more content but, rather, as opportunities for consolidation, application and higher levels of understanding – for probing and exploring the contexts and the limitations, not simply the essentials. We have suggested, moreover, that change is a critical aspect of learning. This generally occurs over longer periods than are required for the simple assimilation of new ideas and information.

Modularity

The modularization of courses into discreet units of study has recently become a widespread feature of curriculum development. It is regarded as an effective way of providing students with more choice and flexibility in their study. It offers students increased versatility to structure their courses in combinations that interest them, at times that fit their schedules, in sequences that suit their learning and in overall time frames that are more appropriate to their lives. Although it certainly has many advantages, it also raises its own problems. Without careful consideration and guidance, modularity often leads to both intellectual and social/personal fragmentation. The integration of the different 'modules' into an overall coherent programme of study can be difficult for students, particularly with respect to making and understanding key relationships and links between the modules.

Students also frequently experience a lack of continuity in developing social and personal relations as a result of constant changes in peer groups. Some of the problems of fragmentation are difficult to solve, but modules can be designed around enabling students to integrate their understanding of the separate modules in relation to each other. Project work may provide an essential element in such integration but has not traditionally been important in this respect. Some universities use examinations for relating different modules, but students can see this as being asked to do what their tutors have failed to do. Peer study and support groups may also help students to avoid some of the intellectual fragmentation, as well as providing opportunities for social and personal development.

Sequencing

Sequencing is closely related to modularity. It is an important principle of teaching that student learning is closely related to what they already know. This is not to suggest that sequencing is concerned with a simple linear addition of blocks of knowledge. From one perspective, it is crucial that modules or units of study which require previous knowledge of the subject should be sequenced after the student has had the opportunity to develop that knowledge and understanding. From another perspective, however, sequencing is concerned with achieving a more holistic approach to a subject. This concept of sequencing considers how course design might develop multiple dimensions for approaching material.

In a 'spiral curriculum' approach, for example, students revisit themes and concepts which they have considered earlier but, in revisiting them, they come from a different perspective, developing both a facility for handling multiple conceptual frameworks and for confronting and/or integrating them to construct new perspectives. Problem-based learning, as we have seen, reverses the usual sequence of giving information to students first and asking them to apply it to problems later. Designing interesting and engaging problems that encourage students to think and solve problems, rather than being told answers, becomes an essential part of course design. While the nature of the problem will diverge widely across disciplines, much in the way of significant teaching innovation will rest in how creative and imaginative teachers are in constructing relevant, appropriate and stimulating problems or tasks for their students.

Projects

Projects, capstone experiences and extended assignments provide another significant dimension to sequencing. Generally they are situated at the end of a course and in some respects this can be sensible and certainly logical. It can also mean, however, that students may go through years without working in a way which seems to be directly related to their life, the career they hope to enter or even their conception of what the course is really about.

Project work can be the focus for a great deal of commitment and personal expression. If this is postponed for a long period it can result in students becoming disillusioned and failing to see the relevance of the course to some of their main concerns. Sequencing projects earlier in the course would help, but it does suggest that there should not be just one project. There should be earlier projects aimed at involving students and developing their initial learning as well as introducing the basics of managing projects. Later projects could then be more in-depth and more capable of being integrated with their earlier learning on the course.

Resources

It goes without saying that the design of courses will need to be structured and delivered within the constraints of the available resources. Table 3.4 gives some of the areas that will need to be considered.

Methods, assessment and evaluation

The teaching methods by which the course will be taught, the assessment methods by which the students will be assessed and the evaluation methods by which the course will be reviewed and improved, all play an essential role in course design. This is particularly the case in terms of their alignment. Unaligned and/or reproductively aligned courses can be particularly detrimental to the development of deeper and richer learning experiences. Course objectives, course content and course structures may,

Table 3.4 *Course design: resource considerations*

Resources	
Staff	Academic faculty, support staff, administrative and managerial staff, visiting staff
Library	Library holdings, multimedia
Reprographic	Printing and publication facilities
Space	Classrooms, lecture theatres, laboratories, clinics, studios, field trips, etc.
Materials	Course packs, key texts, equipment
Guidelines	Course directories, handouts
Technology	Software, hardware, computing facilities
Training	Computer, library, equipment, health and safety, etc.

for example, convey a great deal about a course to the student. How the course engages them, how it is assessed and even to some degree how it is evaluated are, however, much more revealing. They are so fundamental that we shall spend the next six chapters discussing them at some length. It is worth remembering, however, that the same learning considerations raised in Part 2 of this book are also at the heart of our discussion of the following genres of learning and teaching.

COURSE DESIGN AND THE CRITICAL MATRIX

In this section, we explore how course design might play out across the different dimensions of learning highlighted in the critical matrix developed in the previous chapter. The discussion then looks at how course design might address the issue of balance between contexts providing support for students, developing interpersonal skills and encouraging independence. Box 3.1 illustrates how an engineering professor redesigned his materials course.

Box 3.1 *Course design*

In his nanotechnology class, Martin, an engineer, originally used traditional teacher-focused lecturing methods and demonstrations; individual homework assignments; individual projects, such as research proposals and oral presentations; and in-class timed final exams. His students were diverse, drawing from a range of engineering and science backgrounds and bringing with them a wide range of experience and varying levels of expertise.

To engage his students more fully, he completely redesigned his course to make it more learner-focused, using the diversity of learners to the benefit of the whole class. In the new course, he incorporated several non-traditional pedagogical practices, including collaborative group learning, interdisciplinary learning, problem-based learning and peer assessment.

Working in interdisciplinary teams, students developed substantial and relevant projects in nanotechnology, seeking to apply their skills to real-world problems. When each group presented their project to the class, the other teams took turns as consultants and assessors, simulating a professional work experience (a technique described more in Chapter 8). In this way, he was able to support their ability to work independently and in groups.

The intellectual dimension

In terms of innovation theory, the design we suggest here essentially employs an empirical rational strategy, concentrating on giving evidence and reasons as the basis for initiating change. This approach draws upon the more traditional 'intelligences': verbal/linguistic, mathematical/logical and visual/spatial. In relation to learning theory, this design works to develop deep approaches and transforming conceptions which, as we saw in the previous chapter, emphasize meaning, purpose, seeing in a different way and relating one's own experience and the wider context to the course material.

Learning and teaching strategies draw on alternative perspectives and explore the relative strengths and weaknesses of these in different contexts. Adult learning theory and the concepts of reflective practice inform the course activities. The course is essentially problem-centred and learner-focused, rather than content-centred and teacher-focused. The following teaching activities are examples of components that underscore the intellectual dimension of course design.

Background readings/formal lectures

Background readings or formal lectures essentially exist to help students develop their knowledge, and can be a simple and efficient way to present new ideas and information (Lieberg, 2008). Reading background material before class may help orient students to material even before an introductory lecture on a new topic. Formal presentations, such as those by outside speakers, may enable students to meet people whose work they may be reading. Yet, students may be frustrated if there is little opportunity to discuss their ideas. As we discuss more fully in Chapter 4, lectures and presentations do not need to be dull or passive; indeed, there are many ways to engage students actively. When done effectively, such activities provide students with much needed frameworks, which will support their learning.

Small groups

Students can be divided into pairs, triads or small groups to supplement general reflection and discussion on the relevance and use of ideas and concepts (Bligh, 2000a). Such groups encourage personal reflection on what is being learnt and how it applies to the individual problems, a point discussed more fully in Chapter 5.

Syndicate or peer-managed learning

In this method, students are divided into groups of four to six, provided with a resource pack of information and work as a team to look at and cover different aspects of the information (McKeachie, 2006). They then discuss what they learnt in the small group and report back to the rest of the class. This generates a positive approach to addressing relevant aspects of theory and research for practice, while offering some support and more interpersonal development (discussed more fully in Chapter 5).

Project groups

Project groups are used as a focus for integrating learning on a topic into a more coherent framework, which is then shared with the larger group through presentations, posters or formal reports. This type of learning is associated closely with approaches taken in problem-based learning (Boud et al., 2001).

Assignments and exams

These are useful for assessing an individual's retention and application of knowledge, but may be limited if students are asked simply to reproduce the information offered by the instructor in a lecture or acquired from a textbook. When asked to create information or apply ideas in new contexts, students are being asked to be independent in their critical thinking, but are also receiving necessary support and direction (see Chapter 8).

Distributed materials

Much of the intellectual stimulation generated during class may be lost when students leave the environment, particularly if moving to a less supportive environment. Carefully crafted handouts that contain key ideas, concepts, problems, examples and references, and which go beyond what has been covered, will enable students to take away additional resources which will support their learning. Similarly, continued access to materials outside class, either on a course management system or on a website, will enable students to strengthen their understanding and application of complex ideas.

The personal dimension

The intellectual is never purely intellectual and, with courses that have a more practical orientation, energy must be generated to translate the intellectual changes into action. Many traditional courses can be reasonably effective at encouraging students to remember and even to understand, but are not so effective in giving students the ability to act. In the previous chapter, we looked at learning theory which draws on much more than our intellect, stressing the importance of the emotional and personal side of learning, particularly those that emphasize self-direction and self-actualization.

This depends upon giving students a stronger sense of identity and confidence, which can generate an important sense of responsibility and commitment extending beyond the confines of a discrete educational event.

Ownership

One of the essential concepts of innovation theory is ownership. Innovations can fail without a buy-in from participants. This sense of ownership can be undermined by the deskilling of participants through an overpowering emphasis on the teachers' (or other contributors') expertise. The sense of inadequacy can lead to withdrawal, alienation or simply leaving all the serious thinking to the experts. Innovations which stress normative strategies focusing on changing attitudes and approaches, rather than empirical/rational ones focusing on change through the strength of the ideas or content alone, can be truly educational. Ownership is often dependent upon creating the right environment, feelings of support and a sense of trust.

Unfreezing and icebreaking

Another interesting concept of innovation theory is unfreezing. Where current thinking is unyielding and/or even complacent, there is little hope of change succeeding without a prior unfreezing of the existing position. An instructor may use techniques for emotional unfreezing – icebreaking activities to enable students to get to know each other and feel more relaxed and less inhibited – and for challenging some of the intellectual assumptions behind a resistance to our general aims. If this unfreezing is too aggressive, students may resist or resent the activity but, as a general principle of design, it is important to consider the assumptions and resistances which may block the course's aims, as well as the experience students bring to the material (Bligh, 2000b).

The environment: music, space and the visual

The intelligences which this dimension mainly addresses are the intrapersonal and the interpersonal, but we may also think about the relationship of the course to the bodily/kinaesthetic, musical and spatial/visual intelligences. An instructor may use music to welcome students, for example, or to set the tone for the class. The creative use of visual diagrams and written words, using overheads, flip charts, boards and other technology, also helps engage students in the process of constructing their learning.

Brainstorming can be a particularly effective way of engaging students as the production of their ideas and solutions is separated from the often limiting impact of immediate intellectual criticism. Visual expression and intelligence can be engaged in many other ways – as a stimulus constructing complex relationships, for example – and give a sense of contribution and ownership as well. Finally, in the movement of individuals between groups, or in recording discussion and/or making presentations, a class may even engage bodily/kinaesthetic aspects of the learning environment.

Problem contribution

To meet emotional and personal needs, the general atmosphere and environment must feel welcoming to students (Lieberg, 2008). Instructors might ask students to contribute concrete problems in advance, to acknowledge and address in class, perhaps discussing them in small groups or with everyone. Students can feel a sense of belonging and of responsibility for the way the class progresses rather than leaving it all to the teacher, enhancing their feeling of ownership, as well as their learning.

Performance and role-play

To address further the personal and emotional dimension, an instructor might include activities that conclude with some sort of outcome and provide a performance challenge to participants. Role-play sessions, for example, which are followed by a group analysis or debrief, can engage the emotional side of learning as well as enhance self-criticism (Lieberg, 2008). If repeated, with improvement, there can be an important sense of achievement as well. Even where role-play is not the theme, participants can be encouraged to take active performance roles, reporting on the results of group work, or formally describing personally relevant professional or work-based problems.

Reflective pairs and triads

Reserved students may still find groups of five and six difficult or daunting. Pairs and triads (see above) frequently provide an opportunity for students to express some of the more emotional problems common in their learning. To build up confidence and trust, it is often useful to keep these groups constant over the duration of the course, providing extended opportunities to talk about the relevance of what has been happening with respect to the course, their learning and its relationship to their working and personal lives. A useful focus for the final meeting may be a discussion (and planning) of what they are actually going to do as a result of the course.

Feedback and self-assessment

Giving students the opportunity to receive thoughtful and critical feedback from multiple sources – from the instructor, from their peers and from themselves – forms an important aspect of their development as learners and thinkers. This aspect is discussed more fully in Chapter 8.

The social dimension

Of course, our personal and emotional life is strongly bound up with social relationships and many of the issues already discussed are highly relevant to meeting social needs. The frequency and variety of tasks and group sizes and leadership within the activities of the course are important. People need time to begin to work well together. Indeed, groups often go through a period of 'storming' or hostility after the 'forming' stage (see Chapter 5). Even if this is not outwardly expressed, they may, nevertheless, go through a period of intense emotional turbulence.

Generally, such turbulence is considered something to be avoided at all costs but, in fact, crises can be extremely effective in the development of deeper learning and feeling. Provided they do not become destructive, they can lead to radical change (Cox et al., 1981). Unfortunately group work in many courses is often too intermittent for group forces to be particularly valuable, and change and reconceptualization rarely come from very intermittent events.

Leadership

The role of leadership and power is an extremely important issue in encouraging change. An instructor may opt to relinquish much of his or her power to the group, but must realize that the responsibility for structuring activities cannot be completely delegated. Frequent peer discussion and 'buzz group' discussion can encourage more easy social relationships, as will the layout of the furniture and indeed the type of furniture (Bligh, 2000b). Introducing various levels of formality and informality within a course will also establish a balance between leadership and ownership on the course.

Balancing brainstorming contributions, for example, from the group – acknowledging and writing them up on flip charts or boards – with the formal instructions and rules of the activity specified by the leader can encourage that sense of 'ownership' – of both the process and what is produced – at the centre of innovation theory. The various alternative participant perspectives disclosed in such group activities and tasks also reflect important features of learning theory noted in the previous chapter.

Social interactions

Sharing refreshments and meals together is a much valued part of our general social interaction and, indeed, has long been recognized by many institutions as an important feature of education. Yet, within higher education today, this is an increasingly rare part of student–teacher interaction. Still, instructors can build opportunities into a course for students to share in cultural and social events.

The practical dimension

While in many courses, practical outcomes result from considerable time spent in actual practice, practical skills are not all straightforwardly instrumental. Typically, they will represent underlying personal needs and social needs, which can have a very practical dimension to them. Many exercises can result in feelings of inadequacy and so, wherever the opportunity to repeat a practical exercise and improve on it can be introduced, this can result in a substantial gain.

In addition, using linguistic 'intelligences' in small group work, for example, can reinforce practical learning and raises the possibility of future practical changes, as too can an emotional attachment. The integration of many 'intelligences', rather than relying too much on the verbal/linguistic or the logical/mathematical, can make practical outcomes much more significant. Use of our visual intelligence can help to consolidate learning and interpersonal intelligence can give it a strong sense of personal commitment.

Practical examples

Asking students to reflect on specific practical problems and issues beforehand, and then bring them to the class, can be extremely useful. The time set aside on the course to look specifically at these accentuates the practical outcomes of the course in a context that is relevant to practice. Providing time within class for students to demonstrate practical skills with peer feedback can be an exceedingly rich experience for many students. It has the advantage of developing their own practical skills as well as their ability to critique and evaluate the application of such skills.

Learning outside the classroom

Taking advantage of opportunities outside the classroom has long been a very effective way of giving students practical experience, whether in internships, practicals, field trips and clinical or lab work. All these concrete situations offer opportunities for students to engage in the practice of skills and techniques which in the classroom have been primarily academic in nature. More recently increased possibilities for students to integrate their studies with experiences in local (and global) communities through service learning , civic engagement and study abroad opportunities have opened up substantive situations for the development of practical, social and civic skills (Colby et al., 2003).

Project reports and proposals

Creating reports and proposals, especially through working in teams, allows students to experience the work and community standards of a professional in the field.

LEARNING CONTEXTS: BALANCE AND STRUCTURE

Support and independence

While the above discussion has focused primarily on issues concerning the dimensions of the learning matrix, those dimensions were disclosed and described with the range of the matrix's learning contexts. Much of the discussion centred implicitly on, for example, the balance between giving support and encouraging independence. Too much support – either in the form of being told too much information or working within tight and controlling structures – and students may feel they are not taking part, that they have little ownership of what is happening, that it is not relevant to their lives. Too little support, on the other hand, and they may feel too anxious to take risks and/or too inadequate to have much to offer.

Support from teachers (and fellow participants) needs to be matched by challenging tasks, the opportunity to take risks with new ways of working and the opportunity to rethink many of the assumptions which have served well in the past but raise serious doubts for the future. Achieving a better balance of support and independence is often mediated through specific tasks but can be helped by experiencing a wider range of specific roles.

Overall, traditional teaching does not require students to engage in very many different roles. They mainly listen, read, complete exams and other assignments and occasionally do some practical work. This limited range of roles, however, does not parallel what they will have to cope with when they become independent professionals. It certainly does not address the students' future need to develop 'transferable skills' nor their ability to engage in 'meta-learning' and learning how to learn (see Chapter 1). An essential issue in developing these skills includes more emphasis on the interpersonal context of learning.

Interpersonal

The interpersonal context stresses the need to develop abilities through which students are able to contribute to the learning of, and to learn from, others. It is the basis for strong relationships and requires a great deal of sensitivity about the way students are understood by one another both at an intellectual and a personal level. Within the interpersonal context, they will need to be supportive but, to avoid conformity and to ensure the success of the interpersonal situation, they will need to make distinctive and independent contributions.

Many students, even on workshops, do not always expect or even want to learn in such an interpersonal context. They believe they are coming to hear experts tell them what is right and what the best course of action is. On the other hand, one of the most common and positive features of evaluations is how much they appreciate the opportunity to meet and discuss with peers who come from other environments and experiences.

Structure

Common 'icebreaking activities' for getting to know one another are important but, as suggested above, this must also be an 'unfreezing' time in terms of beginning to recognize that some basic ways of understanding and behaving may be serious obstacles to learning new ideas which may be worth trying. If learning in general is more a question of change than assimilation then courses need to recognize that change processes can be difficult. The structure needs to reflect this, not only within the activity itself but also in its preparation and, if possible, within the time during which the learning is applied after the course. It may even include future reunions and reflections upon the problems and success of that application.

Innovations often fail because the implementation is too difficult and the training and sense of ownership of the innovation are not highly developed. Perhaps the processes were only intellectual or the unfreezing was superficial, leaving in place many of the ways of thinking which later under the stresses of the old environment undermined the new ideas and practices. New ideas and information are essential issues in designing courses but they are easily diminished by a lack of deeper integration with behaviour and feelings. Variety in presentation, activities and relationships is not there simply to prevent people from getting bored but is a critical way of integrating what is learnt into a firmer network of reinforcing influences. For some people chatting over a drink at the end of the day may be a more important element of consolidating learning than the more formal consolidation activities.

Evaluations

The evaluation of a course is, too often, tacked on as a bureaucratic feature. If, however, we see evaluation as part of the process of becoming a reflective professional, it needs to display many of the features that characterize the course as a whole. Evaluations should not, for example, simply reflect what students liked and disliked, but how and why they felt affected, and how their fellow students responded. Simple questionnaires may help improve a course, but may not be sophisticated enough to engage participants in very serious reflection, and are often seen as a rather peripheral event.

Much deeper reflection and evaluation need to be built into the learning activities themselves. Deliberations and reflections arising from small groups, for example, may provide a rich source of material for evaluation. Through personal reflection, students may develop a clear sense of gain (or loss), but may also better understand how they have begun to change and adapt to a range of new perspectives. Asking students to contribute written qualitative statements of their individual or group reflections may focus discussion and enhance their learning on the course (see Chapter 9).

ADDRESSING THE IMPOSSIBLE

Some of the features described above may be difficult – even impossible – to use in the context of the expanded faculty–student ratios common to many courses. Creating a learning community, for example, with 200 students may seem unachievable, and providing active practice sessions with teachers supplying analytic feedback may seem entirely out of the question. If these goals are seen entirely as the teacher's work, this will, more than likely, be perfectly true. In an 'engaged' situation, however, the facilitation of learning is not entirely the province of the teacher. Students are engaged in the facilitation of learning as well as the experience of learning. Indeed, they are often the same.

Broadening responsibility

The focus on developing abilities for learning how to learn, for internalizing a 'lifelong learning agenda', requires students to take a great deal more responsibility for their own learning earlier on: both as individuals and as members of a group. In Germany, for example, students on courses with extremely high faculty–student ratios have spontaneously formed working groups to compensate for the lack of faculty attention. This can provide substantial opportunities for reflection and comments from peers.

This creation of active peer-learning communities is essential to developing a sense of individual and group responsibility in students. Some medical education programmes focusing on problem-based learning approaches to their curriculum are already encouraging the development of such peer groups. There will be a role for teacher support in initiating such groups but certainly not in terms of the teacher doing the work for them.

Student contributions

Faculty may find it challenging to address the specific problems, concerns and interests of students. Splitting larger groups into smaller groups to help them interact more easily can enable them to formulate problems and issues that are more directly related to their own experiences and concerns. Such groups may start, for example, with individual thinking extended through contributions from others as the groups expand. Again, this offers opportunities for more students to contribute, but also provides a key route for exploring solutions to common problems.

The teacher role in such sessions is less focused on transmitting a higher concentration of material but rather on facilitating and bringing together material and issues for discussion in the larger groups. They will focus on commenting on and comparing the different issues and solutions arising, contributing material where there are substantial gaps and adding more sophisticated and critical perspectives on the topic.

In many cases such groups offer students an opportunity to go away and do extensive reading of their own which is shared within the group in later sessions without the direct or immediate involvement of the faculty member. This can mean that students have a far greater opportunity for choice than is usually the case. Unfortunately, the more courses become excessively burdened with required work the less scope there is for student choice, which as Ryan and Deci (2000) point out, is fundamental to learning and motivation. As content overload is one of the most significant pressures towards surface learning, reducing the content or, perhaps, distinguishing between 'mastery' content and 'acquaintance' content may give students the time to develop their own thinking and, indeed, extend their own knowledge of the topic.

Balancing support and independence

This provision of space for student contributions highlights what may be the most serious feature to incorporate into undergraduate teaching: establishing the optimum balance between support and independence. Students are often very ambivalent about needing support from staff. They often want to be told the answers and be directed, especially in conditions of high anxiety, but if this becomes the dominant experience of the course, it can have a very serious effect on motivation.

This ambivalence is a crucial aspect of even those students who appear the most submissive. It reflects a need to become independent of the pressures of family and school life and to become fully adult. Acquiescing in a state of dependency may be unacceptable to both the student and teacher. It is as important in science and technology, which often require a great deal of conformity to extensive curricular demands. The opportunity for choice and challenging independent work should be introduced early and not left to later years.

Problem and task-based learning

The development of specific skills is another area where it is difficult to adopt the teaching-intensive pattern characteristic of workshops or short courses. Problem or task-based learning is an approach where highly structured resource-based and computer-based learning can be acceptable and appropriate. Teaching staff may not need to be heavily involved; it is essentially a question of setting up processes and enabling students to go through them at their own pace. They will, however, need to receive formal feedback mediated either by senior students, mentors (Swarat et al., 2004) or through computer-generated responses. Within some contexts this may be quite difficult but in others such resource-based learning approaches are very effective.

Follow-up

Finally, the opportunity for follow-up sessions may be difficult to arrange with large undergraduate courses. With support and encouragement from teachers, this, again, might be something students could organize. Teaching staff could play an important role within such an initiative without being overly directive and without it becoming an unreasonable demand on their time. It can also become an important source of information to draw upon for course evaluation, particularly as it relates to student career progression following the completion of their studies. Inviting previous course students back for a session can become a regular and effective feature of a course. Current students can gain useful insights with respect to their learning and teachers can acquire interesting perspective on the impact of their course.

CONCLUSIONS

In many ways, course design is the integrating genre in the language of learning and teaching. In this respect it may be regarded as a kind of meta-genre in which the other genres dwell. Such a perspective has the advantage of emphasizing the core feature of design – its role in integrating or aligning (Biggs et al., 2007) the various aspects of learning and teaching into a comprehensive and coherent practice informed by and drawing upon a substantial body of knowledge and conceptual understanding of learning.

We have suggested that a useful way of engaging practice with this body of knowledge is through the learning matrix, a conceptual tool which we shall refer to throughout the following chapters. The following genres, however, dwell within course design only, so to speak, on paper. The practice of design is not the practice of assessment, nor the practice of lecturing. However intimately they are linked, these genres are distinctive and can be usefully differentiated for separate consideration.

Final questions: in so far as the elements of course design reflect, to return to our opening quotation, 'a sense on the part of the educator as to what counts as a genuine act of knowing', the critical questions which a teacher might want to reflect on are not simply concerned with knowledge but also with the opportunities raised for students to engage in 'genuine acts of knowing'. What is a genuine act of knowing for the course? Am I asking students to construct new knowledge, or to reproduce knowledge that I already have? How am I helping students to discover such acts of learning? Across what dimensions of learning? How well do my assessments and my teaching methods align with my learning objectives?

chapter 4

LECTURING: LARGE-GROUP TEACHING

I was in a state of panic throughout the lecture. I never looked at a face in an audience for fear it might smile, or frown or yawn. I've always lectured to the top right-hand corner of the room. I spoke very fast in order to get to the end. It was rather like crossing a narrow bridge over a causeway with lions on the right, tigers on the left. At the end of the lecture I always felt 'Now they can see through me and I'm no good'. (Isaiah Berlin cited in Ingrams, 1997: 2)

The authority of those who teach is often an obstacle to those who want to learn. (Cicero)

In this chapter, we focus on the lecture as an opportunity to stimulate critical thinking and promote reflective engagement on the part of students and the teacher. We contrast two models of lecturing – the traditional and the engaged – focusing on the integration of lecture content, structure and performance with key questions of student understanding and learning.

INTRODUCTION

When one thinks of teaching and learning in higher education, one invariably thinks of the lecture. The lecture and lecturing are almost synonymous with what higher education is about, particularly for undergraduates. It is what higher education teachers do; indeed, in the UK, it describes the title of the profession – lecturer. Significantly, it also describes a way of human communication that would not be acceptable in most other forms of social interaction. The statement 'you are lecturing me' in almost all other social situations would not be a positive statement. It would be regarded as dehumanizing and unnatural, if not condescending and offensive. Yet, as a method of communication aimed at large groups of students (even at small groups), it thrives in higher education.

The large-group context makes the lecture an acceptable form of addressing others, just as it makes the speech or the sermon acceptable. In addition, the 'efficiencies' which the large-group context is purported to provide higher education support its continuing institutional popularity. Assuming adequate space, voice and technology, the lecture can 'teach' the student multitudes.

The lecture, however, has been increasingly and severely taken to task, as swelling student numbers have kept it a highly visible mainstay in undergraduate education. The educational assault of the lecture has mainly targeted its traditional or conventional form, which Bligh (2000b) describes generally as ongoing periods of exposition by a speaker, before an audience who is seeking to learn from that speaker. Some commentators have even called for its total abandonment (Barnett, 2000). In his now classic review of the extensive research literature investigating the achievement of the lecture, Bligh (2000b) found that lectures are:

- no more or less effective than other methods in transmitting facts and information;
- not as effective as discussion methods in promoting thought;
- relatively ineffective for teaching values, inspiring interest in a subject or for personal and social adjustment; and
- relatively ineffective for teaching skills.

In terms of the gap schema presented in Chapter 2, the research suggests that traditional lectures are as effective (but no more so) than discussion-based and other teaching methods in helping students reach the acquisition/recall of information stage in the first gap. It is, moreover, less effective in aiding students to overcome the other gaps. Given the strength of this research it is not surprising that educational scorn has been heaped upon the lecture and questions as to its continued use raised (Bligh, 2000b).

In defence of the lecture, however, Biggs et al. (2007) suggests that the lecture does have significant advantages over both group work and books, for example, which rest in the lecturer's unique scholarly mind and integrate their role as teacher and researcher/scholar. The lecturer can bring to the lecture both her own critical perspective or angle on the subject and the most recent developments which books may not have had time to provide. In this, the lecturer becomes not only a facilitator for helping students transform and construct knowledge but also in the very practice of the lecturing can model that transformation for them.

More ardent champions of the lecture have suggested that the traditional large introductory lecture works particularly well for freshmen because they are still in the process of forming their adult identities and, as such, do not yet possess the ability to create knowledge for themselves. The anonymity of the lecture hall shields them from the embarrassment of sharing a 'wrong' answer and from being bored by the 'wrong' or meandering responses of their peers. Instead, these defenders suggest, the lecture provides impressionable undergraduates with the opportunity to see impassioned master learners articulate knowledge that has already been created for them. As Burgan (2006: 33) contends: 'Teachers are irreplaceable as models of knowledgeable adults grappling with first principles in order to open their students' understanding'. While these are admirable and necessary objectives for the lecture, alone they are not sufficient to justify the use of lectures. Such approaches and objectives can be achieved (and usually are achieved) more easily in small-group teaching situations.

To justify lecturing educationally, its one overwhelming advantage over all other methods of teaching must be acknowledged: that unique combination of incorporating live, face-to-face contact with large-scale student numbers. The former feature, of course, is common to most teaching and learning sessions in higher education, be they seminars, tutorials, workshops, lab settings, clinical work, etc. The latter feature is common to much distance and open learning where technology and media can aid in large-scale teaching projects. Only the lecture, however, combines both.

To be seriously justified, the lecture must exploit this combination. Unfortunately, this combination has been traditionally and rather feebly justified as being 1) a good way of delivering content to 2) a large number of students 3) cheaply. The first point is mainly true for the teacher as 'transmitter', much less so for the student as 'learner'. The second and third points probably provide the main reason for the lecture's longevity, but they are not integrated with the educational issues implicit in the first point. They do not address the critical aspect of the lecture as a method of live human contact, cost and numbers potentially achieved more efficiently by new technology. Both the justification for and description of the lecture, here, are couched in the linear (or monologue) model of human communication. Lecturing is fundamentally a one-way traffic of information in which the lived human dialogue quality of the situation is unimportant.

Understood and practised within such a model, lecturing has little educational justification. Moreover, no matter the perceived benefits of lecturing, for students for whom the lecture is in a second language, these benefits may be lost as they struggle to comprehend the lecturer's expert reconstruction of the material (Miller, 2007). This chapter, however, looks at how the practice of lecturing might be repositioned within an dialogical and interactive model and, in doing so, take advantage of the tremendous potential of the live plus large-group experience.

BEING WHERE THE ACTION IS

Higher education is full of exceptional lecturers who inspire, provoke, stimulate and fuel the mind with new ideas, thoughts, feeling and the desire to learn. It is a very unfortunate student who has failed to be enthused or stirred by at least one lecture. These lecturers achieve with a wide range of styles and approaches, sometimes employing a wide range of techniques and other times captivating with the very simplicity of their methods. Most experienced lecturers will probably be able to recall at least one lecture which they gave where the combination of material, presentation, location, audience and so on seemed to come together into a wonderful shared experience of mutual learning and appreciation. Where it worked! It is possible. The problem is that these occasions are too rare and they are extremely difficult to repeat.

This quality is also the quality of lecturing which is generally regarded as somewhat mysterious and unknowable. Some lecturers can inspire; others cannot. It is a form of artistry; something you either have or do not have, a quality of birth, so to speak, which can neither be taught nor learnt. Consequently, it is often simply noted in discussions of lecturing with no serious attempt to understand it.

The best that one can do for the lecturer unfortunate enough to lack such qualities is to smother him or her in a range of tips, hoping that some will stick and be of benefit to their students. It is an additive approach. The lecturer remains essentially unchanged. While there are lecturers who undoubtedly take to lecturing more easily and successfully than others, it is not because they have added bits to their lecturing behaviour and personality, but (whether instinctive or learnt) is primarily a consequence of a different way of thinking about lecturing and 'being' a lecturer. Moreover, what is probably the case in the vast majority of occasions when 'it worked' is that the vitality of the achievement was grounded to a large degree in the situation being live, large and engaged.

The wider experience of dialogue

Being *live* provides a wonderful opportunity for engagement and dialogue. Being *large* gives that dialogue the potential for a tremendous sharing. This should not be underestimated nor devalued. That feeling of sharing in large numbers can provide a wonderful feeling of intellectual security and exhilaration, of being part of a broader dialogue, a higher intellectual conversation that extends substantially beyond me into an extensive and inclusive network. It is the same feeling enjoyed at huge sports events, or cultural events or festivals. It is the feeling of relevance and of 'being where the action is'.

'Being where the action is' is a feeling often most fully enjoyed in large numbers. It can be enjoyed in smaller number but normally only when such numbers enjoy the authority and support of large numbers, such as being with social, political or cultural celebrities. A few lecturers enjoy such status and their very presence is often enough to engender such feelings.

For students, however, the experience of 'being where the action is' may simply rest in the opportunity to participate within a 'larger' higher education community, sharing with academics and a large number of their fellow students the various aspects of a new 'academic' language and new ways of thinking. This may consist of sharing the lecturer's comments about a reading list, or indications about what is central in a particular topic, or a new use of particular terms and vocabulary, or key remarks about the assessment/examination procedures, or hints about how to approach their studies in this discipline.

More extraordinarily, it will include the shared experience of being on the threshold (Meyer et al., 2007) or at the entrance to a new conceptual framework, a network of new ideas and concepts along with the opportunity to explore them and test them out. In all these the authority and weight of larger numbers can increase confidence and facility in new ways of thinking, understanding and practising. 'Being where the action is', of course, has its potential dangers. Numbers and authority can amplify confusion and insecurity, even become a form of intellectual tyranny, if badly managed, facilitated or directed.

All too frequently, however, lectures are neither directed nor facilitated. They are avoided. For reasons that we address below, the lecturer is often not fully engaged as a person. The result of such a lack of engagement is the opposite of the feeling of 'being where the action is'. It is the feeling of being where the action is not: of being in a remote, impersonal situation replete with the feelings of irrelevance, anonymity, insignificance and disorientation.

Many students frequently realize that they can miss the lecture without missing anything of critical import. Others suffer on in the vain hope of relevance and meaningful connections, often yielding to what Carbonne (1998) refers to as 'internal noise' – those internal dialogues and mental tangents which transport them out of the lecture situation. Without a break, the maximum attention span of students in such lectures is about 10–15 minutes, after which learning drops off dramatically (Bligh, 2000b). The student is, at best, in reception of 'unmediated' content in which the lecturer's personal presence is almost invisible or even unhelpful. For some students, the better students, it is just about adequate. For most students it is not, and it certainly does not justify the lecturer's presence. While necessary, content is not in itself sufficient.

The experience of relevance

In an innovative study of students' experience of the relevance of lecture content, Hodgson (2005) found that students experienced relevance in qualitatively distinct ways. For some students their experience of the relevance of the lecture content was 'intrinsic', expressed in terms of their understanding of it and the meaning it has for them personally and linked to deep learning. The experience of others, however, was 'extrinsic', expressed in terms of assessment or even in terms of a merely hoped-for potential use and linked to surface learning.

Her main finding, however, was of a third kind of relevance, a *vicarious* experience of relevance which she describes as a 'bridge between extrinsic experience or a surface approach and intrinsic experience or a deep approach' (2005: 171). This vicarious experience, moreover, is related to the lecturer, to the way they lecture, to their enthusiasm, their use of illustrations, the ways in which they engage students.

Content is, then, not the problem. It never has been. It is the use and 'context' of content that is the problem. There is nothing inherently wrong with $e = mc^2$ or the idea that Hamlet suffered from an oedipal complex or that Thatcher came to power in 1979 or the theory of evolution. Whatever one's view of them, the existence of facts, ideas, concepts and theories to talk about is not inherently problematic – challenging perhaps, but that is not the point. It is how we talk about them – how we help students encounter knowledge – that is problematic. In lectures, we rarely talk in the way they first made sense to the teacher but rather in ways that often do not make sense. We rarely design deep or meaningful encounters with lecture content and knowledge. As the stuff of human dialogue, content and knowledge reign supreme. As the stuff of monologue it clatters on deaf ears and disengaged minds and vanishes. When this happens, all too often the lecture as a method is blamed.

Models of lecturing

The issue here is not so much lecturing but rather the way in which it is envisaged and realized. As a practice with the potential to ignite that sense of 'being where the action is', the traditional lecture needs to be re-envisaged as a dialogue in which the lecturer and the students are genuinely engaged.

Table 4.1 notes some of the characteristics of such an 'engagement' model, contrasting them with those of more traditional 'restricted' models of lecturing. The restricted category of lecturing can be divided into two sub-models. The models closely echo the general distinctions observed with respect to both the models of communication and the conceptions of teaching described in Chapter 1. The models are distinguished in terms of two sets of descriptive features. The first set describes the essential structure of the lecture. The second set describes the nature of the lecturer. They are not meant to be mutually exclusive but, rather, descriptive and will become clearer when we describe the practical aspects of lecturing.

Restricted 1

The first restricted model of lecturing focuses on the content/material of the lecture exclusively. The lecturer is generally viewed as an instrument for transmitting information: head to 'carry' the material, body physically to transmit it. The approach is essentially prescriptive: improvement is restricted to communication tips being added to the lecturer, like fiddling with the dials and buttons of a television set to adjust the picture, sound, colour, etc., until the quality is sufficiently loud and clear. Lecturing is essentially separate from learning which is entirely the domain of the student and has very little to do with the lecturer.

Lecturing consists here of little more than the reproduction of tips to transmit the material. Its aim is to get the information 'out' clearly: to send it. The implicit assumption is of a linear monologue: that, given the lecturer can be properly heard, the success of lecturing lies in the quality of the information or material presented.

Table 4.1   *Models of lecturing*

Restricted 1	Restricted 2	Engaged
Teacher-focused	**Student-focused**	**Learner-focused**
Structure		
Lecturer agenda	Student agenda	Learning agenda
Lecturing is 'separate' from learning	Lecturing 'causes' learning	Lecturing is 'by-product' of learning
Content from teacher	Content for student	Content for learning
Linear structure	Linear structure	Non-linear structure
Monologue (conceptual transmission)	Monologue (conceptual explanation)	Dialogue (conceptual exchange and change)
Lecturer		
Head and body	Head and body	Head, body and self
Severed persona	Cognitive persona	Engaged persona
Personal focus	Personal-other focus	Interpersonal focus

Restricted 2

The second restricted model also focuses on the content of the lecture but is also concerned that the student receive and acquire the content. As in the first model, the lecturer is essentially a head and body to provide the content, but there is a focus on the student. Improvement of lecturing goes beyond communication tips but is restricted to the acquisition of performance techniques and strategies for delivering the content as the lecture presents it. There is still an implicit assumption of the lecture as a monologue and, given the quality of the instruction and/or explanation of the material, the lecture causes a transfer of content (and hopefully understanding) and will be remembered on the strength of the content and the explanation.

Engaged

The engaged model focuses on the lecturer as a person committed to engaging with other people in a dialogue focused on particular content. This approach considers the lecturer as the pre-eminent instrument for engaging with and communicating to other people. It regards issues of voice, body, movement, use of technology, etc., as aspects of the lecturer's personal engagement with the audience and the relevant content in the learning situation. It aspires to a deep integration or transformation of both the self and the lecture material in terms of the audience (students) to which both are directed. Its aim is to engage the audience: to facilitate both conceptual exchange and conceptual change in the students.

The view here is of the lecture as dialogue – that lecturing (and, indeed, being heard) is the by-product of learning and understanding. If the students learn, then the lecturing has occurred and has been successful, success being measured by the strength of the engagement as constitutive of the whole lecturing and learning situation. Throughout the rest of this chapter, we consider the practical issues of lecturing in terms of moving away from a reliance upon the restricted models and towards the development of an 'engagement' model of lecturing.

DESIGNING THE LECTURE

Designing a lecture from the perspective of the above 'engagement' model is essentially a question of designing a human encounter. In this respect, it is a professional performance addressing a range of issues with respect to both external and internal conditions. By these we mean, respectively, the overall teaching and learning context and design to which the lecture is contributing and the conditions or parameters of the specific lecture(s) itself.

Designing the internal aspects of the lecture needs, of course, to take into consideration the reasons why the lecture is being employed and what its role is within the overall learning and teaching context in which the lecture is situated:

- What general aims and objectives is the lecture method addressing?
- What contexts of meaning are appropriate and what dimensions are to be addressed?
- How does this relate to the other methods of teaching used, to the forms of assessment being employed, to the issues of evaluation being raised?

In other words, it needs to be designed within the overall context of the course and curriculum strategies that we explored in the previous chapter, including the appropriate context and dimension of meaning.

The three primary features describing the internal conditions of the lecture are:

- the lecturer;
- the student group to whom the lecturer is lecturing; and
- the material/content which the former is 'sharing' with the latter.

(We shall come to the environmental situation in which the lecture is taking place in a moment.) In the traditional 'restricted' models, the

Figure 4.1 *Traditional/'restricted' lecture*

commonly regarded configuration of these three features is given in Figure 4.1. It is, as suggested earlier, linear in structure, placing sub-stantial constraints on all three features.

The positions of the lecturer and the student group are essentially separate from one another. Their relationships are primarily defined with respect to the lecture content. The latter, moreover, is generally given in a textual format – knowledge as written – reducing its potential with respect to both the lecturer's presentation and the students' reconstruction of it. In terms of the structural matrix describing the teaching and learning environment, the conventional lecture has generally tended to focus on the intellectual context of student learning, drawing primarily on this content feature at the expense of the social, personal and practical. In addition it has primarily been con-structed as a method of support to student learning – the materials and con-tent chosen and structured with respect to what discipline 'knowledge' students should have at the appropriate level. This support, however, is usu-ally conceived and delivered as a stream of facts, concepts, theories, etc.

The lecture does not have to be so constrained, either in terms of the roles of the student and lecturer or in terms of the structure of the learn-ing matrix employed. In order to diminish some of these constraints the three primary features need to be reconceptualized without a centrally priv-ileged or dominant feature. Figure 4.2 depicts the underlying structure of the engaged model of lecturing in which the material neither defines the relationship between lecturer and student nor remains aloof to change as a result of the relationship between lecturer and student.

In Figure 4.2, the lecture integrates the three features equally. The rela-tionship between the lecturer and the student group is a human relationship potentially capable of addressing a much broader range of the aspects of the matrix describing the learning situation. It will also have repercussions on the way in which the content is chosen and structured. From this perspective the design of the particular lecture or series of lectures is not simply a ques-tion of designing a lecturing 'text' – determining and structuring the material to be presented – but rather designing a lecturing 'voice' or 'mode of being' which integrates material, students and self. By this we do not mean the

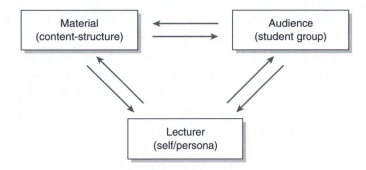

Figure 4.2   *Open/engaged lecture*

actual speaking voice but rather the way in which the individual lecturer is engaged with all the elements making up the lecturing situation. It encompasses the nature of the general learning matrix being used as well as more specific issues of lecture preparation, performance and management.

EXPANDING THE LEARNING MATRIX

As noted above, lifting the constraints on the relationship between the lecturer and the student group allows the lecture to address a much wider range of the learning matrix. Where, for example, a passive relationship almost by definition eliminated the potential for developing the social and practical dimensions of learning and commonly the personal dimension, a more active or interactive approach opens up the possibility for developing these learning dimensions. It goes beyond the few minutes for questions at the end of a lecture, providing time and a structure for students to become actively engaged throughout the lecture. The following activities illustrate the increasing range of such interaction:

- *Reflect*: provide time during the lecture for students to reflect upon the material presented, to digest it and begin to construct their own personal knowledge from it. This may simply consist of a few minutes out for reflection. It might be focused around a question posed by the teacher verbally or on a slide, such as: 'What is the main point of the lecture so far?'
- *Share*: provide time for students to share the main ideas and points of that part of the lecture with a neighbour. Again, this may be focused around a question or even a problem they address together. They may be asked to think of a pertinent question for the teacher or the class. They may, moreover, be encouraged to keep the same partners from lecture to lecture and to share out of class as well.

- *Discuss*: provide time for students to form small groups in which they can take the material raised in the lecture further. This may range from a free-flowing discussion to a set task or problem that they address together. Groups may be asked to elect a chair/spokesperson to feedback questions, points and concerns raised by the group to the teacher and/or to the main group plenary. Such groups may also be asked to work together outside the lecture.

These activities for encouraging interaction can, of course, be used separately or together, one leading to another in a *snowball* fashion. They may be used several times during the lecture depending on time and can be effectively linked to a series of pre-readings as well as the lecture material.

Students need some preparation in the acceptance and development of such interactive techniques. Teachers need to develop and practise their own practical and creative skills in initiating them and managing them within the constraints of the lecture hall. These activities, and others, can be extremely effective and successful for engaging students. They also provide the lecturer with feedback on how well their students understand certain key ideas or concepts by assessing their learning. Such activities – called classroom assessment techniques or CATs (Angelo and Cross, 1993) – can be used in very large groups and in a wide range of spatial configurations (CATs are discussed more fully in Chapter 8).

Managed well, interspersing teacher exposition with student activities offers opportunities for students to develop the social dimensions of learning with others and opens up the potential and time for practical learning in the form of task- or problem-focused group work. In addition, it goes a long way towards addressing key problems associated with traditional lecturing, chief among those being the student's lack of engagement with the situation and the content, and the distracting internal dialogues ('internal noise') disrupting their concentration and attention. It permits the development of a focused and pertinent dialogue, dialogue which, moreover, can be internalized and developed into active and constructive approaches to the content and material.

In this respect interactive techniques of lecturing encourage the development of the 'double-arrow' nature of the relationship between the lecturer and student group in Figure 4.2 above, extending its dynamic and potential. Such techniques, moreover, also sanction the personal dimension of learning and, at the same time, extend the relationship between 'student' and 'material' in Figure 4.2. In providing the space for students to contribute their own personal material to the lecture situation, material from their readings, personal experience, reflections in the form of ideas, concepts, illustrations and so forth, the interactive lecture is able to enrich the material/content aspect of the lecture immensely.

While the lecture is primarily regarded as a method for supporting student learning, the open/engaged model permits the possibility of developing the lecture as more of a process for facilitating an interpersonal context of learning. Here, interactive learning techniques are extended to overall leadership of the lecturing session. Individual groups of students or the whole group itself may be given the authority and role of deciding the content/material, the objectives and the learning methods of particular lecture sessions or even a series of lectures. Structured guidelines for such student-led sessions and training in their operation may be necessary but they have been found to result in wider-ranging discussions and more complex learning outcomes (Tang, 1998; McKeachie, 2006). Lectures might also be used to encourage the development of such peer-run groups outside the classroom.

The lecture, moreover, need not confine itself to supporting learning or facilitating interpersonal learning. Lectures or substantial parts of lectures might be designed to encourage independent learning. This does not simply mean devising innovative methods for interactive group work. It requires methods by which they are encouraged to develop an independent curriculum in certain topics, with guidelines and strategies for self-direction in their out-of-class reading, use of the library, exploration of computer-mediated resources, electronic bulletin boards and so forth. It may include – particularly for more mature students and part-time students – sessions that encourage a critical self-exploration of appropriate social, cultural and work-related activities. Each provides potential access to the range of intellectual, personal, social and practical aspects of their learning.

The context and dimensions of student learning are here intrinsic to the lecture, guiding the development and complexion of the matrix on which the lecturer will develop their design. How the lecture matrix is structured will ultimately depend on the overall course matrix (Chapter 3) and includes subject matter, the level and experience of the student group, the learning objectives for the lecture sessions, the other teaching and learning activities and methods, and so forth. It will also have significant implications for preparing the lecture, its performance and management.

LECTURING PREPARATION AND PERFORMANCE

Preparing for a lecture is both more important and more multifaceted than is often imagined, particularly if one is preparing an 'open/engaged' lecture. All too frequently, lecturers will regard themselves primarily as the writer of

Matrix shape	Lecture objectives	Content and structure	Teaching and learning activities	Resources, space and technology	Self-persona

Figure 4.3 *Key areas of preparation*

a lecture and, sometimes, albeit reluctantly, as an actor delivering lines. In truth, they are writer, actor, director and producer, responsible for all aspects of a performance and its preparation. The main function of these roles is to ensure that the key links between the lecturer, the students and the material shared between them are integrated, aligned and working together. In this respect, preparation should focus on the development and relationship between six key areas (see Figure 4.3).

The arrow in Figure 4.3 suggests that decisions and consequent links will tend to go from left to right, although this is not strict. There is typically a recursive aspect to preparation which entails a back and forth movement across the features. Limits and constraints in the resources and space available will have repercussions on what can be effectively accomplished. Generally, however, it is useful to decide on the shape of the learning 'matrix' that the lecturer wishes to address and then design the specific objectives and content/structure for the lecture in light of that shape. Much of this part of the preparation may already have been undertaken in the overall course design (see Chapter 3). The precise teaching and learning activities that the lecture will employ, the nature of the resources used and the personal style or approach which the lecturer adopts, ideally will be composed to realize these objectives.

Lecture matrix and learning objectives

In designing the shape of the lecture matrix, one has to be realistic and take into consideration the overall shape of the course matrix and associated objectives (Chapter 3). While the lecture can address more issues of learning than generally acknowledged, it cannot achieve everything. Nor should it be expected to do so. Within these parameters, the specific objectives should be realistic and achievable for the students, and may even be negotiated with them.

Content and structure

The main question here concerns the relationship between the specific content of the lecture – which needs to relate coherently with the overall

Table 4.2 *Lecture structures*

Traditional – linear
Problem-oriented
Comparisons
Thesis
Sequence – development
Network
Concept map
Case studies

general topic/subject of the course or lecture series – and the structure of its presentation. A well planned lecture allows the instructor to:

- summarize vast chunks of material succinctly;
- present cutting-edge research not found in a textbook;
- provide students with necessary background or a conceptual framework;
- present key concepts, ideas and principles clearly; and
- model how scholars approach or solve problems.

Lecturers, however, routinely take a linear and/or textual approach to the structuring of lecture content, an approach often derived from their own experience, from the textual nature of their own engagement with the material and from not reflecting on the alternatives. Yet, lectures are primarily an oral experience providing the opportunity for a range of more non-linear structures. Table 4.2 presents just a few options which lecturers may wish to consider.

While a charismatic instructor certainly can get students excited about the material (McKeachie, 2006), these alternatives illustrate just a few possibilities for approaching material in ways designed to facilitate student learning. They include helping students make connections, challenge preconceptions, relate the material to concrete problems and/or real cases and critically analyse hypotheses and interpretations. They can also aid students to develop higher-level conceptual tools – models, maps and networks – for exploring and developing ideas, concepts, facts, skills, attitudes, personal and social interactions and so on.

Choice of structure will, crucially, include how the material is introduced and concluded, be that with a problem, an illustration, a quote, an object, a picture or even with an explanation of an unfamiliar structure itself – all of which might be used as introductions or conclusions. As cognitive psychologists have found, effective processing includes attention, interpretation, elaboration, generation and retrieval practice. A lecture, then, that is carefully structured in such a way that both repeats and introduces new material across the term, will enable students to focus, draw on and connect with prior knowledge and experience, elaborate and build knowledge, and ultimately retrieve that knowledge in new contexts (deWinstanley et al., 2002).

Teaching and learning activities

Opening up the possible lecture structures that can be used also opens up the range of teaching and learning activities, as indicated above, which may be employed. Ideally, the structure and activities will be developed together, complementing one another. A problem-oriented structure may, for example, begin with a demonstration: concept maps with group discussion, case studies with role-play and so on. The design of this relationship between lecture structures and activities provides the key location for creativity and innovation in lecturing. Even given the usual academic constraints of what is 'permissible' as well as those of space, time, resources and so forth, the permutations and possibilities available to the lecturer are limited primarily by their imagination and confidence.

Problematizing teaching

The most effective lecture structures often share a common and critical characteristic: they problematize the student's encounter with the lecture content. According to Ken Bain (2004), the 'best' or most effective college teachers were distinguished from their less accomplished colleagues in how they engaged their students with questions in their teaching, especially their lectures. In a study of 63 college professors from a range of disciplines, he found that the lectures of the more accomplished lecturers problematized their lectures in five separate ways. They regularly:

- began with a question or story that raised a problem;
- found ways to help the students understand the significance of the question (by helping them connect it to other larger questions or their own experience);
- asked their students to answer or engage critically with the question;
- answered the question for the students; and
- ended the lecture with a related question.

The only step they did not do, on occasion, was to answer the question. This, ironically, is often all that most lectures actually do: provide answers (in terms of facts and content) for questions which have not been posed to the students, and the relevance of which has not been articulated, and which the students do not get a chance to answer or grapple with in the classroom and which are not related to further questions or problems. While these excellent lecturers will often simply pose questions directly to the students, more often the students are encouraged to come up with their own questions and to construct the meaning of course content (Bain, 2004). The problematized lecture structure gives students a model for how to raise critical questions and actively engage with the course content in their study individually or with peers (see Box 4.1).

Box 4.1 *Lecturing to large groups*

Elisabeth, a professor of cardiology in the medical school, has been asked to do five linked lectures for a large group of second-year medical students. More used to teaching in rounds and in small clinical settings, she was a bit daunted about speaking to 100 staring faces. Having sat in on some passive lectures given by her peers, and recalling her own experience as a chronically tired med student struggling to stay awake in class, she knew it was necessary to engage the students. She decided to structure her lectures to promote critical thinking and engaging student learning without sacrificing crucial content.

Importantly, she sought to problematize each lecture, by asking them initially to reflect critically on a key question pertinent to the topic, to underscore the relevance and application. She then broke up her presentation by asking students to form small groups and to predict responses or generate answers, and simply to take a few moments to reflect on how they could apply what they had just learnt to clinical settings. By varying the length, time and type of student response breaks, students remained engaged in the lecture throughout, and felt comfortable asking questions. Elisabeth also gauged student comprehension of difficult concepts by asking them to answer a simple question or to generate a new question about the material. This gave her instant feedback on her teaching and their learning. She often had them do this in groups or pairs, to promote the interpersonal, as well as to enhance their individual learning.

Resources, space and technology

Preparing for a lecture also requires an imaginative examination of the technological resources available and their integration with the lecture's structure and specific activities. In the first instance, this might entail what the space will look like for both lecturers and student groups. Lecturers exist in three dimensions but often stand or sit in a one-dimensional spot and deliver in a straight line out to a student body. What possibilities exist for movement: both among students and in front of them? Can they be developed? Can the students easily move or slide into groups? Has the lecturer positioned herself in front of a lectern or next to an overhead projector so that movement is inadvertently (or even intentionally) limited? Is he maximizing the potential of the space?

What resources are available: projectors, computers, Internet access, conferencing facilities, video equipment, laboratory apparatus, pictures, maps, objects, whiteboards, blackboards, flip charts? Are they familiar

Time	Learning objectives	Content and structure	Teaching and learning activities	Resources, space and technology
0–10 mins				
10–30 mins				
30–50 mins				
50–75 mins				
75–90 mins				

Figure 4.4 *Sample lecture script*

with and able to use the equipment? Can it be configured in ways that will help, not hinder the lecture? Can personal resources augment the available resources? These questions need to be carefully addressed and integrated within the overall preparation. How, what, when and where might resources be effectively exploited?

It is not a good idea to become overly complex and technical just for the sake of it but, on the other hand, it is unwise to avoid using resources that may add significantly to the lecture out of fear, unfamiliarity or a lack of skill in their use. Good preparation will include becoming skilled and innovative in the use and deployment of relevant and appropriate space and resources, ranging from ensuring that slides are interesting and easily read, to 'reconstructing' the space to encourage movement, interaction and alternative learning activities.

One useful way of preparing for a lecture is to write out a lecture script. Figure 4.4 gives a simple example setting time guidelines against learning objectives, content and structures, teaching and learning activities and resources to be used. Such scripts provide a guide to making effective relationships between these areas and permit the lecturer a quick guide or summary of what she is doing. Lecturers may draw up their scripts in a variety of different ways, expanding, condensing and experimenting. A script may even provide a useful resource for students.

Self-persona

So far, we have primarily been discussing the lecturer in his role as the writer, director and producer of a lecture. Lecturers, of course, have a critical role as actor or performer – a role often neglected to the detriment of both themselves and their students. The area most often neglected is what might be called the lecturer's inner self or persona. The lecturer's intellect is called upon, as is her physical presence, but her inner self often is not. This is understandable and underpins the general performance dilemma that

Isaiah Berlin describes as being 'in a state of panic throughout the lecture. I never looked at a face in an audience for fear it might smile, or frown or yawn.' Box 4.2 describes an embellished version of this dilemma.

Box 4.2 *Lecturing performance: the dilemma*

Nervous and anxious, the inner self does not actually enter fully into the situation. It leaves the self's presence up to its intellect and body. This is the key problem. Without a self to regulate it, nerves get in. There is an empty 'place' for them to inhabit. From this position, they begin to manipulate the situation rather mischievously. They begin to play with the voice: too high, too fast, too breathy, too laboured. They begin to play with the hands: in the pocket, by your side, behind your back, crossed arms, etc. They begin to play with movement: pacing repetitively, entirely static, back to audience, shuffling, rocking, etc. They begin to play with eyes: not looking at anyone; skidding away; looking over the top; trapped on one person. They begin playing with time: too fast, too slow, with objects. They fiddle with pens, combs, paper, glasses, watches and rings. They play with machines: switches do not work, slides and transparencies appear upside down and screens wobble. They begin playing with the space: tables, chairs and lecterns suddenly surround and constrain or, alternatively, look miles away; the floor is a menacing void. Not content simply to play with these aspects of the lecturer's actual performance, nerves then rather maliciously begin to make the lecturer hyperconscious of what is happening, setting off a debilitating succession of feelings of panic, fright, alarm, dread, frenzy, terror and hysteria. The intellect all but collapses and the body all but freezes. The tiny fragment of the self that may have been there has long ago fled.

This, of course, is an exaggerated version of a lecturer's worst nightmare. The solution is rather simple, if requiring some practice and preparation to implement. Bring yourself into the lecture! More accurately, do not let yourself depart. Maintaining a lecturing self or persona in performance is the key to developing a lecturing 'voice' and the secret to cultivating an encounter 'where the action is'. It requires the lecturer to decide the kind of person he wishes to be for the lecture. This should not be something counterfeit or insincere but, rather, should be informed by positive and appropriate aspects of the lecturer's own personality and extended for the engagement with students. It might, for example, consist of being:

- open and friendly;
- expert and authoritative;
- emotive and enthusiastic;
- relaxed and dry;
- reflective and analytical; and
- unpredictable and challenging.

Such selves or personae are best tailored to particular times and audiences. A matrix shape concerned with support, for example, may be open and friendly, whereas a matrix shape focusing on encouraging independence might be more analytical and dry. These are, of course, not mutually exclusive.

Critically, a teacher should not feel compelled to adopt a persona that is unnatural or seems to go against the grain of his or her personality. 'But I'm not an entertainer,' many teachers protest. 'I can't run around the room, telling jokes or being dramatic.' This may be true for many of us, but we can still dig down and reflect on what it was about the material that inspired or engaged us, and seek to share that enthusiasm with our students. Such selves should normally also incorporate a willingness to enjoy oneself within the central concern of engaging students.

Preparing the self adequately, moreover, usually requires a degree of 'rehearsing' with the material, space and resources, particularly if these are unfamiliar. Even two or three minutes spent preparing both the lecturing self and the space can be immensely effective.

Finally, it is worth remembering that a lecture is not a monologue starting from nowhere but rather a dialogue responding to a tangible comment or question or expression of interest evidenced by the very presence of the student group. The nature of that interest is precisely that which the lecture is addressing and which is embodied in the lecture's objectives. Preparation, however elaborate, is then preparation for a response. The degree to which one prepares will depend on the lecturer, the lecturing style he or she develops, the environment and so forth, but providing time for preparation can make all the difference to both the students' and the lecturer's learning.

DELIVERING AND MANAGING THE LECTURE

Lecturing 'tips'?

How the lecturer delivers her lecture will depend largely on how the above issues have been developed and prepared. The idea of an *engaged* encounter focused on dialogue and student learning addresses a wide range of key delivery issues often provided as communication 'tips' in a rather additive way. These include:

- taking care that you can be heard by everyone;
- making eye contact with the whole student group;
- ensuring that your visual aids and handouts are clear;
- using humour, anecdotes, illustrations;
- stressing important points; and
- being prepared to be flexible and change/add/delete aspects of the lecture.

Such general 'tips' are important but must make sense to the lecturer and not be slavishly implemented for reasons the lecturer is not sure about. All the above points are largely common sense and, in each case, their effective use is a result of an 'engaged' lecture.

If, for example, a lecturer genuinely wants to engage and communicate with his students he will naturally want to find ways to ensure his voice is heard (using microphones if necessary), to make eye contact and stress the important points. This is not simply a question of raising one's voice to the minimum required of a monologue or staring at students or underlining points for the sake of it. Similarly, the design and clarity of visual aids and handouts are to enable engagement, not simply for the transmission and simple acquisition of content. Humour, anecdotes and illustrations, moreover, may be prearranged but their use is most effective when they arise naturally and are not merely inserted into the lecture (e.g. 'Tell joke here'). Be prepared not to use them or to use others where appropriate.

Likewise, be willing to improvise – to change, delete and add material – if this encourages an engagement between lecturer, students and material. Lecturing tips and communication advice should not be simply added on without thinking through their intention but, rather, integrated within the lecturing 'voice' or 'way of being' and practised only in so far as they promote engagement and learning.

Management styles

If the range of 'lecturing voices' behind the delivery of lectures is broad and diverse, there is also considerable latitude in the general management styles employed in lectures. They range from the complete 'laissez faire' to seeing the classroom as the 'sacred temple of learning' (Carbonne, 1998: 77–8), with many shades in between. They each have their respective responses to such issues as: attendance, arriving late or leaving early, reading non-classroom materials at the back, checking email, using the Internet, side talking and so on. Some lecturers will accept just about anything; others will accept very little.

There is no right or wrong as such. What is appropriate for the class is usually for individual lecturers to decide, but should develop from the relationship between their lecturing self, the nature of the student group and the material. Moreover, the instructor should address disruptive or offensive behaviours, but should identify those behaviours upfront, in class and in the course syllabus. It is unlikely that one set of rules or expectations will be appropriate for all situations. The key issue will be the effect of the behaviour on the quality of the engagement and student learning and this may, in many cases, be effectively shared and negotiated with the student group.

Evaluation

Finally, developing and improving one's lecturing is an ongoing process. As a semi-public practice, lecturing allows for feedback from a variety of sources other than one's own reflections and judgments (see Chapter 9). These will primarily consist of colleagues and students and may include the use of student evaluations, peer observations, digital recordings and teaching observations (see Appendix 1) and so on. Evaluations and feedback will provide a wealth of data and useful comments, information and suggestions.

Reflecting and implementing the results of this feedback needs, again, to be considered within the context of the full scope of lecturing as a process of engagement. A small number of teachers will, for various reasons, be unable to develop lecturing approaches in which they are engaged with their material and their students. These teachers should, if at all possible, look to alternative methods of teaching.

CONCLUSIONS

In many ways, the lecture is the classic scapegoat for attacks on the quality of higher education. These attacks may be warranted – they are certainly not surprising. Regarded by society at large as almost synonymous with what the university does, when quality is challenged, the lecture will be first in the firing line, protected only by its embedded traditions and its sheer efficiency of working with large numbers of students. It does suggest, however, that widespread and substantive change in the way in which academics approach the lecture may profoundly change how the university is viewed, by all those who work in, and are served by, higher education.

Final questions: The emphasis on coverage – and the perception that one must not sacrifice content or waste course time with alternative learning strategies – continues to make its mark. Reflective professionals may want to consider: what are there barriers that I must address in promoting interactive and learner-focused lecturing? How many of these barriers are due mainly to my discomfort with a new approach? Are there other, non-lecture-based teaching methods that might be more appropriate for meeting my learning objectives? What strategies can I use to engage my students in actively participating in the presentation of the lecture? What activities and/or lecture-related assignments might assist students in the active construction of new knowledge? Addressing these questions will help change the very nature of the lecture as it has traditionally been regarded.

chapter 5

FACILITATING: SMALL-GROUP TEACHING

Of a good leader when his task is finished, his goal achieved, they say, we did that ourselves. (Lao Tzu, c. 600 BCE)

In this chapter, we explore the significance of small-group learning in higher education. Drawing on a wide range of theories and practices of small-group teaching, we examine keys aspects of group teaching, including the overall purposes of groups, group leadership and phases of groups. We then carefully explore how different types of group activity might address the learning issues raised by the critical matrix, providing a diverse range of possibilities and activities for achieving the different outcomes which teachers may have established for the students on their courses.

INTRODUCTION

Lao Tzu's ancient observation resonates with many contemporary ideas in teaching in higher education. Earlier, we discussed the importance of innovation theory in course design, and a key aspect of this is encouraging our students' sense of ownership in the learning process. We have also suggested that learning is more a process of change than of assimilation. In other words, learning is innovation.

In today's context, however, Lao Tzu's words may seem manipulative, even coercive. Are we setting up our students to do what we want them to do, rather than helping them develop a strong sense of responsibility for their own learning? Are we helping them view their programmes as a joint venture with their teachers, rather than as a course of study imposed upon them? The reality is we must be sensitive to our own tendencies to transmit in group work; otherwise students will hardly feel they did it themselves.

The opportunity to come together in small groups to change conceptions and explore theories and insights provides students with one of the most important learning experiences higher education has to offer. Research has shown that small-group work can help students construct meaning more deeply; enhance critical thinking skills; provide opportunities for feedback and self-reflection; promote social and emotional development; enhance an awareness and acceptance of diversity; and even lessen student attrition (Cooper and Robinson, 2000a). Interacting with their peers can help students develop and construct their own conceptions – partly by having to think through and even defend their own ideas, but also when they question or clarify the views held by others (Webb and Mastergeorge, 2003). When worked into large classes, small-group activities can also reduce anonymity and promote student accountability (Yazedjian and Kolkhorst, 2007).

Small-group work can also develop the interpersonal and collegial interactions among students; promote leadership, teamwork and collaboration; and enhance practical problem-solving, decision-making, presenting and other professional skills. Research on millennials has suggested that students entering college today are more team-oriented than ever before, having gone through their youth and adolescence moving from one structured team activity, project or sport to the next, winning or losing as a team, not as individuals (Howe and Strauss, 2003; DeBard, 2004). This generation of students is said to be more rule-abiding and compliant than previous generations, and are comfortable with (and may even expect) learning situations that stress co-operation and collaboration over competition (DeBard, 2004).

While there is a strong student demand for teaching through tutorials and seminars, and other forms of small-group learning (Bligh, 2000b), not all students, or the faculty who teach them, are satisfied with the experience. Teachers may find teaching in small groups to be demanding, particularly if they have not learnt strategies for engaging their students effectively. This may also be the case for our students who, despite years of primary and secondary education aimed at developing interpersonal skills, express the same kind of feelings prevalent years ago: 'Classes are purgatory for [faculty] and purgatory for us. They're boring because everyone just sits there and everyone else's silent and I feel it's incumbent on me to speak but I don't like to unless I am sure of myself. I don't like to express half-formed ideas' (Cox, 1976: 40). We might say that expressing half-formed ideas to develop in dialogue with others is an important part of the whole learning process, but our students may still need to be convinced.

Teaching in small groups is not without its challenges. Issues, such as domination by individuals, a lack of trust among group members, hidden agendas and private aims can subvert what the group is trying to do and pose substantial problems for achieving learning. They also include distractions that may be much more than a healthy form of testing out and/or 'scapegoating', which can not only ruin the atmosphere of a group but also prevent any understanding of the underlying problems (McKeachie, 2006).

Teachers, too, may be sceptical of small-group work for other reasons as well. For many, employing small-group activities may mean that they must reject lectures, an approach they would not want to abandon. Others may assume that using class time for small-group work means they must sacrifice time to cover important material, while others may question how well students learn in small-group contexts. Still others have resisted small-group work for reasons related to the perception that learning is a solitary venture; the idea that students must be adequately prepped to work in groups; perceptions of student resistance to group work; real or imagined negative reactions from fellow faculty members; and simply the perception that classroom logistics are ill-conducive to small-group work (Cooper et al., 2000).

In this chapter, we first explore some of these general problems and issues and consider the roles and purposes of group work. Then we give the practical dimension in terms of how they apply to the different areas of the matrix and what might be done to improve teaching in these areas. Unfortunately, problems within groups are not solved by reading advice, no matter how useful. Changing behaviour in this context involves some deeper assumptions, expectations and even values that do not change easily through acquiring a little extra knowledge.

A serious difficulty is the discrepancy between expectations and what actually happens. Usually when we come together in groups, as distinct from crowds or audiences, for instance, we do so either to seek pleasure in other people's company, in a pub or at a party for example, or because we need to join together to do something or to produce something. On the one hand, students may expect to experience a sense of belonging and enjoyment, and to share ideas and experiences. Alternatively, when a group is really nothing more than a collection of individual learners, even when some learning happens, students may feel threatened by the group experience. If individuals

Table 5.1 *Small-group work and the critical matrix*

Intellectual	Personal
Developing cognitive understanding Appreciating other perceptions, points of view Changing conceptions Questioning assumptions Developing oral and written skills Providing feedback to faculty	Providing opportunities for practice in self-expression Developing self-awareness Encouraging autonomy Encouraging commitment Weakening defensive attitudes Improving attitudes to the subject
Social	**Practical**

Encouraging co-operation and an awareness of
  others
Developing a sense of social identity
Developing a sense of belonging and
  community
Enhancing communication
Developing leadership
	Developing teamwork skills
	Developing entrepreneurial skills
	Solving practical problems
	Carrying out specific tasks
	Creating artefacts or designs
	Writing reports
	Collecting samples
	Describing environments
	Presenting/reporting knowledge

feel that they have not engaged with, or meaningfully contributed something to the group, they may feel frustrated, powerless or even alienated. Understanding the nature and dynamics of the small-group experience can do much to enhance learning.

GROUP WORK

Purposes

In Table 5.1 we present some common purposes of group work, which we frame within the categories of the critical matrix. As with any genre of teaching, great skill and determination are needed to see these purposes achieved.

Many faculty believe that the essential purpose of teaching in small groups is to ensure that students understand what they try to convey in lectures, although this view may be changing (Bogaard et al., 2005). Careful questioning, some would argue, may bring out major misunderstandings and difficulties, which can then be clarified by the teacher. Given that teachers often feel extreme pressure to cover ground effectively, this view is understandable. Yet, if this purpose is pursued vigorously, other purposes of group work may be ignored or actively discouraged, to the detriment of student learning and professional development.

When they leave the formal supportive structures of higher education behind them, students will likely encounter new structures in the workplace, but may have little ability to cope with new learning contexts. Many professionals, for example, now find themselves working in teams, and an important function of group work in higher education is to enable students to work both independently and co-operatively within a team. Such teams may or may not have formal leaders. Moreover, students entering the workplace are unlikely to encounter the leadership style of the traditional seminar leader who controls the activity of the class in such a way that students may not feel any sense of responsibility for what happens in the group.

The group experience can, in fact, be extremely important in achieving freedom from dependency if the students learn to play a variety of roles in the group and begin to develop a sense of responsibility for the group's success or failure. In the process of learning these roles they will need to develop more acute self-understanding; to become aware of their own inhibitions, defences and assumptions; to be able to recognize the difficulties that other students experience; and to begin to help themselves to overcome these difficulties. In learning to become more sensitive to different points of view and ways of thinking, and to work co-operatively with others using the varied skills of the group, they may begin to develop a surer sense of social identity and a feeling of belonging and commitment. This can not only encourage enthusiasm in the subject but also a willingness to reveal abilities, which are frequently hidden, even from themselves. Students' oral skills, moreover, are unlikely to develop very much more simply in response to probing questions.

There needs to be a genuine sense of opportunity for self-expression and this may be difficult in a context where the main object is to increase understanding and correct misconceptions and faulty reasoning. Such a restricted conception might limit other important uses of small-group work, such as enabling staff to understand more about how students respond generally to their educational experience.

Most faculty would agree that it is important for them to know why their students are taking their courses, and what sort of deeper satisfaction and disappointments they are experiencing. This will depend on the quality of the personal relationships established with the students but, if the roles played by the students and faculty in their group work are highly restricted, it may be difficult for good personal relationships to develop.

It is important to note, however, that students many not necessarily perceive the value of group work in the same way as their teachers. Bogaard et al.

(2005), for example, found that many instructors did believe that small-group teaching was important for building students' communication skills and helping them acquire the confidence to express their ideas. Less important was their need to disseminate more information to their students, or to lecture during the small-group session. Interestingly, while students enrolled in those classes agreed that developing their communications skills was important, they valued the small-group sections because they allowed them the opportunity to clarify lecture points, improve their understanding of the material and receive help with their written work.

Leading groups

Student participation in small groups has frequently been described in general terms that look something like personality characteristics: the 'friendly helper', the 'tough battler' and the 'logical thinker'. Their respective worlds might be described as mutual love, affection, tenderness and sympathy; conflict-flight, assertiveness; and understanding, logic, knowledge and systems. They will have different task-maintenance behaviours, different ways of evaluating others and different methods of influence, and will suffer from different personal threats (Kolb et al., 1994).

Many student roles will, in this respect, be dependent upon the leadership styles that teachers adopt, so it is especially important for teachers to recognize both 1) the range of different leadership styles they might effectively employ to improve student learning; and 2) that they are not personally limited to a small range of styles. Indeed, as will become apparent in the next section, teachers may need to alternate leadership styles as a group progresses.

In a now classic study based on Kurt Lewin's work on small groups (Lippet and White, 1961), for example, teachers were asked to run a group teaching session, each teacher employing three very different leadership styles – autocratic, democratic and laissez-faire. While the democratic style was deemed most effective in the teaching context of the study, it was also found that, despite their different personalities, the teachers were all capable of operating the three leadership styles effectively.

Figure 5.1 provides a useful way of mapping leadership styles with respect to two general dimensions: a directing dimension which describes the degree to which a leader is telling the group what to do (learn) and how to do it; and a supportive dimension which describes the degree to which the leader is supporting the group members in doing what they are doing (learning).

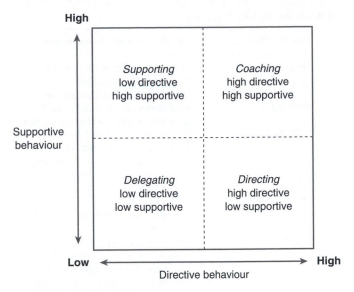

Figure 5.1 *Group leadership styles*

The traditional role of the teacher in a small-group setting is that of a directive leader – exhibiting differing degrees of support – who initiates proceedings with a short statement or summary, and then tries to draw out students' thoughts, periodically linking those perspectives together, redirecting the content of the discussion as appropriate. Students and teachers may come to depend on this process, in which the teacher retains the voice of authority and expertise. While this may seem effective, since the instructor may be able to elicit the precise responses she is looking for, this process may inhibit the creativity and originality of the group. To counteract this dependency on the instructor, this role has recently included fewer directive styles of the teacher as facilitator, in which she encourages interaction without dominating the group (Curzan and Damour, 2006).

Within the structure depicted in Figure 5.1, leadership styles can include a wide range of roles, suggesting a range of teaching behaviours or strategies that teachers might display in small-group work. They might include 'devil's advocate', 'chairperson', 'consultant' and 'counsellor', the latter indicating a concern for the social and emotional needs of students. In addition, the teacher may sometimes need to be an observer or commentator or, at other times, if the group is divided into subgroups, even a 'wandering minstrel'.

Heron's (2001) 'six category intervention analysis' offers a useful way to understand the variation in instructor behaviours across the range of these leadership styles and roles (see Table 5.2). These may be arranged along

Table 5.2 *Teacher behaviours in groups*

	The teacher can	Related verbal behaviours	
Inform	PRESCRIBE	Provide a topic or raise an issue Re-route the discussion Direct the student's responses	Teacher-focused
	INFORM	Summarize, inter-relate, clarify Give knowledge and information	

	CONFRONT	Challenge by a direct question
		Disagree with, correct, critically
		   evaluate a student statement
		Raise student consciousness about
		   the material	

	RELEASE TENSION	Arouse laughter Stimulate an emotional response to the topic	
	ELICIT	Draw out student opinion/ knowledge/problem-solving Facilitate student interaction Encourage self-directed learning Approve, reinforce, affirm the	
Elicit	SUPPORT	value of student contributions	Learner-focused

Source: Adapted from Heron, 2001

polar axes from teacher-focused behaviours, in which the teacher informs and tightly prescribes and directs the discussion, to more learner-focused behaviours where the teacher uses discussion to elicit and support students in the development of their own knowledge and contributions. It is worth noting, as Bligh (2000a) suggests, that the omission of these latter behaviours in discussion groups can also contribute to the persistence of interpersonal barriers between students.

Phases in groups

It can be important for teachers to realize that groups, like people, have life stages with important implications for leadership. Some group behaviour can be very worrying for a teacher unless they realize it is normal for it to be happening at various phases or stages. There is considerable agreement on how to describe these phases with, however, some interesting differences (Chidambaram and Bostrom, 1996; Jaques and Salmon, 2007). Research on groups suggests that they may work either sequentially or non-sequentially (see Table 5.3).

Tuckman's classic study (1965/2001), for example, describes the sequential phases as:

Table 5.3 *Comparison of models of group developement*

Sequential model		Non-sequential model
Tuckman *Without teacher facilitation*	**Johnson and Johnson** *With teacher facilitation*	**Gersick** *Without teacher facilitation or group leader*
Forming Members meet Test limits of acceptable behaviour	**Defining and structuring** Identifying procedures Becoming oriented	
Storming Conflict within the group Expression of individuality resistance to group influence	**Conforming** Getting acquainted Conforming to procedures	**Alternating periods of inertia and inactivity; revolution and conflict; stability and productivity** Stability accentuated by abrupt changes in group behaviour
	Trust building Recognizing mutuality Building trust	
	Rebelling and differentiating Student or group may challenge authority of teacher	
Norming Members accept group Develop more cohesiveness, more comfortable with one another Able to express opinions	**Committing and owning** Committing to goals of group 'Owning' group and other members Dependence on other group members Personal commitment to the group experience Reliance on group members	**Midpoint realization** No universal pattern, but activity level might change at midway point of process Equilibrium destroyed Group becomes aware of task at hand and/or deadline New behaviours established
Performing Task-related work increases as group supports grows; more constructive activity	**Producing** Functioning maturely and productively Increased commitment to the group Controversy handled constructively Problem-solving through consensus Shared leadership Harmonious division of labour	**Producing** Group realizes it must complete task at hand Committed to finishing task Still may have intermittent bursts of inertia or conflict
Adjourning Can create anxiety; disengagement with group	**Terminating** Potentially sad/upsetting Collaborative groups will feel sense of accomplishment	**Completion of project** No uniformity in group separation

Source: Adapted from Tuckman, 1965; Chidambaram and Bostrom, 1996; Feather, 1999

- forming;
- storming;
- norming;
- performing; and
- adjourning.

Tuckman's research, however, was based on groups with little or minimal facilitator interaction; the groups essentially lacked guidance and had to figure out how to work together on their own. Other sequential models might work differently when a facilitator is more directly involved with the groups. Johnson and Johnson (cited in Feather, 1999) describe the phases as:

- defining and structuring;
- conforming to procedures;
- trust building;
- rebelling and differentiating;
- committing and owning;
- producing; and
- terminating.

While groups may intend to work towards a more co-operative and functional way of operating, they can get a fouled up on the way. They may even break up if the hostility, storming or rebellious phase is too dominant. Some groups do not experience storming or a great deal of hostility, but it certainly seems to be the case that there is an important time of greater emotion which may come about a quarter of the way through the expected life of the group. With a group that is together over a long period, this might come much nearer the beginning.

These models are similar in their linear and sequential progression towards completion, but the points of conflict and conforming occur at different times. In a one-week course for general practitioners, for example, we found that, on the second or third day, participants were more emotional. The course leaders capitalized on this by introducing the more emotional-oriented learning activities of the course – such as role-play and dealing with patient hostility or bereavement – at this time. While it did result in some very emotional interactions and even tears, the activities would not have been so engaging and useful in the learning process if they had come on the first day or even on the last.

A group could also develop non-sequentially, as in Gersick's model (Chidambaram and Bostrom, 1996). This might occur if students have no clear leadership for their group, either from the teacher or a strong peer. Although there are no uniform phases or stages in this type, groups usually will spend the first part of their allotted time in alternating periods of inertia/inactivity or rebellion/conflict, before realizing at the midpoint that only half their working time remains.

For example, students in a business class may know they have a month to work on a project which asks them to research and present a formal marketing report to the class. Without guidance, it may take the group a while to settle on their topic and the means for gathering preliminary data. In early meetings they may spend a lot of time talking aimlessly, arguing or challenging one another's approaches. At the midpoint, they may suddenly realize the project is due in two weeks. At this point, they may begin more earnestly to produce, but there may still be intermittent stretches of inactivity or bursts of conflict without any guidance.

It is important that the earlier dependency phases are not prolonged. It is also important that the opening phase, where it appears to be necessary to give a great deal more direction, does not set a pattern for the rest of the life of the group. Expecting students to be independent when they are uncertain both about themselves and the group might create serious difficulties. On the other hand, when a teacher is very directive at the beginning, this can be a learning phase for the group indicating that their role is to sit and listen. Setting ground rules for the group at the beginning may be particularly important where there is a danger that students might develop the wrong expectations about how they should proceed and behave.

Ground rules

If the ground rules for working in groups are neither written nor discussed, students are likely to imagine their own. They may, for example, begin by assuming that:

- they should leave it to the teacher to lead, direct and summarize the discussion fully;
- it is the teacher's job to determine the objectives and procedures;
- one should not express one's feelings openly;
- one should not interrupt someone making a presentation;
- a period of silent reading for the whole group is inappropriate; and, even
- breaking into smaller groups or writing is disruptive.

Ground rules which are simply imposed, on the other hand, may have little influence on group behaviour. If the group has a relatively long life, working them out with the students can be helpful and can encourage commitment

(Lieberg, 2008). Ground rules that are worked out with the group or class might include:

- treating one another with respect;
- listening to one another;
- considering each student's opinion;
- tolerating each other's viewpoints;
- being polite when challenging each other; and
- in the case of sensitive topics, agreeing to keep one another's opinions and comments within the confines of the classroom (Davis, 2001).

Ground rules might also include that students come to the class or group prepared and ready to engage in the work.

Giving students some choice and control may make them less inclined to endure 'purgatory' and feel they have responsibility for modifying rules and developing them during the life of the group. Sometimes, individual students may become overly preoccupied with their own behaviour and the group processes, which can distract them from the main group activities. This issue will need to be carefully considered by the teacher. On the other hand, where it is of particular interest for the group to understand better how groups function, learning from the direct experience of the group can be much more effective than being told about it or simply working it out intellectually.

We have raised a number of key general points about group teaching. In the discussion below, we will develop these points further – in terms of the learning matrix – in order to consider in more detail how different approaches can be related to the different purposes of working in groups. Box 5.1 illustrates several of these principles in practice.

Box 5.1 *Facilitating small-group work in a lab setting*

Chris regularly works with six advanced undergraduates and postgraduates in his chemical engineering lab. While he has been satisfied with the overall productivity, he has wondered from time to time if his team works together as effectively as they could, and whether his students, especially his undergraduates, would be able to apply their skills to new contexts. He has also wondered if his postgraduates should be getting more leadership and supervisory experience necessary for their careers either in academia or in industry.

This year, he restructured his labs so that his two postgraduates were each in charge of guiding and training two new undergraduates working in the lab. To support their interpersonal development, each week the lab held a 'journal club' in which undergraduate–postgraduate pairs took turns leading a discussion about a relevant recent article they had all read. Together, they discussed the research, pulling apart the structure of the article better to acclimate the whole lab to the professional expectations and requirements of the field. To develop their independence, he had them take turns presenting different aspects of the research findings and process to one another. The undergraduates were also involved in writing up the results for professional papers and conferences.

THE INTELLECTUAL DIMENSION

Supportive teaching

We have suggested that using small groups primarily to cover material, to increase understanding and to correct misconceptions and faulty reasoning may overshadow the other important purposes of small-group work. Yet, in large groups, teachers find it difficult to explore and understand student problems in coping with difficult parts of the course. Small groups can offer teachers an opportunity to learn more on why students may be having the problems and how they might help solve them.

The first of our intellectual purposes might be approached through essentially supportive teaching, selecting tasks for the appropriate level and exploring where students have misconceptions which prevent them from progressing. If this is the dominant pattern, however, the result may be intellectual dependency and a failure to develop as creative, independent learners and productive team members. Teachers can be quite directive in terms of group processes and enabling students to understand these without telling students what to think or doing their work for them. Clarifying criteria and resources will help indicate how teachers can support their students' independent and interpersonal learning.

We suggested in Chapter 3 that prior reading could be a very important way of covering the content without wasting the learning potential of interacting in small groups. In many disciplines, teachers have integrated active learning activities into their classes by expanding their lecture notes to provide the content previously covered by lectures and used class time to break their students into small groups to solve problems associated with these notes and other key course readings (Bligh, 2000a). These small groups and the lecturer can, then, look at the strengths and weaknesses of the diverse solutions generated, engaging one another in higher-level dialogue and discussion. Mazur (1997) describes the comprehensive development of just such an active learning method called peer instruction. Originally pioneered in physics at Harvard and aimed at engaging students in science (Rosenberg et al., 2006), it has been widely used in a range of disciplines and types of institutions (Fagen et al., 2002).

Promoting discussion and debate

Traditionally, small-group teaching was designed to enable the student to 'think for himself [sic] and work on his own' (Hale, 1964: iii). But small groups can also help students to:

- co-operate and work in teams;
- develop, articulate and share their ideas as individuals;
- challenge the ideas of others;
- learn to assess their own strengths; and
- critique the strengths and weaknesses of their peers and themselves as a group.

Teachers have developed a wide range of techniques (Cooper and Robinson, 2000b; Smith, 2000) to ensure that students are exposed to alternative perspectives, which students learn to evaluate, without assuming they will find the right answer.

Discussion

To ensure that the whole group is involved in discussion, students must be encouraged to do more than simply express their ideas in response to probing or challenging questions from the teacher. Early on, students will need to know that they are expected to respond to each other (constructively) and to develop a sense of responsibility for the group. The kinds of questions that are most effective for generating discussion and critical thinking are usually open-ended ('how' and 'why' rather than 'what' or 'who'), and they do not presume a right or wrong answer, or ask the students to 'guess' the discussion leader's point of view (Curzan and Damour, 2006).

In effective discussions, too, students can be asked to generate solutions or counterpoints to their peers' points of view. Occasionally stopping to summarize key ideas or what has been learnt so far is another effective strategy, as are helping students view their own gaps in their understanding and make larger connections between ideas (Curzan and Damour, 2006). Students can also take turns generating discussion questions and leading discussions, either individually or in small groups.

Debate

Holding a debate can be another effective way to provide support for learning, to encourage independence and to foster the interpersonal. A debate might consist of small groups who are asked to tackle different sides of an issue. They may have to prepare ahead of class, doing research or reading, and develop not only their own argument but also identify points to counter the arguments of their opponents. They may not know the group they will be in ahead of time, or be asked to take the opposite perspective of what they would like to argue, to ensure that they can grasp the alternative point of view more fully (Lieberg, 2008). Other students can take different roles, serving as the moderator, the audience, panellists, etc., to ensure that two students do not dominate the discussion and that many students will have the opportunity to express themselves.

Think-pair-square-share (also called pyramiding, snowballing or progressive doubling)

Another way to engage students in a conversation is by first introducing a problem or task and then asking the students to jot down their thoughts before the discussion begins ('think'). After a few moments of quiet reflection, students will then share their thoughts with a classmate seated near them ('pair'). This ensures that quieter students are not dominated by their more assertive peers. They may then join another pair ('square') or return to the full group and discuss their ideas ('share') (Cooper and Robinson, 2000b). The ideas of individual students are then more likely to be followed through on their merits rather than through personality and domination. Students can gradually be introduced to alternative ideas and have the ability to compare them with their own and perhaps to see a gradual development of these within the group.

The change process, which we have emphasized in earlier chapters, can become a real practical possibility. The progressive doubling structure is also particularly helpful in creating a more personal and co-operative atmosphere and so enabling us to integrate ideas into a wider understanding rather than only progressing by eliminating the apparently weaker ideas. It is often effective to put the ideas of the four or sometimes eight on to flip charts and spend part of the session assisting students to understand the variation between the different solutions and integrate them into a richer and more complex approach.

Buzz groups

This is another method which works informally to get students to share their opinions and ideas with their classmates, supporting the interpersonal. Here, students simply talk to four or five students who sit near them – a particularly useful strategy for using small groups in large lecture settings – to discuss a problem quickly. For example, they may be asked to generate a potential solution, anticipate results or hypothesize an application. They may have to come up with one idea that they can then share with the rest of the class (McKeachie, 2006).

Sharing in rounds

A somewhat less developmental way of introducing independent thinking is to ask for a 'round' where the teacher goes around the group encouraging students to express their ideas and comments individually. This can be threatening unless it is made clear that there is no obligation on the students to say something every time. They may simply pass which is, generally speaking, completely acceptable.

Like progressive doubling, rounds are a useful method of enabling quieter students, especially students whose first language is not English, to contribute. Rounds can offset the limitation of otherwise stimulating and lively discussions, in which there are often no pauses between contributions, which, again, can be particularly difficult for those students who are less assertive or less sure of their own linguistic and intellectual abilities.

These activities address the concern that academic interaction is frequently conducted in an adversarial style, in which ideas are perceived as being in perpetual competition. De Bono (1994), for example, criticizes this style of academic interaction and the overly critical ways of thinking it often inspires. He points out that this style does not always allow us to arrive at the best of different perspectives and suggests that discussion will be enhanced by engaging in processes of 'parallel' thinking, keeping open a range of parallel ideas and drawing from them. Yet, each of the processes described above allows time for ideas to be developed, but also enables them be consolidated into new ways of thinking.

Collaborative learning

Encouraging interdependence through collaborative forms of learning can still be focused on ideas and the intellect. Enabling students to interact within groups of different sizes is important both for intellectual expression and for learning to appreciate the way people can interact, co-operate and collaborate productively. Early research with leaderless groups indicated that, while the distribution of talk in groups of three and four is not shared equally, it is not particularly wide. As soon as there are more than four or five people in a group, the distribution starts to change, with just one or two participants contributing more than the others. Even with relatively small groups of eight, there will start to be a number of participants whose participation is very small (Bligh, 2000a).

The dynamics of this finding are addressed rather easily. The simple process of dividing groups into smaller groups of three or four will guarantee that almost all the participants will have a good opportunity to contribute. For the teacher, this can also be a much easier task than continually trying to encourage reluctant students to participate in the larger group or preventing more talkative students from dominating the discussion through a range of gestures or even a direct verbal intervention (Davis, 2001).

Research has shown, too, that students learning or receiving assistance from peers who are near their own educational level or level of development encourages both student achievement and positive attitudes towards learning (Swarat et al., 2004). Similarly, a recent study of peer-facilitated discussion, in which students enrolled in introductory science, maths and engineering worked substantially with peers who had previously taken and achieved in the course, showed that this helped improve student performance and retained under-represented groups in the sciences (Drane et al., 2005).

Syndicate or peer-managed learning

This method features a team-based system of learning, where students are divided into teams or syndicates (McKeachie, 2006). This division can be spontaneous, in response to a very animated discussion, or it can be deliberately planned, as where a task is introduced and materials are either provided or referenced for students to explore themselves either in libraries or electronically.

The tasks for these groups can be designed to cover areas of the syllabus in which the selection of materials is central. They are, however, more effectively presented through individual and group processes than directly transmitted by the teacher. The group, then, has a responsibility for planning peer activity, for sharing individual reading and for communicating and initiating discussion of the results of this individual work. The final communication can be given in written form or presented orally in a presentation.

As with the progressive doubling, this offers an excellent way to enable students to work on alternative solutions and learn to combine different perspectives and develop the skills of working together. A variation of this method is called jigsaw but, in this case, the groups do not present to the entire class but, instead, each group member represents and presents their work to a new task group. In this way, every student can learn from all the other students (McKeachie, 2006).

Games and simulations

The use of carefully constructed games and simulations can also help address material a teacher may wish to cover in a course. For example, a professor of Spanish and Portuguese created 'bingo'-style games and versions of popular television shows to help familiarize her students with common vocabulary, without having to resort to repetitious memory exercises. Similarly, a professor of history requires his students to play a complicated game of 'Lords and serfs', where students take on different medieval avatars and seek to survive the Crusades, the plague and other medieval events.

Such activities can be highly motivating and compelling, but can also introduce ways of dealing with a changing dynamic context. It is very difficult to teach students the ability to make decisions in the context of change and uncertainty, without them having actually to be in these situations. Merely telling students about how others have coped may not develop the flexibility required to live and work in our changing world.

THE PERSONAL DIMENSION

Creating supportive group-learning environments

The most important issue here is for the teacher to establish a supportive and secure environment – a safe space in which students can learn and thrive (Lieberg, 2008). As in any learning context, students may feel concerned about expressing their ideas, but this may be more common in small-group settings. As one student once remarked: 'I've always resented making an idiot of myself' (Cox, 1976: 45).

As we suggested above in our discussion of ground rules, the fear that students experience, even in apparently friendly peer groups, may not be dispelled by simply saying 'we are friendly ... please feel free to express half-formed ideas'. With many groups, the emotional learning might take much longer than the intellectual learning. As the French poet, Paul Valery, has observed: 'Long years must pass before the truths we have made our own become our living flesh.' Some approaches for establishing a supportive environment follow.

Making connections with students

Intellectual change is often delayed or prevented by emotional resistances which may stem from early experiences. Teachers can find themselves being treated as parent figures where independence becomes the issue rather than an intellectual problem. Students can be very anxious and ambivalent about both control and support, and many students, particularly in the first years, feel that university life is impersonal and would welcome a closer relationship with lecturers similar to that which they had with their teachers in secondary school (Cox, 1987; Light, 2001).

University students, however, are adults and part of being an adult at university is relating to the teachers as equals in a way not possible at school. This does not mean that, intellectually, students are on the same level as their teachers, but it does mean that, in talking about more personal matters, it can be a more balanced relationship.

Locating alternative learning environments

Geologists and botanists often comment, for example, on how they get to know their students better and relate more fully on field trips. Although it is more difficult for teachers in other subjects to do this in the same way, there are, nevertheless, ways of relating outside the seminar room. These might be combined with visits to exhibitions, museums or even outside lectures and, for arts students, theatres and galleries can be obvious ways of combining intellectual with personal interests. Some programmes include residential short courses and these can be especially useful in breaking down barriers.

Responding with empathy

In Chapter 3 we mentioned reflective triads which can help students to personalize what they have been learning on their courses. Here, teachers build upon a student's idea without taking it away and making it purely their own. Empathy, the key characteristic, provides students with the sense of real participation in a very personal way. Similarly, asking students questions, which they can actually respond to, might help.

Often students are intimidated by questions that may seem appropriate to the teacher but which require both conceptual levels of thinking and a broad range of knowledge that are inappropriate. For example, a group of first-year students were asked to relate the Hegelian theory of tragedy to a difficult line in a complex Samuel Beckett play. The silence that ensued was predictable. On the other hand, asking questions which simply require short, right or wrong answers may make students feel they are being interrogated, rather than taking part in an intellectual discussion.

As mentioned above, if students are asked open-ended questions, they can then reply in a way that is more closely related to their personal concerns, but not be clearly 'wrong'. Gentle encouragement to continue, moreover, can help students to take more risks, especially if they are not immediately corrected when they make a mistake.

Encouraging self-knowledge

One of the elements of the deeper approach to learning is relating what we have learnt to our own personal experience, but sometimes students feel this is not a legitimate thing to do within a serious seminar, so it may need to be encouraged. An important aspect of learning is that experience is valued. This is especially true with more mature students who can feel rejected when they think their experience is ignored. Independent thinking can be more risky in larger groups and the opportunity to talk in pairs or threes, as we have stressed, can be particularly important for beginning to explore ideas that are more independent.

Encouraging self-knowledge is an important feature of group work, and reflecting on the impact of our words on the other people in the group can be very helpful. Providing space in a session to take time-out from the topic and engage in activities in which the topic is dropped, and examining various issues of the group process and its impact on individuals intellectually and emotionally, is still rare in higher education. Yet such strategies can be extremely useful in supporting learning. It may be emotionally risky or difficult for the teacher, but as it becomes part of the normal way of working in groups, supported by ground rules, it can be an important aid for developing student independence.

Role-play

Another activity where students can take risks in expressing other aspects of themselves, often those which are guarded and concealed, is role-play. This activity can be incorporated into many types of classes, not just those subjects concerned with personal relationships. The purpose is to help students reflect individually on a specific perspective with an assigned role, and to extend creative thinking to the character's attitudes, opinions and responses (Lieberg, 2008).

When students take risks in this way it is important to have debriefing sessions which enable the students to work through any embarrassing anxiety they may have had as well as relating role-play to the learning issues. Role-play can be very enjoyable as well as challenging and, if students enjoy learning, they are likely to become more independent as well as more highly motivated.

Interpersonal knowledge

Discussing interdependence within the context of small-group teaching could include almost anything that makes the group function more effectively. We want to emphasize, however, that such a heading involves developing self-knowledge. This is a general aim of education but it can be particularly helpful for developing effective group work.

Giving students opportunities to observe themselves as part of a group can be essential for developing their self-knowledge. As observers, students will begin to see the nature of their own role in a learning session – how far, for example, they may be serving themselves rather than the needs of the group.

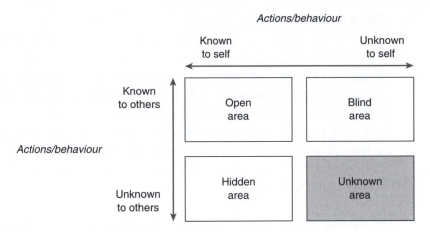

Figure 5.2 *A classification of behaviour in groups*
Source: Adapted from the Johari window (Luft, 1984)

The reports on them as the observed in the group activities, on the other hand, can assist them in becoming aware of qualities and ways of working – blindspots – which they were not aware of in themselves. These areas have been referred to in a renowned framework for classifying group behaviours – the Johari window – as the 'blind' group behaviours (Figure 5.2).

In the 'blind' category, other members of the group can help individuals see things about themselves which they did not know about. At the same time there is an opportunity for hidden behaviours, known to themselves but not to others, to become more public and to offer the opportunity for constructive learning. The area, which is both unknown to the self and unknown to others, is normally not the province of group work in higher education and is best left to a different, perhaps more therapeutic context. A few methods of observation follow.

Fishbowl
One way of encouraging this is to set aside time for individuals or groups to observe the group as it works. For group observation, a fishbowl arrangement is useful. The group is divided into two, an inner group doing task-orientated work related to the course, and an outer group focusing on the process, observing the way the group is working. The groups can switch, to maintain student interest and enthusiasm (Lieberg, 2008). Providing students with an observer rating form can be useful (see Chapter 9). This cultivation of self-knowledge, together with understanding how groups function, might also be encouraged by watching visual recordings of the whole group in action.

Peer teaching

Another way of encouraging students to develop self-knowledge can be provided through opportunities to peer teach, with feedback from the group and a chance to reflect (Boud et al., 2001; Swarat et al., 2004). This may be effectively accompanied by watching visual recordings of the session. As the old adage suggests: 'To teach is to learn twice.'

Given the opportunity to teach their peers, students will report gains across all four categories of the critical matrix. Micari et al. (2005), for example, report student gains on a large peer-facilitation programme in the sciences which include:

- intellectual growth in terms of consolidating knowledge in the discipline, enhancing conceptual understanding and developing problem-solving skills;
- interpersonal growth in terms of communication skills;
- practical growth in terms of pedagogical skills; and
- personal growth in terms of increased confidence.

THE SOCIAL DIMENSION

Establishing a welcoming environment

The beginnings of group life are often very important for establishing the supportive atmosphere. Traditional introductions with a simple round of each participant giving a brief self-description can be somewhat tense and perhaps boring. Instead, individuals can talk to their neighbour, find out a few interesting details and then share what they learnt as a means to introduce one another to the group. This can be both more engaging and more useful as a way of introducing each other since it involves both listening and talking. These functions are important in group work and this way of beginning sets up expectations about the way the group will be run; participants will be expected both to talk to and listen to their peers and not merely listen and respond to the teacher.

It is important to organize the layout of the room carefully. Ideally, the students will all be able to see the instructor and each other and to maintain eye contact which, in turn, fosters good interpersonal communication. Many classrooms do not permit everyone to see each other, when the class is particularly large or the physical structure is hard to change. Certainly, this is another side-effect of poor teacher–student ratios. Breaking into smaller groups can help significantly here.

Yet, eye contact is not the only issue. Everyone might see each other but the teacher might be seated behind a big desk – an indication of distance or of a detached authority relationship that can inhibit student participation. The relationship between students that are more talkative and quieter students is also a feature in encouraging and enhancing even more participation within groups.

In a broad discussion about group participation, Bligh (2000a: 176–7), for example, reports research indicating that students across from one another are more likely to respond to one another and those side by side less likely. A teacher sitting opposite a talkative student may make it more difficult for others to participate. In a now classic study, Abercrombie (1966) found another expression of the importance of environment. Two groups were working independently in separate rooms and one group had red chairs, the other green. When they came together in another room a circle of chairs was set out with alternating red and green chairs. When the two groups came together, each group – without realizing – sat on its own colour chair, but talked to their own group across the other group. This rather surprising finding illustrates how subconscious influences can be important within groups, in particular when bringing smaller groups back into a larger-group discussion.

Finally, the supportive side of the social dimension may also be enhanced through generating enjoyment, on the one hand, and a lack of anxiety about what might be happening on the other. It needs to be said, however, that while the lack of clear group guidelines might generate anxiety, a degree of confusion or puzzlement, as we suggested earlier, is often a good starting point for the achievement of understanding. The issue here is that guidelines should not become a straitjacket and clear expectations not a recipe for dullness.

Working with ambiguity and confusion

A sense of ownership in the group may, indeed, be generated out of working this sense of confusion through into constructive co-operation. We saw in discussing phases in the groups that effective working is often preceded by intra-group hostility, but confidence is often a condition for independent work. Overcoming difficulties is frequently important in achieving a sense of ownership of one's learning. The autocratic style did not leave much scope for this, but neither did the laissez-faire style. Democratic and/or coaching styles of leadership can be important in generating a real sense of independence within the group.

Encouraging peer interaction

As mentioned above, peer teaching may be one of the best ways to encourage interpersonal and social skills. Teachers often say they have learnt things most effectively when teaching, but rarely give their students a chance to do the same – to learn by teaching. Problem and task-based learning approaches to teaching involve both teaching by students and the need to work in an interdependent way. It is important, however, to give our students a full range of different tasks and structures so that what they learn in this respect is more easily transferable to new situations. In addition to peer-teaching experiences, what is learnt may also be reinforced by serious reflection on, and evaluation of, the process of learning.

One learning activity which may have more general application is this respect is the *consultants and assessors* game (see Chapter 8 for a full description). Briefly, a task or problem focused on the course or session topic is given to different groups of students who act as teams of consultants developing solutions. They will need to draw upon course materials as well as using their own initiative to hunt down others which they share with 'colleagues' to produce a solution. These are presented to a student group of assessors who devise criteria for evaluating the quality of the solutions and decide how to apply these to the consultants' reports or presentations. This can raise interesting issues of inter-group and intra-group relations in conditions of success and failure. In the process it also raises issues of giving and taking criticism in the context of developing their own assessment and evaluation abilities. It has the important advantage of directly addressing substantial areas of course content.

More broadly it should be noted that peer interaction is essentially a product of meaningful *learning communities* in which students take a high degree of ownership. These communities come in various shapes and sizes and may include the kind of peer-facilitated workshops reported above (Swarat et al., 2004; Drane et al., 2005); first-year seminars often linked to writing courses; and course-linked and/or clustered learning communities (MacGregor, 2000; Smith and MacGregor, 2000). They also include informal peer study and friendship groups which students form outside class. Indeed, in his study of students at Harvard, Light (2001) reported that students appreciated, even enjoyed complex and challenging homework assignments if they were permitted to co-operate and collaborate with peers in completing them. Many felt that such 'assignments increase both their learning and their engagement with a class' (2001: 9).

THE PRACTICAL DIMENSION

Supporting practical skills

Much of what has been said already is in fact about the practical dimension of encouraging students to work effectively within groups. It was suggested that field trips and other practical work can provide a very good context for exploring teamwork and interpersonal skills and the quality of the relationships can often be very much better than that in the seminar rooms. Working in teams may, for example, also help develop such practical skills as rehearsal, practising, writing, reporting and presenting, although such skills will vary in different disciplinary contexts.

The rich variety of ways of relating in practical work needs to be exploited. This is best done by a combination of quiet individual reflection, often with reflective diaries, and in the sharing of these with the help of teachers who can encourage students to integrate these experiences into a coherent framework. Within this dimension, a balance needs to be achieved between helpful direction and the freedom to explore, to take risks, to fail and learn from these experiences. Strenuous attempts to avoid risk and failure may undermine independent and deeper, long-lasting learning.

The nature of the practical task given to a group, Bligh (2000a) reminds us, will have a significant influence on the dynamics of that group. Members may, for example, have serious differences about how to proceed, or conflicting values guiding their decisions. These plus a sense of urgency, which may be imposed from the outside, can play havoc with group performance. He suggests that students in such practical groups need to be aware of the difference between the group task goals and the group maintenance goals, and to spend time addressing both: 'groups that spend longer on group maintenance achieve more. That is to say, discussions about group processes accelerate achievements on content. Why? Because groups that don't maintain themselves spend much longer disagreeing' (2000a: 121).

CONCLUSIONS

Small-group teaching in the past has often promised much but achieved far less. It is popular in theory but often unpopular in practice, even if not universally considered 'purgatory'! It can be difficult, however, for teachers who have been appointed primarily for their ability as thinkers and writers to develop interpersonal skills and an understanding of complex and often disturbing group processes. Part of the problem for teachers is that many of the social conventions, which can have a deep-seated influence on our behaviour, are contrary to what teachers believe needs to be done to achieve efficient practice.

If we were to suggest that a dinner party be split into groups of three or four to record interesting points of conversation on a flip chart or to reflect on a video-recording of their interacting, we would probably have to find new guests for our future parties. If, on the other hand, we prevented our guests from forming small groups of two or three, again future parties would be rare. Similarly, if our seminars have absolutely nothing of the friendly smiles, the sensitive introductions, the attention to the importance of values, beliefs and diversity, they, too, might begin to dwindle and disappear, especially as there is rarely anything to eat or drink, and absolutely no music!

In other words, groups are groups wherever they come together. Mere collections of individuals may learn something together, but may lack the personal involvement that can be both memorable and lead to a change of behaviour. In their social lives outside the university, teachers are generally very sensitive to behaviour that can enhance social relationships as well as behaviour that can create bad feeling, hostility and withdrawal. It is not always clear that these skills are actually being transferred into their teaching.

If we want to transfer some of the important features of our enjoyable and interesting social lives to our group teaching, we need to be aware of not only the intellectual dimension but also of the personal and social activities and relationships which can make this possible. Parties are not obvious models for seminars but they do have features from which we can learn. Academics do not need books to tell them the key topics, skills and even attitudes which are all important in their discipline, but they may need to be reminded of the personal and emotional problems which can get in the way of students' learning.

Young people, and mature students, too, want to feel they are in a community of adults who relate to them as adults and not as parents or a remote intellectual elite that can undermine their own identity as adults or as developing professionals. Creating the conditions for them to engage in the variety of roles that are the context of adult life today is itself important for the role of lecturer. Group work has the potential to enrich the different roles that stimulate engagement and learning. It can give students a wide range of experiences, provided we are willing to go beyond the usual boundaries and encourage students to learn how to learn from observing the group and comparing the reactions, ideas and feelings generated by these experiences.

Final questions: The integration of content tasks with process tasks in small groups is often difficult and keenly resisted by teacher and student alike – but, with thoughtful encouragement, can itself become a valuable group task. What are my broad goals and expectations for this group work? Am I structuring my groups in such a way that my students will meet the more specific learning objectives? How will I ensure that the group process offers a meaningful and engaging learning experience for my students? Ideally, students should be able to look back on the experience and say, as Lao Tzu suggests, 'we did that ourselves' and be proud.

chapter 6

SUPERVISING: PROJECT, DISSERTATION AND THESIS GUIDANCE

> *The independent research experience changes people, not simply in terms of technical expertise and knowledge in their field, but also in terms of the ways they value themselves and their work ... A self forged through tackling the difficulties of research, especially when stress from other sources is high, is a new self. So is the self that overcomes the doubts about ability to do the work. (Hazel Francis cited in Graves and Varma, 1997: 18)*

In this chapter, we look at the role of supervising in higher education, particularly how it encourages independent learning, as well co-operation, collaboration and the development of new roles and relationships. Supervising has relevance to teaching in general as well as projects, reports, dissertations and theses where maintaining the balance between support and independence is crucial to allay anxiety while fostering independence. The emotional is stressed as well as the greater intellectual demands in contributing to personal and professional identity. We discuss problems in assessment in relation to the need for individuality, creativity and originality.

INTRODUCTION

As we discussed in Chapter 2, research on conceptions of learning suggests that the most sophisticated conception of learning is 'changing as a person'. In undergraduate courses – where much of the research on student conceptions has focused – the aspect of study with perhaps the most potential to change people is the project or undergraduate thesis. The Master's dissertation[1] offers even greater opportunities for change, and the PhD thesis has the greatest potential. Wherever an educational experience offers great promise, however, there can be great disappointment. Such disappointment may be traced directly to shortcomings in the supervision (Rudd, 1986).

By 'supervision', we are referring to the process by which a teacher directs or guides a student – whether at the undergraduate or graduate/ postgraduate level – through a significant research or clinical project, thesis or dissertation. As such, supervision has three widely accepted functions – support, education and management – which have generally been seen to be unidirectional processes (the supervisor provides; the student receives), although this may be changing (Carrington, 2004). Although we draw some ideas from the vast body of research on 'mentoring', a concept used more extensively in the USA, our focus here is on the supervisor's facilitation of the project as a teaching genre, and the student's experience of that project. The projects we refer to are extended research projects, which often serve as the final assessment of a student's programme. While the descriptions of these projects may vary, they share certain characteristics:

- They are intended to be learner-focused (students usually determine their own research questions, although the supervisor might shape the focus and methodology).
- They promote independence and self-directed learning (students are expected to complete the work on their own, but the supervisor may guide the process of data collection, analysis and interpretation of primary and secondary data, depending on the student's expected level of expertise).
- They provide students with a substantial and deep exposure to a research area that gets beyond normal coursework (Todd et al., 2006).

Although interpersonal skills are quite important when conducting seminars and even when lecturing, in supervision (as to a large degree in personal teaching) a clash of personality or even insensitivity towards the feelings of the student can lead to disaster. A supervisor who is willing to help with the emotional turmoil of the process, sharing its pleasures and pains, is as important for researchers as is the tutorial supervision of their work (Grant, 2003). As Francis (1997: 19) explains: 'most is gained from the research process by finding a balance between individual drive and autonomy and the engagement and support of others'.

In this chapter, we consider the key issues in supervision, as well as the roles, responsibilities and expectations of supervisors and students, and explore some common problems with supervision. We then consider supervision as it relates to specific elements of the learning matrix, concluding with an examination of the often thorny issue of assessment.

KEY ISSUES OF SUPERVISION

We have frequently stressed the importance of achieving a balance between providing support, encouraging independence and developing the interpersonal. In supervising, this is much more than an intellectual achievement on the part of the supervisor. Supervision involves a constant interaction between the supervisor and the student and, since this is a one-to-one relationship, crude stereotypes of each other can destroy deeper learning. With larger groups, to some extent, we have to work with generalizations rather more, even if they do not amount to stereotypes. But with supervising, sensitivity to individual differences, the ability to accommodate these differences and to accept changes in mood, motivation and even intellectual approach are crucial to the developing relationship as well as to the quality of the research.

In many respects, the supervisory relationship offers a useful model for teaching in general. While supervisors might transmit information on occasion, they are more likely to expect students working on an independent project to engage deeply in the learning process and construct their own knowledge. They are more likely to view themselves as facilitating learning and expect students to embrace and 'own' their research.

Yet, supervisors do not usually receive much training or instruction on how to supervise effectively, and may often rely on their experience being supervised, which may not have been particularly effective or positive (Brew and Peseta, 2004; Calkins and Kelley, 2005; Calkins and Light, 2007). This is starting to change, however, with more faculty programmes and short courses on effective supervision practices and the professional development of research supervisors (Pearson and Brew, 2002; Brew and Peseta, 2004).

Relationships and roles in supervision

The relationship between supervisors and their students is complex and varied, and the roles that each takes can change, especially through an extended period of supervision. Table 6.1 sets out a range of different roles and relationships which supervisors and students might take.

Table 6.1 *Range of roles and relationships between supervisor and student*

Supervisor	Student
Director	Follower
Master	Servant
Guru	Disciple
Teacher	Pupil
Expert	Novice
Guide	Explorer
Project manager	Team worker
Auditor	Client
Editor	Author
Doctor	Patient
Senior partner	Junior
Professional colleague	Colleague
Friend	Friend
Mentor	Mentee
Adviser/counsellor	Seeker
Consultant	Customer

Source: Adapted from Brown and Atkins, 1988: 121

At times, any of these might be appropriate, but the important and difficult issue is achieving the right balance over the whole supervisory period. Each one relates to a reciprocal relationship on the part of the student. Some of these may not feel like acceptable relationships but they are helpful in reflecting on and reviewing our relationship with our students. They help us ask: are we flexible in the way we are meeting the needs of the particular stage of supervision?

In an in-depth research inquiry into the nature of supervision, Gardiner (1989) focused on trying to understand how supervision styles relate to deep and surface approaches to learning, and how conceptions of knowledge relate to the approaches to learning and styles of teaching discussed earlier (in Chapters 1 and 2). From his studies, he developed a complex model identifying three levels of interaction. The first level focuses upon the content of learning and is linked to reproductive conceptions of learning. At this level, 'Supervisors believed that the right way to supervise was to reflect the hierarchy casework relationship with clients, and to maintain control, not only of what the student should be learning but also the single right path to achieve it' (1989: 131).

At the second level, the focus is on the process of learning with a recognition of diversity and the active involvement of a learner in the learning process. There is a shift from the reproductive to the constructive/transforming conceptions of learning. Students take increasing responsibility for setting the agenda, for supervision, and for assessing their own work and learning.

The third level focuses on meta-learning, learning to learn and the demonstration of versatility. Here students and supervisors use their own learning processes as the basis (content) of further learning (process) of a higher order. Gardiner (1989) suggests that this meta-learning can promote the transfer of the content and process of learning to contexts other than those in which the original learning arose.

A matching of levels between supervisor and student is very important, especially if the supervisor is operating at the *reproductive* level (level 1). The effect of mismatches, however, is dependent on the level at which the mismatch occurs. If students and supervisors are capable of operating at the highest *meta-learning* level, they are able to reflect upon and discuss the way in which they are interacting in a mutual engagement which should be able to adjust to any mismatches. If they are not, the potential for dialogue and engagement about both the learning and the interaction is reduced.

Gardiner's work has interesting parallels with Schon's (1983, 1987) two models of interpersonal behaviour. In the first model, the values are 'to achieve the object as I see it', 'to strive to win and avoid losing' and 'to avoid negative feelings'. Its strategies include unilateral control of the task and the environment and unilateral protection of self and others. It is a very restrictive, 'single-loop' model of interaction where assumptions are not questioned and private dilemmas are concealed.

The second model is a 'double-loop' model in which the participants are learning about the values and assumptions that drive their own and/or other people's behaviour. In this model learning involves the governing variables that underlie behavioural strategies. Participants are willing to share difficult and sensitive matters that may be getting in the way. In supervising students we need be willing to express our disappointment with each other's performance. Both sides need to explore how far it is possible to share issues of doubt and mistrust that can so easily remain private and undisclosed.

Styles and Radloff (2001) provide another way to think about the supervisor–student relationship through their self-regulatory synergistic model of supervision (see Figure 6.1). While this model was created to understand the postgraduate experience, its principles can be easily applied to the undergraduate experience of supervision. Self-regulation encompasses learner autonomy, self-efficacy, adaptability and a sense of control over the learning that is achieved. This model integrates four important elements of the supervised research experience:

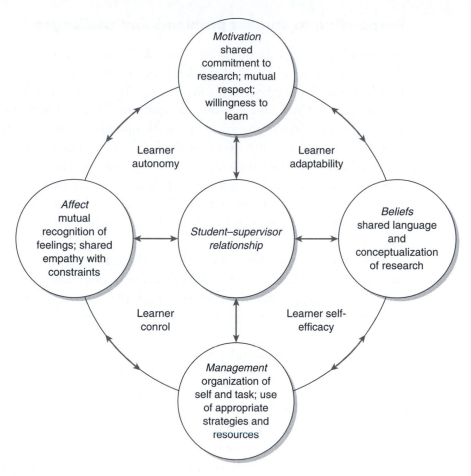

Figure 6.1 *Self-regulatory synergistic model of supervision*
Source: Adapted from Styles and Radloff, 2001

- *Motivation*: shared commitment to the research, a mutual respect, the willingness to learn.
- *Beliefs*: requires students and supervisor to share language and conceptualization of the purpose of the research project.
- *Management strategies*: organization of self and task; use of appropriate strategies and relevant resources.
- *Affect*: recognition that positive and negative changes in supervisor and student's feelings will occur; empathy with constraints and problems each person faces.

Although these aspects may not be harmonious at the outset, ideally they will develop synergistically over time (Styles and Radloff, 2001).

Responding to student problems and challenges

Students bring many diverse problems and challenges to their supervisors that emerge from all areas of the learning matrix (see Chapter 2). Each problem must be engaged on its own terms; there are no necessarily 'right' ways to respond nor 'one size fits all' solutions. Teachers must make professional judgements in the way they handle or address a student challenge. Figure 6.1 provides a continuum of the kinds of approach which supervisors might choose when students encounter problems. They range between taking the problem out of the student's hands and solving it to sympathizing but not addressing the problem at all. Each response has its advantages and disadvantages, and each can be appropriate or inappropriate according to the situation.

Supervisors may seldom take either of the extremes but, on occasion, may come quite close to one or the other. Some may listen to the student and offer advice, provide the solution or tell the student where to find it. Occasionally this might seem to be a reasonable thing to do but, if this becomes the general pattern of the supervision, then it may impair that student's ability to learn independently. On the other hand, other supervisors might reflect back to the student what he or she seems to be saying, in an attempt to help the student to examine the implications and come to terms with the problem. While this may sometimes be a good way of encouraging independence, if the meetings are always like this it may actually discourage the student or send him or her on the road to failure.

Generally, supervisors will feel they should be operating somewhere near the supportive end of the scale, getting students to list possible solutions and suggest bases upon which they feel the choice should be made, and then exploring any difficulties the student might have in making the choice (Woolhouse, 2002). In practice, however, supervisors will find themselves confined to one or two kinds of response, often offering advice and suggesting what the student might do. In their anxiety to retain control lest students make mistakes, they may persist with this approach long after its sell-by date.

Supervisors and teachers will better serve themselves and their students by developing and sustaining a wider repertoire of responses to employ as the circumstances require. As one supervisor from the social sciences commented on his role in the undergraduate thesis process: 'I think that my role isn't [to get involved in the writing of content] but you're looking for ways to facilitate what they're doing and that might mean, for some of the weaker students, some direct intervention' (cited in Todd et al., 2006: 169).

THE INTELLECTUAL DIMENSION

Establishing learning contracts

We have stressed, especially in supervision, that support is essentially concerned with helping students to learn and make decisions, rather than transferring knowledge and deciding for students. All innovation, change and creative work involve risk-taking, but risks are very difficult to take if students are feeling very insecure. At the undergraduate level, projects are perhaps the only area where students may consciously feel they are taking risks. But even graduate students may not be very practised at relating to their lecturer as a supervisor who is not going to do all the explaining and clarifying and direct-ing that they may have come to expect. In recalling her own postgraduate experiences of being supervised, one teacher recalled painfully: 'I was basically just thrown into the deep end ... I had to teach myself, had to give myself my own kind of emotional and intellectual support, and generally they were quite aversive experiences where I was basically left alone' (Grant, 2003: 176).

At all levels, setting ground rules or even learning contracts (Phillips and Pugh, 2005) and clarifying them is an important first step. It should not be assumed that because these have been carefully discussed at the beginning they will not be forgotten later under the more stressful conditions of trying to write up the project or dissertation for a deadline. Part of the more sup-portive side of supervising will be to help students understand a wider range of possible roles and what they actually mean in terms of the supervisor's behaviour as well as their own (Todd et al., 2006). It is unlikely that students will initiate a discussion about the wide variety of roles and relationships outlined earlier (Table 6.1). And while confronting the student with all ten possibilities may not be the best way to begin a supervision experience, it may be useful to make clear in the early stages that coming to terms with a new way of working is an important part of the working relationship.

Roles and relationships are not the only important part of setting the ground rules. It is important to negotiate the actual practical side of what each can expect of the other. These are more likely to be set out in course documentation. Although an expectation that these might be read before the first meeting may be reasonable, it is useful to spend time interpreting what they mean and perhaps modifying and suggesting new elements which suit your particular relationship. Now, there are pressures to formalize the duration and frequency of supervision meetings but we need to bear in mind that this is an area in which there are important individual differences and working to a mythical average may not always be appropriate.

Table 6.2 *Supervisor and student expectations*

Supervisors expect their research students to	Students expect their supervisors to
• be independent, even though some aspects of the research process may require conformity • follow their advice, especially when requested by the student • produce written work that is fairly polished • have regular meetings • be honest when reporting progress • be excited about their research	• supervise them • read their work well in advance • be available when needed • be friendly, open and supportive • structure sessions to support an easy exchange of ideas • have good knowledge of the research area • have sufficient interest in their research to put more information in the student's path • be sufficiently involved in their success to help them get a good job at the end of it all!

Sources: Adapted from Woolhouse, 2002; Phillips and Pugh, 2005

We should not assume that written ground rules will get in the way of a close personal relationship. It is easy for discussions about processes to be seen as personal criticism. Ground rules, statements of responsibilities and written criteria can more easily become a subject for discussion than can particular issues troubling the supervisor or the student. Phillips and Pugh (2005) describe what supervisors expect from their research students, as well as what their research students generally expect of them, which might provide useful guidelines for supervisors (Table 6.2).

Student expectations of their supervisor

While student expectations of their supervisor may vary in different learning contexts, research has shown that there are many similarities. Students expect their supervisor to:

- be friendly and supportive;
- read their work ahead of time and provide feedback;
- have relevant experience and knowledge of the research field;
- help them locate resources; and
- ultimately, to be involved and interested in their development (Woolhouse, 2002; Phillips and Pugh, 2005).

Interestingly, when supervisors were interviewed about what they believed were their actual responsibilities to their students, they identified similar expectations. These included:

- supporting students by helping them identify and define their research question;
- determining the feasibility of the student's proposed research (whether necessary resources are available);
- questioning – even challenging – the student on research decisions;
- requiring the student to justify the research approach and methods;
- advising the student on appropriate methodologies (assisting with methods when appropriate);
- helping the student plan work and meet targets; and
- attending to technical or mechanical parts of the research project (writing, grammar, citation, etc.) (Todd et al., 2006).

Students usually find it helpful to know that other students share their expectations and that they are not expecting too much. On the other hand, these expectations need to be interpreted in context. It may be reasonable, for instance, to feel that their supervisor should have the courtesy not to answer the telephone during a meeting. Given the pressures on supervisors it is often easy to forget to put telephones through to support staff or turn them off. If the supervisor were expecting an urgent or very important call, however, many students would agree that this is perfectly acceptable if it were mentioned beforehand. Similarly, how much help, realistically, to expect from a supervisor in finding a job at the end of the research is worth addressing. Guidance, references, contacts, some 'inside' information and so on may be reasonable but pursuing or hunting a job down for a student is not.

All students expect detailed comments on their written work but there is disagreement as to how far these comments should be directed at telling students what they should do and how far they should raise questions and suggest alternatives. Whereas the latter might be the more useful general approach, there are occasions when students might expect straight answers to straight questions. The range of possible responses to students' work (Chapter 8) is not only concerned with the quality of comments. The quantity can also be quite problematic as staff–student ratios deteriorate. Some supervisors write very little and rely upon the tutorial discussion while others write a great deal. Either way, as Cox (2007) notes, extensive feedback is a valuable feature of higher education with a substantial impact on student learning (see also Chapter 8).

Supervisor expectations of their students

At the same time, supervisors would do well to reflect on their own expectations of the students they supervise, to explain those expectations at the outset and to review those expectations throughout the supervision process. Again, expectations may be individual and specific, but research has shown many similarities. Supervisors often expect students to:

- become familiar with and adopt the practices of the research community;
- make original contributions to the field (although not necessarily at the undergraduate level);
- develop a 'critical and reflexive intellectual stance'; and
- believe deeply in the value of the project at a personal level (Anderson et al., 2006: 156).

Most expect their students to attend meetings on time, to come prepared (with something tangible to discuss), to help establish and meet target goals and to bring passion and enthusiasm to the project (Todd et al., 2006). They also expect students to be honest when reporting their progress and simply to be excited about their research (Phillips and Pugh, 2005) (see Table 6.2).

As Brew and Peseta (2004) have suggested, such expectations may be more or less student-centred. For example, they examined how a professor's ideas of 'competent autonomy' shifted to become more student-centred and relevant to the current higher education context after participating in a faculty development module on supervision. Before his engagement with the programme, his old ideas of competent autonomy included such things as being able to design experiments; to interpret the literature critically; to analyse data; to know lab and field techniques; and to know scientific writing. After the programme, he expressed new ideas of competent autonomy, which included being able to write for refereed journals; to prepare research grant applications; to cope with and respond to peer review; to speak publicly; to work in teams; to supervise; and to understand the professional standards of the field (Brew and Peseta, 2004). The overarching expectation is that a student will become a part of the community of scholars, a process which greatly transcends acquiring knowledge and new skills.

Self-directed learning

Promoting self-directed independent learning and the acquisition of meta-skills (learning to learn and the transfer of learning to new contexts) is a critical aspect of supervision. Meta-cognitive learning skills focus upon self-management and what the learner does in new contexts, which is the ultimate aim of university teaching. Good traditional teaching – and developing learning – involves going beyond the information given. Here, direct instruction is followed by thought-oriented activities that challenge students so that they apply, generalize and refine their understanding (Biggs et al., 2007). Like the experience of problem or inquiry-based learning, students are encouraged to raise critical questions, to reformulate problems and to test new solutions. The supervising case study in Box 6.1 illustrates this process.

Box 6.1 *Supervising postgraduate work*

Kate, a new faculty member in English and fresh from her doctoral studies, has learnt she must supervise three Masters' students. Although her own experiences of being supervised have varied, she recalled often feeling unsupported and distanced from supervisors, and she did not want to replicate that experience with her own students. She wanted to offer her students guidance and support, but also to let them wrestle with the research process as well.

She decided to meet with each student to get to know them as individuals, but also to get a sense of their abilities and interests. With each student, she helped them set up an individual research plan, where she outlined her expectations about the final product, and let them explain the kind of support and supervision they thought would personally work for them. Two of the students, Margarite and Henry, preferred to meet monthly and send her drafts as they completed sections, while Ronan preferred to meet weekly and get more feedback as he developed his ideas.

She occasionally had all three meet together, as a research group, to share their progress and setbacks, to support their interpersonal development and growth as researchers. She helped all three shape their specific projects, working with them through the research process. She reined in Henry, for example, when the scope of his question grew unwieldy. When they ran into problems, she offered guidance when they seemed to stray off course, but asked them to think through possible resolutions to the problems they encountered, to encourage independence and self-directed learning.

Biggs, here, takes a more purely intellectual slant on some of Schon's requirements for working effectively within his model 2 described above. Schon values the willingness to explore assumptions and inhibitions that we may not know we have. It comes closer to encouraging a more therapeutic approach. And in many respects good supervision requires us to explore what we have called learning gap 4 (see Chapter 2), where the student may know what to do and want to do it and yet not actually do it. The student may be more worried about it not being good enough and feel that the risks are not worth taking. On the other hand, the consequences of not taking the risk might be even more damaging in the end to a sense of personal and professional identity. These are important issues in the more creative activities associated with theses, dissertations and even undergraduate projects. The project, as an undergraduate student said, 'is the only real opportunity for your own ideas'.

Some students, but certainly not all, may begin their research in a state of considerable dependency, and must be encouraged to be independent and accept responsibility for their own learning. Whereas for some students the release from severe time constraints can mean that they feel free to take risks and explore ideas now that they have the time to research and back up their ideas, for others, this open-endedness can be threatening. Fear can be quite a common response to freedom but, although more support may be necessary at the beginning, it is important not to set up patterns and expectations that mean that students remain in a state of dependency.

On the other hand, in trying to avoid this, we may find ourselves behaving as if our main purpose is to point out all the faults and difficulties to the student and fail to see that this can be very damaging and may make them retreat into even greater dependency. Phillips and Pugh (2005) have reported how students interviewed in their study sometimes burst into tears when discussing some of the difficulties they had in relating to their supervisors, even many years after they had actually gained their PhDs. At the time they had not revealed their feelings and felt in retrospect that perhaps their supervisors did not realize just how badly hurt they had been. A sensitive interview provided the opportunity to express the feelings that they had hidden at the time.

Unfortunately, supervisors often get very little help in coping with the more emotional aspects of giving criticism, but they may need much more than helpful advice and role-plays can be a very useful addition to supervisor workshops. In encouraging independence, the language of alternatives and different perspectives is likely to be more effective than the language of right and wrong or good and bad. Edward de Bono's (1994) approach in terms of parallel thinking provides a useful non-adversarial approach to encouraging more constructive and creative thinking. Different perspectives and arguments need to be kept in mind to see if they might contribute to a richer and more integrated approach rather than eliminating each one because of its particular failings.

Self-criticism can be extremely inhibiting where it undermines self-confidence. Opportunities for students to present their work in a rough form and use rough drafts can help them to take more risks and be more independent. It can help get past the feeling, as one student put it, that they 'don't like to express half-formed ideas' or write unless they are sure of themselves.

Another way to lessen the threat of self-criticism and encourage more independent thinking is to encourage students to keep an intellectual diary. This is not necessarily seen by the supervisor but is a place where a student can express guesses, opinions and hypotheses without necessarily immediately having to justify them. This has some parallels with the very useful device of brainstorming. Students may need to be encouraged to try out new ways of writing and being productive as well as new perspectives and alternative solutions.

Encouraging dialogue

Supervision is predominantly about dialogue. There is a need for constant adjustment to what each participant is saying, and the balance between giving and taking, listening and talking is crucial if the session is not to become a lecture in disguise. Although supervisors can and do learn a great deal from supervisions, the dialogue is not simply a friendly conversation. Nor is it an interrogation or even a Socratic dialogue.

Initially at least there may be a considerable imbalance of power and intellectual sophistication, but an important function of the supervision is to reduce this imbalance and to enable the student to become an independent researcher. There may be times when interrogation and serious challenging are appropriate, but if the general pattern is one of unilateral judgement and assessment rather than constructive dialogue it may be difficult to develop the professional skills of self-criticism and critical reflection.

The issue may be less one of supervisors not thinking about supervision in these terms, than that it is easy to let development not happen. In ordinary conversations we may avoid dominating the discussion but, in general, if we have interesting things to say, we say them. We do not see it as one of our aims to encourage the other to say those ideas we feel are our own. In fact, it is easy to slip into either a didactic mode of telling or a conversational mode of enjoying giving our opinions.

In supervision, maintaining a subtle balance of talking and listening is not simply a question of letting the other person have their say and listening with interest. There is a more active, searching process involved whereby you become clearer about both the strengths of what the other is saying and about the hidden assumptions and misconceptions. It is essentially an exploratory process, which can be enjoyable but does not benefit from the self-expression that comes from good friendships.

Supervision is not just about one-to-one interaction; it may involve a wider involvement in the student's personal and social life. Loneliness is a dominant theme in many of the books on doing a research degree, although there is now much more interest within universities in creating learning communities not only for undergraduates but also for graduate students (Lave and Wenger, 2000b; Smith and MacGregor, 2000).

Science research students have often benefited from being able to interact with their peers and to learn from them in the laboratories. Now research students generally are able not only to express their own discoveries and new ideas but also to talk about the problems of their research and its methodology.

Sharing perspectives and approaches is an important part of most research students' lives. Perhaps the most valuable part of this is the semi-formal environment of student seminars that are often attended by supervisors. The more formal courses can also be a new area for students to interact and learn the skills of becoming professional researchers. If these are too remote from the student's own perspectives and approaches then they can appear to be increasingly like being subject to undergraduate control. There is now a wider realization that if these courses are to become part of the transition into professional life, they need to become less authoritarian and remote and more responsive to the needs and ideas of students.

THE PERSONAL DIMENSION

The influence of personal relationships in supervising is extremely important but it is still rather controversial just how much the relationship should be a friendship. Most would now agree that it is important for each to get to know the other and very often this is difficult if the only relationship is in a study or in a seminar room. Although there is very little discussion of this in the literature, many supervisors feel it is important to be able to relate within a more informal social dimension. The ways in which groups get to know each other better (Chapter 5) can also be relevant to groups of research students.

Supporting the research journey

It is within the more personal one-to-one relationships where boundaries become an important issue. Research students often go through difficult periods of confusion and a loss of confidence, not only in the quality of what they are doing, but whether it is worth doing at all. Unlike their undergraduate lives, when they have many areas of interest and many different and quite close relationships, research students find they are very influenced by their view of how their research is going and how the most significant other person in that research, their supervisor, is feeling about it.

We saw earlier that undergraduate projects can become a very important focus of students' lives; this is very much magnified for research students. For supervisors, maintaining the balance between support and independence in the personal sphere can be rather more difficult than in the intellectual. With research students, the supervisor is much more bound up with the success or failure of the research and often there is a very strong shared interest in the topic. Trying to make the student more independent might be seen as being uncaring and not supportive.

In many fields, a PhD may seem more of a 'personal journey' than a process of research training (Salmon, 1992). Becoming lost on this 'personal journey' can be quite frightening and disturbing for students if they feel more dependent on their supervisor and want to be given firm direction. Helping students find direction is certainly an important role for supervisors but, if they become too dominant in this respect, then the ownership of the project begins to pass away from the student and towards the supervisor. This might provide some temporary relief for the student but in the long run the question of whose research it is can become in itself quite disturbing. Science PhD students often only meet this problem when they are doing their post-doctoral work; their PhDs are frequently much closer to research training where close direction from the supervisor is expected. With arts and social science students these ambiguities and ambivalence can create tensions which may need an outside professional to help resolve.

Even experienced supervisors often encounter serious problems from having been drawn into personal problems that directly affect the student's work. This can make the more academic aspect of supervision very difficult, and it is important that there should be other academics in the department who have some responsibility for students when supervisors find it difficult to cope effectively. In some departments, it may be difficult for a research supervisor to be able to share responsibility for all the research students. Small supervisory committees are, on paper, supposed to be able to cope with this. In effect it is very difficult to take responsibility for another supervisor's students as well as your own unless this is taken account of in resource terms as an important extra responsibility. Supervisors themselves can benefit from being able to share anxieties and pleasures with other supervisors. Some highly stressed professions take care to set up supportive relationships among the faculty.

Research styles and professional identity

Encouraging independence (in the personal sense) will, to a large degree, depend on the supervisor's understanding of the range of styles and ways in which research may be approached. Supervisors may regard their own approach as the only one and convey it – tacitly or explicitly – through the supervisory relationship. Gough and Woodworth (1960) have, for example, identified eight stylistic variations among professional research scientists that are still instructive for their diversity:

- the zealot;
- the initiator;
- the diagnostician;
- the scholar;
- the artificer;
- the aesthetician;
- the methodologist; and
- the independent.

This is not an exhaustive list and other categories of variations will exist among the social scientists and the arts, although it is amazing how many transcend discipline and professions.

Enabling research students to develop their own appropriate style(s) of research is crucial to their independent development. There are also concerns as to whether a more uniform and formalized system of research training will encourage and further expand such diversity. Such training programmes often justify research methods courses in terms of introducing students to a variety of research approaches. This might help students to discover what sort of researcher they want to be.

Supervisors have a key role in guiding and developing individual understanding and confidence in this respect. Reflecting, for example, on how the master's dissertation can get beyond the intellectual, a faculty member from the social sciences commented: 'I think beyond that, something which is less tangible but gives evidence that the student has been excited by it and values it and really wants to carry it further forward, so it's meant something personal to the student beyond the requirements' (Anderson et al., 2006: 154).

Achieving a sense of independent personal and professional identity is an important aspect of higher education, especially for advanced postgraduate/ graduate students. Many research students do not particularly want to be researchers but see a doctorate as a necessary qualification for becoming a teacher in higher education. With the rapid expansion of higher education throughout the developed world, this may be a bigger problem in the future and it could be that some of the problems which our research students face relate to this issue of professional socialization. Certainly no teachers in higher education should be ignorant of research methodology, and indeed research practice, but it may be that many PhD students should be doing professional or practice-based doctorates. Their research is personally important but is not their prime orientation.

The significance for supervising is that we – individually and collectively – need to understand more about why students are doing their research in higher education and how far it enables them to develop a sense of professional identity. Even for students who do want to become research academics, the development of a particular research style can be a crucial aspect of their development. At the same time, some teachers are critical that the research project will lean too far towards application, rather than seeing it as an opportunity for students to pose, rather than solve problems, and transform their conceptions of professional development (Anderson et al., 2006). It is not clear, however, that supervisors address these issues very coherently.

THE SOCIAL DIMENSION

The challenge of social isolation

Although the situation has improved in recent years, social isolation can still be a problem for research students. This is still partly a question of poor facilities for research students (Becher et al., 1994). Science students may be able to identify quite closely with their space in a laboratory, but arts and social science students may have little sense of belonging, without a sense of geographical personal identity other than a shifting library seat and the opportunity to use a communal computer.

Supporting students in their quest for space within the academic research supervision is important. The issue is now being addressed more seriously and may become less of a problem as graduate students are more integrated into the teaching staff. Cryer (1996) highlights the social dimension of graduate education and promotes the development of more personal student and staff networks. Email and web-based social network systems are unlikely to provide all the social contact that students may need, although they can certainly help reduce isolation and can provide a valuable channel of communication based on the intellectual side of being a research student, as well as fulfil more personal and social needs (Oblinger, 2003).

For a long time, it has been common for scientists to work in teams, but now the value of developing interpersonal and teamwork skills has been recognized much more widely both for industry and for social and personal benefits. Certainly, students coming to college today expect to work in teams, both at university and in their careers (Howe and Strauss, 2003).

Many universities now recognize the need to help research students develop their teamwork skills and their communication skills more widely. Conference, poster and seminar presentations are more valued for both content and process. Journal clubs and thesis groups, a standard in the sciences and social sciences, are becoming more common in other fields. These provide opportunities for students to meet with their peers to discuss recent scholarship and to share their own research. This new emphasis upon the social dimension of graduate studies can make a valuable contribution to developing confidence and independence.

THE PRACTICAL DIMENSION

Encouraging problem-solving

Providing support to students developing their practical research skills may be confined to supporting their practical and technical need for access to equipment/apparatus, appropriate physical spaces/laboratory/clinical/field, relevant services (library, media, computing, etc.). More often than not, it will also include support in the practical use and application of these. Considerable support for the above can be given to students through the provision of clear:

• guidelines, structures and timetables;
• support documents/material/equipment; and
• criteria for their use, together with close supervisor/tutor and technician supervision and feedback.

Fostering independence and accountability

Supervisors will need to be careful in the extent to which they provide such explicit support. There is the danger of undermining the student's developing research independence. As with the undergraduate practical work, there needs to be plenty of opportunity for choice in deciding, defining and carrying out tasks and problems. This may include:

• involvement in planning and decision-making;
• the opportunity for students to find and provide support materials;
• involvement in setting criteria for progress and for self-assessment;
• time and opportunity for development and risk-taking; and
• accountability for the research and completion of the project.

A difficulty with PhDs in both the sciences and social sciences is that often the supervisor is responsible to specific fund holders for ensuring that a particular research project is designed and completed successfully. Issues of independence can be difficult to balance with the supervisor's own research responsibilities. Rudd (1985) found that many research students – particularly in the sciences – feel that the research is not their own, but rather almost entirely their supervisor's. In those circumstances, it is difficult to develop student independence. Careful planning, however, can help supervisors arrange for both their own needs as project directors and those of their students to be accommodated. Research students are not simply research assistants. They are often engaged in the two equally, and both roles need to be recognized in terms of their developing independence.

Part of being independent is being accountable for the completion of the project as well, whether speaking of the undergraduate or postgraduate research experience. Reflecting on his early experiences supervising undergraduates, a faculty member from a science department commented:

> I expect them to be much more independent than they are. One of my students needed to do an extremely complex statistical analysis, which I had only theoretical interest in. I encouraged her to go and see an expert in that field. She did not. So I arranged the meeting for her. The format of the meeting was to be the student giving a talk on her work, and then getting some advice on the analysis. She failed to prepare for the meeting. It was awful. (Brew and Peseta, 2004: 14)

In this case, the teacher had taken steps to solve one problem (the student's lack of experience with the required specifics), but had not addressed the underlying problem: the student had chosen not to be, or had not known how to be, accountable for her own learning in the project.

Developing the interpersonal

Interpersonal practical skills can be developed in the relationship between student and supervisor but it will be restricted. They will be more fully enhanced by being part of either a research team or a group of researchers focusing on mutually beneficial processes of general and specific practices. This will include the negotiations of tasks and roles, setting criteria for progress and involvement in peer and group assessment and evaluation of practice. Such activities will be enhanced if group social relations are considered as an integral part of good team working. Many universities also foster professional links, visits and even exchanges which enable students to gain a wider view of research practices and to improve their collaboration and communications skills within them.

ASSESSING RESEARCH

Formative assessment

For the supervisor, research assessment is essentially an issue of formative assessment, concerned primarily with feedback and helping students to learn and develop their research rather than with summative assessment that is concerned with the final examination (see Chapter 8 for a full discussion of assessment). Supervision may be defined as a process of formative assessment (albeit with a focus on the final examination). In many ways this constant reflection upon the quality of the work the student is producing is a more important feature of the total educational process than it is with undergraduate education. It maintains a much more important role in learning than in ordinary courses since, unlike many aspects of undergraduate assessment, it is constantly integrated into the learning process.

The analysis of comments on assignments in terms of both possible purposes and styles of comment (see Chapter 8) is one way of gaining insight into research student assessment. The purpose of enabling students to become more aware of their implicit conceptions of the task is highly relevant (Brew and Peseta, 2004). How far, for example, do they understand it as a transformative process, emphasizing in their writing the 'argument' and 'cogency' presented by the material, rather than simply as a telling process with an emphasis on merely the relevance of the material and its textual arrangement?

Sloboda and Newstead (1995) provide a useful analysis of the process of assessing research students, which has been of great use to both research students and supervisors. The main interest here is in the criteria to be used for assessing the written submission – central criteria also in giving feedback to students for developing their learning. They divide these into four general attributes and five sectional attributes (Table 6.3). Their appendix contains notes of guidance for examiners concerning the criteria to be applied when assessing each of these nine attributes but with the caveat that they should be considered as indicative rather than definitive.

Creativity and originality

These criteria say very little about creativity or originality, an important element within all the universities' criteria for examining PhDs. Phillips and Pugh (2005) and Cryer (1996) give interesting reviews of the very diverse conceptions of originality currently in use. Originality can be a rather worrying criterion for research students and their supervisor could help them

Table 6.3 *Attributes of research project assessment*

General attributes	Sectional attributes
Presentation and clarity	Review of relevant literature
Integration and coherence	Statement of the research problem
Contribution to knowledge	Methods of inquiry adopted
Originality and creativity	Analysis of data
	Discussion of outcomes

to review the different ways in which a thesis might be considered to be original. Such interpretations as 'saying something nobody has said before' or 'carrying out empirical work that has not been done before' leave a lot unsaid about just how intellectually challenging each needs to be in order for them to count as an original contribution. Designing a new questionnaire, sending it out and analysing the results can be original, but a vital question to address is whether or not it is worth doing and whether it has anything important to say (Anderson et al., 2006). Similarly, making a new synthesis or a new interpretation or trying out in one country what has only been done in different countries, or taking a particular technique and applying it in a new area, are all potentially interesting for their originality but by themselves may guarantee very little.

Being very prescriptive about originality may be somewhat contradictory and create new problems. The context and the levels of sophistication are critically important in judging whether a cross-disciplinary study or new methodologies or reinterpretations of someone else's ideas or carrying out original work designed by a supervisor present difficult questions about how far the student really is making an original contribution.

Like many other issues of supervision, the best policy is to look at different examples and discuss these with the students. Ongoing discussions with colleagues within individual disciplines and departments are also essential to ensure a critical consensus. This might usefully be covered in research seminars at early stages in the research process. Abstract descriptions of what is required can often be difficult for students who may have different assumptions and expectations from the supervisor and may interpret criteria in a very different way.

Summative assessment

In general, there is a fair amount of agreement among examiners in the assessment of research, but in some cases the differences are striking. In her qualitative study of 51 examiners' evaluations of doctoral theses, Johnston (1997), for example, reports this agreement, but also highlights the disagreements that can occur. One examiner enjoyed reading it and felt in no doubt that it should be passed. Another said: 'this is a genuine and admirable doctoral work, well worthy of the degree at any Australian university.' The third examiner, however, recommended it fail: 'It falls short of the key criteria for a PhD... I do not think that the idea or the way in which it is deployed in this thesis displays sufficient originality or makes a significant enough contribution to learning to merit the award of a PhD.' Johnston suggests that such cases may arise where there is an ideological incompatibility with the content of the thesis. She feels that there is a need for more openness in the examination process and for more formal training of examiners.

Supervisors can help to open the process through more thorough-going departmental and institutional discussion and the sharing of good practice. The organization of mock vivas or defences and providing the opportunity to observe other students going through mock vivas can also be extremely useful and helpful to both supervisors and students. Like many aspects of higher education, being told about processes or even having them demonstrated might be far less important than enabling students and supervisors to become actively engaged with the process.

Past PhD theses can be an important source of information for students. Reading these could be combined with an assessment exercise (however simple) with the supervisor or in company with other students who have an interest in the area. An interesting feature of Sloboda and Newstead's (1995) report is the suggestion that students should be encouraged to include a section in their thesis on their learning. This would discuss what they have gained from the research process, personally as well as intellectually, and how they might change and develop their approach if they were to start anew.

In many ways, assessing a dissertation or thesis is more demanding than assessing coursework assignments. Knowledge of the field is reasonably straightforward to assess, but assessing the higher levels of academic work – including originality, analysis, synthesis and evaluation – often within ideologically incompatible contexts – can be very difficult to assess reliably.

CONCLUSIONS

Supervising can be a model for teaching in general. It combines not only sharing and developing a high level of intellectual interest, but does so within a very personal and emotional dimension where students' whole lives become intimately bound up with their intellectual expression and development.

Many years ago, a student was being interviewed in her final year about her response to the assessment system (Cox, 1975). Although initially focused on assessment, the interview soon became an exploration of the changes which students go through in their transition from school to university. The assessment system was seen to be an important element in this transition from dependency to independence. Towards the end of this very long interview, the student said that, despite being in her final year, this was the first time that she had thought seriously about what being at university really meant to her. Her academic work had not been well integrated into her personal life and development. Another student, slightly earlier in her academic life, said 'I'm finding my feet, I don't care so much about the work.' Perhaps today's students think more about what being at university means to them, but often there is no particular encouragement to do this. Even if not everyone wants to take their place in the research community, the experience of engaging in a significant research project can be an important formative period in their lives.

Thus, supervision can be an essential part of a student's development and 'changing as a person' that we discussed in Chapter 2. Transferring our own learning from supervision into more traditional teaching can be a very valuable development if we encourage students in general to cope with the unexpected and the supercomplexity of modern life (Barnett, 2000). The process of supervision, however, even at undergraduate level, should not be viewed as one-directional. It can be a great opportunity for reciprocal learning: the experience can remind supervisors that there are still new things to learn; that they can gain new insights and perspectives; that they can gain a fresh understanding of old material; and that there are new questions to consider (Carrington, 2004). Certainly, it can provide a much stronger relationship between personal identity and academic work (Brew and Peseta, 2004). Francis (1997: 19) puts the personal side of supervision strongly:

Helping to cope with the emotional turmoil, sharing the pleasures and the pains, is as important for researchers as is the tutorial supervision of their work. Friendship helps a great deal – so does the opportunity to bounce ideas and feelings off others also engaged in research. Work with a supervisor is the richer if there is a strong shared interest in the work and in each other's ideas about it; and most is gained from the research process by finding a balance between individual drive and autonomy and the engagement of support of others. One of the most satisfying aspects of the process for both supervisor and student is the emergence or strengthening of a competent researcher, personally wiser and more confident in their work, and fit to take their place in the research community.

Final questions: Supervision allows us to learn a great deal more about the importance of the learning process and personal relationships in teaching. The end product is obviously of great importance in research, but we might want to concern ourselves less with end products and reflect more on learning processes. As such, supervisors might ask themselves: how can I foster a learning environment that will allow my students to integrate the creation of knowledge with critical reflections on their process? How can my students produce research which allows them to develop and change as people? How can I assist my student to develop the ability to transfer the skills and strategies they learn as novice researchers to other contexts? Fostering this independence, while offering support and guidance, is crucial for their students' development as researchers and as lifelong learners.

NOTE

[1] The UK and the USA use different terms for these substantive projects. In the UK, at the postgraduate level, Master's students complete dissertations and doctoral candidates theses, while at the graduate level in the USA it is the other way around: Master's students usually complete Master's theses and doctoral students complete dissertations to earn their PhDs. At the undergraduate level, a range of terms are used, including projects and dissertations in the UK and independent studies, senior projects, senior theses and honours theses in the USA.

chapter 7

INNOVATING: TEACHING WITH TECHNOLOGY

We cannot ignore the transformation taking place in our world today – the fact that the new technologies and the associated dramatic changes in the relationship between people and information are creating the cultural signature of the world. We are in the midst of a revolution that will profoundly alter how we learn, work, and communicate, and conversations emerge about philosophical considerations inherent in the use of these technologies. (Watts, 2003a: 5)

In this chapter, we examine the innovative potential for enhancing learning and teaching that occurs when new technology is integrated into a learning context. First, we look at a range of frameworks or conceptual dimensions to describe the use of new technology for learning and teaching. Secondly, we explore the diverse range of pedagogical applications for the available communication and information technologies. Finally, we look at how these technologies might be used for extending the learning matrix described in Chapter 2.

INTRODUCTION

Innovation is not constrained to teaching with the aid of new communication and information technologies (Hannan, 2005). Opportunities for being innovative can be discovered, developed and seized upon in all the practices and genres of teaching that we describe in this part of the book. Developing reflective teaching practices that address the wider range of needs identified in the learning matrix will require more innovative approaches to teaching. We associate the term with new (and newer) technologies here because the recent upsurge in their use by students provides increasing opportunities for teachers in higher education to be more 'innovative' in their learning and teaching practices.

Certainly, university students today – millennials specifically – are extremely comfortable with technology, and generally view its existence as part of their natural living environment. Computers, the Internet, email and social networking systems (e.g. 'Facebook', 'MySpace') are considered an expected part of everyday life; as such, students may be quicker to experience or see the potential application of new technologies than their teachers (Oblinger, 2003). Students' ease with technology, and seeming impatience with older or outdated technologies, may intimidate faculty unnecessarily. Pressured faculty may either seize on technological 'bells and whistles' in the hopes of catching their students' attention, or ignore technology altogether, clinging to traditional assumptions about learning.

We do not suggest here, however, that technology in itself *transforms* learning, as many faculty and administrators are urged to believe (Surry and Land, 2000). Instead, we suggest that technology, especially emerging technologies, such as multi-media, the Internet, distance education and online learning environments, as well as specific technologies such as student response systems, can *encourage* or *enhance* learning (Hall, 2002; Aravamudan et al., 2008). Throughout this chapter, then, we offer a conceptual framework for understanding technology in teaching, focus on the tensions surrounding the successful integration of technology, consider the diverse range of applications and consider how these technologies fit within the learning matrix.

Flexible strategies

This chapter will focus primarily on the potential of new technology for innovative contributions, alongside more traditional lecturing, facilitating and tutoring approaches, but will touch on the implications for distance learning. This may be called a 'flexible learning' strategy (Moran and Myringer, 1999; Khan, 2006) or a 'close-distance education' (Mason, 1998), although as Watts (2003b) has urged: let's take the 'distance' out of education. A flexible learning strategy is applied to teaching and learning wherever they occur (on campus, off campus, cross campus); frees up the place, time, methods and pace of learning and teaching; is learner-centred rather than teacher-centred; and seeks to help students become independent, lifelong learners (Moran and Myringer, 1999).

We are not suggesting that fully comprehensive systems of teaching – designed, delivered, assessed and evaluated primarily or fully with new technology – cannot address the full range of 'matrix' issues. There have been some highly successful examples, which have moved from a cottage industry phase and into more wide-scale systematic ventures, most notably the Open University in the UK and the University of Phoenix in the USA (Kirp, 2003) and new strategies in the developing world (Kember, 2007b). Strategies that use new technology as part of a more flexible programme are increasingly characterizing the general evolution of distance technologies (Harry and Perraton, 1999: 9).

CONCEPTUAL DIMENSIONS OF USING NEW TECHNOLOGIES

Although there are faculty who are still suspicious of any technology newer than chalk and board, or simply lack the time or resources required to innovate (Gandolfo, 1998; Bass, 2000; Watts, 2003a), the introduction of new technology in education continues to exercise the educational imagination and to open opportunities within more traditional learning and teaching practices in higher education. It draws upon a variety of ways of speaking and thinking about learning and teaching, generating a substantial and continually expanding body of educational literature.

Lecturers have recently been adding a plethora of new expressions to their learning and teaching vocabulary. A selection of these includes distance learning, open learning, flexible learning, hybrid and blended learning, dual-mode teaching, online education, virtual classrooms, global education, computer-mediated communication, technology-mediated knowledge and so on. The addition of new terms with older ones and the swift ability for writers in the area to develop new permutations of these terms are rapidly increasing this vocabulary. Indeed, even the metaphors we commonly employ to describe certain technologies such as the Internet ('surfing the Net', 'travelling the information superhighway', etc.) may not have a shared meaning for all users (Taniguchi, 2003).

While it is not feasible to keep abreast of the theoretical nuances and implications of every new addition, it will be useful to have a broad conceptual overview of the area. In this section, we briefly sketch out some of the dimensions characterizing such an overview. We do so in terms of some

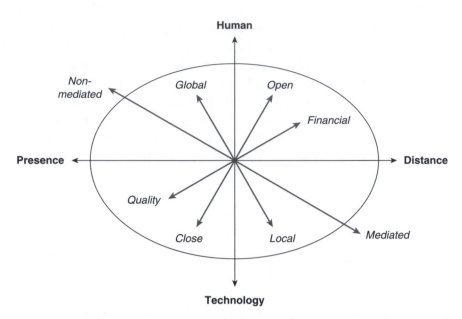

Figure 7.1 *Using new technology in learning and teaching: conceptual dimensions and tensions*

of the important polarities that have come to describe much of the development and discussion.

Figure 7.1 illustrates this conceptual overview in terms of two categories. The first category describes two broad dimensions, emphasizing 1) the technology *v.* human character of this approach to learning and teaching; and 2) its critical role in expanding the physical and geographical 'distance' between teacher and learner. The second category consists of a number of pairs of conceptual tensions which have been associated with new technology.

Engagement and dialogue

The use of technology should not necessarily be associated with increases in distance; much of this new technology enhances traditional face-to-face learning and teaching. Recent technologies, however, have been increasingly associated with their ability to achieve effective teaching and learning at a distance, providing access to expanded and more diverse communities of learners.

These two dimensions are often erroneously conflated. 'Human' is habitually associated with being physically present and technology is increasingly associated with learning at a distance. This association undermines the essential 'human' quality of teaching. There is no intrinsic reason why the lack of physical presence should be dehumanizing. The telephone, for example, is almost a universal distance technology and is advertised as a 'humanizing' instrument. Take time out to call a family member, a friend, just to talk. Some people also find it easier to 'open up' and 'speak' with the use of technology. As Hensley (2003) has suggested, too:

> Technology works best when it is used not as a device to get to some place but, rather, as the destination itself. Technology as a destination is not the only environment for learning, but it is effective as a learning environment when it is applied to the process of learning as the learning place.

The conflation of these two dimensions can also easily be associated, if we are not careful, with another pair of terms: transmission *v.* engagement models of teaching. It does not take a huge leap of the imagination to see that, if presence is conflated with the 'human', human engagement will follow closely behind. Similarly, conflating distance with the technology consigns engagement to face-to-face modes of teaching, linking new technology to transmission modes of teaching. This would be a critical mistake and undermine its effective use as a mode of teaching.

The 'human' aspect of interaction rests ultimately on why and how we use technology. Its effectiveness in improving learning will depend on whether teachers use it genuinely to engage with students in an intersubjective dialogue of shared meanings or whether they regard it as a medium for transmitting content and through which the student can be avoided.

Aravamudan et al. (2008), for example, found that novice instructors understood the integration of technology as either content-oriented (with the focus on the students' acquisition and organization of course content) or process-oriented (with the focus on the students' ability to collaborate or communicate with others, or to enhance their students' learning). And Ellis et al. (2009) reported contrasting teacher conceptions and approaches to the use of learning technologies, ranging from tools for access and information delivery to ways of providing interactive learning opportunities and assisting students to build knowledge. The development of genuine 'human-presence-at-a-distance' engagement is the main challenge that the growth of this new technology presents to learning and teaching in higher education.

Roberts et al. (2007), moreover, found that the meaningful and engaged adoption of new technology in their teaching was determined by a range of factors. Social factors (e.g. peer support, shared values in the department, friendship networks and student perceptions), physical resources (e.g. ease and reliability of technology) and personal factors (e.g. interest in enhancing student learning, interest in improving teaching, interest in instructional technology) were all very important in the decision to adopt new technology in teaching. Engaging students in meaningful dialogue and learning experiences with new technology often requires meaningful development and change in teachers, their departments and the institutional resources available.

A set of tensions

These two dimensions are supplemented in the framework by a set of 'tensions' that are not confined to the sphere of new technology, but are highlighted by its expansion. They include:

- financial *v.* quality considerations;
- the global *v.* the local classroom;
- open *v.* closed learning; and
- technology-mediated *v.* non-mediated communication.

This set of tensions is not an exhaustive or defining list. It illustrates the more general themes associated with the development and use of new technology in learning and teaching. There are other closely linked and more specific tensions – such as synchronous *v.* asynchronous learning – which we shall discuss later in the chapter. While we will briefly consider the above themes individually, as we shall see, they closely intersect one another in a variety of ways and in a variety of different social, cultural, political, institutional and disciplinary contexts.

Financial v. quality considerations

Perhaps the most widely and recently voiced arguments for investing in and developing new technologies in higher education have centred on financial considerations. Financial and efficiency rationales are often a significant force behind the increasing development of flexible strategies integrating new technology within more traditionally taught, face-to-face programmes and courses (Kirp, 2003).

It is clear, however, that the use of new technology is not yet as cost-effective as some might wish it to be. There are substantial upfront investments in the technology, course preparation, teacher training and support, which cannot necessarily be spread over long periods of time as each of these needs to be updated regularly. While it provides opportunities to access new markets, real cost savings and other gains in these areas it often comes at the expense of educational quality (Hannan, 2005).

The global v. the local classroom

The tension between financial and quality considerations intersects here with issues of access at both a global and a local level. While the benefits of new technology – through both its distance and technology dimensions – provide access to both a wider number and diversity of students, accessibility is also paradoxically constrained by these dimensions (Conceição, 2007). They can open the learning and teaching environment and close it down.

The very technology itself, for example, excludes those persons with no or little access to the relevant technology. It also excludes those without the relevant technological skills, people who are not technologically literate. This is particularly acute in many third-world nations where the technology and the associated training are expensive and limited. This may also be true in the local context, even when used alongside traditional face-to-face courses, but particularly when aimed at students at a significant distance.

Open v. closed learning

If the means of studying becomes highly technology-centred – to the point where it is critical to the successful completion of a course – more traditional students may also find the course closed to them (Conceição, 2007). This tension of open v. closed learning environments which has been a feature of new technology from the beginning extends also to issues of academic, language and cultural considerations.

While new technology opens access to courses previously limited to face-to-face delivery, access is usually only open to those students who have an adequate command of the delivery language and who meet the prerequisite academic standards for entry. This need not always be the case – auditors pursuing open independent study may be permitted access as in many traditional courses – but it requires careful consideration.

Technology-mediated v. non-mediated communication

The fourth tension of the conceptual framework concerns the growing distinction between technology-mediated and non-mediated communication and knowledge. The mediation of information and of the modes of human exchange between teacher, knowledge and learner through new technology transforms the nature of both information/knowledge and of human exchange (Watts, 2003b; Conceição, 2007). This does not limit itself to the skills of using new technology, but includes closely associated ways of 'writing' to and 'reading' from it – and ultimately of thinking.

What is important in mediated communication is 'that intellectual energy must be devoted to the real task at hand. What matters is no longer to massively store facts, but to sort them, integrate them and reveal their relationships' (Moro, 1997: 73). The learner is empowered to choose 'knowledge' that is relevant, useful and appropriate and is liberated from the necessity of having to accumulate and 'store' it. Mediation in this context contributes significantly to more autonomous and independent learners: 'Work with new technologies invariably involves the delegation of responsibility to learners and successful learning outcomes will depend on learners' ability to work independently and autonomously from the teacher and, increasingly, to take control of the learning process themselves' (Noss and Pachler, 1999: 205).

Such claims, however, need to be tempered by the potential loss attributed to technological mediation. These include suggestions that technology contributes to the breakdown of linear, narrative thinking, of traditional notions of knowledge and truth and associated losses of quality and standards. It has also been argued that technology can diminish our sense of community and undermines our fundamental assumptions regarding identity and free will (Watts, 2003a). As Watts (2003a) suggests:

> Contrary to the enthusiasts who declare immersion to be inevitable, like the bee's immersion in the life of the hive, technology can be a catalyst that implements our free will. We do have a choice about whether and when to log on, or what to do when we get there. So free will and individual moral responsibility are not virtues that can be ascribed only to Luddites, any more than they are quaint notions to be left behind by the enthusiastic explorers of cyberspace. Responsible choices will lead us into some quarters of cyberspace, and they will lead us out again, enriched, instructed, and better equipped to be agents of constructive change.

In addition, the very global character associated with new technology has been attacked as contributing to a global homogenization of education, undermining local education initiatives and, even, of generating a new version of imperialism and colonization by western values (Spring, 2008). These potential risks, as well as the enormous benefits of using new technology, present a challenge to teaching in higher education. It is a challenge we should neither ignore nor uncritically pursue. This conceptual overview provides a general map of some of the broad issues underlying these benefits and dangers, many of which we shall be returning to later. In the next section, however, we should like to address the kinds and range of available technologies themselves.

INTEGRATING TECHNOLOGY INTO TEACHING AND LEARNING

Given the rapid developments, adaptations and subtle variations in the range of technologies that can be used for a pedagogical purpose, we will only be able to touch the surface of the wide and diverse range of the technological possibilities available to teachers in the space available. These technologies are the subjects of continuous research and change. Generally, however, we can group them usefully by their common application and integration into teaching and learning. Although they may overlap, these categories and technologies include:

- organizing course content;
- engaging students;
- fostering communication; and
- assessing learning.

Organizing course content

Course management system

One recent and substantial innovation for instructors hoping to organize and maintain their courses more effectively is the course management system (CMS). While the specific features may vary, most systems provide instructors with basic administrative and record-keeping tools. Most contain course rosters, including relevant student and instructor details, and offer space for instructors to post course materials, assignments, audio and visual materials, and links to websites and other resources, as well as to record attendance and grades (Bongey, 2005). They offer faculty a rather comprehensive opportunity to providing support for student learning.

As the features of the CMS develop, so too has how students access and use the system, expanding interpersonal support and encouraging independence. Stephens (2005), for example, has his psychology students use wireless laptops in class to connect directly to the course website during class so that they can organize course information, assignments and materials, and connect their own notes to the class outlines more effectively.

While the CMS may be used most regularly for administrative or management purposes (Morgan, 2003), many instructors are taking more advantage of other features offered by the system, in order to support learning, by using online quizzes, discussion boards, peer grouping and other assessment measures (described more fully below). McGee and Leffel (2005), for example, used the CMS to promote ethical decision-making in a business ethics course, which offers both intellectual and social support and promotes independence.

PowerPoint

Essentially replacing transparencies and overhead projectors, slides and carousels, PowerPoint – the most well-known and ubiquitous of presentation software – is almost synonymous in higher education with lecture and organization. In its most basic application, PowerPoint can easily convey the instructor's key points in a bullet-point fashion, while at a more sophisticated level this can link to interactive websites, play video-clips and manipulate images through custom animation.

Faculty can also provide slides to students, either as handouts or electronically, before or after the class. This may be valuable for students, especially if they miss a class, but, of course, the instructor needs to make sure that the slides do not make him, or the textbook, obsolete. He might opt to leave some parts of slides out to ensure that students fill in the missing areas and construct meaning.

Even more importantly, while using PowerPoint has great potential for providing intellectual support, there is a danger, too, if the professor simply uses PowerPoint to transmit vast amounts of information to her students, or if she gets so enthused with its tricks and gimmicks that she loses the interest of her students. Despite these concerns, skilful and innovative uses of PowerPoint can, however, be used effectively to improve student learning in the classroom (Craig and Amernic, 2006).

Engaging students

Personal response systems

Instructors from a wide range of disciplines have increasingly sought to engage students through wireless handheld response systems, commonly called personal response systems (PRS) (known also as student response systems, individual response systems or, more colloquially, as 'zappers' or 'clickers'). The variety of ways that the PRS can be used is extensive and ever growing. At its most basic level, the PRS can be used simply to determine attendance but, at a more sophisticated level, the PRS can be used to poll students instantly about their attitudes, conceptions, beliefs and knowledge in a particular area or about a specific topic (Barrett et al., 2005), providing intellectual support and encouraging independence.

It can also be used to predict student answers, provide feedback, build student consensus and assess learning, either among individuals or in groups (Barrett et al., 2005). Bode et al. (2009) report on the positive impact of using PRS technology to promote interpersonal interaction and learning in the teaching of calculus by giving one 'clicker' per group rather than per student. Since student responses can also be kept anonymous, an instructor may use the PRS as an evaluation tool, to gauge teaching effectiveness or to determine student satisfaction about the course or instruction.

This resource can be invaluable, particularly in large lecture settings, where hundreds of students can be easily polled, and the responses tabulated and available for viewing within a matter of seconds (d'Inverno et al., 2003). While simply using PRS does not mean that learning will enhance learning – indeed, a recent study has shown that there is no clear difference between the learning that happens with PRS and that associated with low-tech flashcards (Lasry, 2008) – the PRS has been shown to help engage and interest students in the topic at hand (Martyn, 2007), although its effectiveness likely depends on how the system is used or the types of questions asked (Morling et al., 2008). Moreover, student responses can also be readily stored and retrieved, which allows instructors the option of comparing student answers over time (Lasry, 2008). Box 7.1 explains how one biology professor used the PRS in her large lecture class.

Box 7.1 *Case study: using 'clickers' in class*

Elsa, a professor of biology, was dissatisfied with the level of student engagement in her large lecture class. Mostly passive, her students rarely responded to her questions. To make her course more interactive, she began to use a personal response system – clickers – in her large introductory biology classes. The clickers allowed Elsa to track both individual and group responses to the questions that she posed, but also, as she soon found, they provided her with immediate feedback on her students' learning.

To maintain student interest and to stimulate them intellectually, she varied the types of questions and the activities associated with each question. The questions allowed her to address misconceptions, gauge students' prior or current knowledge of a subject, or to test assumptions or hypotheses. Sometimes, she has her students work together in teams to solve problems collaboratively, sharing one clicker between them. At other times, she asks her students to respond individually and then predict or hypothesize the class responses. By first deciding on a response, and then being able to compare that response with those of their peers, students can assess their own knowledge. Moving beyond the clickers, Elsa often uses the responses as a starting point for more discussion or as a means to clarify lecture content.

Wikis

Another recent innovation with significant pedagogical potential is the wiki. A wiki is a communal, collaborative web-based application which allows students to contribute and edit information, collectively building a website on a given subject or set of subjects. Wikis usually allow students to pose questions to one another about the material, as well as comment and revise one another's work.

While there may be some questions about the attribution and understanding of authorship, and how 'accurate' the knowledge created is on a wiki site (Calkins and Kelley, in press), as a pedagogical tool, the wiki has great potential for offering personal and social support of students' learning, facilitating independence and self-directed learning, and promoting interpersonal and social interactions among students.

GPS applications

An interesting innovation to engage students and support student learning is the use of Global Positioning System (GPS) software, used most often in a lab or field setting. Found most commonly in the geological sciences (so far), students use tracking devices (even their own mobile phones, in many cases) to locate and report the position of different objects (Johnson and Guth, 2002). Students could track, for example, certain types of rocks and then log the information into a central database that tracks plate tectonic shifts. Such innovations can offer practical support and help students to work both independently and collaboratively in groups.

Fostering communication

Email

Email is by far the easiest and the most commonly used communication technology in developed countries where almost all faculty and increasing numbers of students have extensive access to it. Teachers normally tend to use it for one-to-one exchanges with students concerning a range of issues and questions regarding a student's individual study. The facility for attaching documents to email messages is also being used more extensively. In addition, email systems afford the possibility of one-to-many exchanges between teacher and students and of many-to-many exchanges and interactions between students, and can be used in conjunction with many of the other technologies, such as course management systems, described above.

Computer-conferencing systems

Discussion boards, chat rooms and blogs also provide opportunities for students to develop discussion groups and subgroups on a variety of aspects and issues of the course. These may be formally structured around specific

course assignments, individual or group projects and tasks or more informally established and free-ranging group discussion, including real-time chat
rooms. In some cases they may require additional client software but can also
be effectively established within existing email systems (Pincas, 1999). In
addition, course websites and bulletin boards accessed through the Internet
provide students access to a range of textual material, such as course and programme details, readings, handouts, notices and so on.

Podcasting

Developed in 2004, podcasting is another new technology whose potential
has not been completely realized. At this point, instructors seem mainly to
use podcasting to post their lectures to the web, which benefits students by
helping them access missed coursework, reinforce difficult course concepts
or review for an exam, and which benefits instructors (potentially) by min-
imizing the re-teaching of a lecture and providing the opportunity to reflect
on teaching practice (Roberts, 2008). Podcasts could, however, be used to
supplement the course lecture with additional material or to assess student
learning by asking students to create their own podcast as a class project
(Roberts, 2008).

Digital-based systems

Digital, video and audio-based systems vary in term of the degrees of the
complexity of the technology that may be involved. They range from using
videos, audios and DVDs in class, to the more advanced use of conferencing
systems for interactive teaching. They also include the use of video on websites and related Internet sites for enhancing and providing wider resources
and materials. Again, these technologies provide opportunities for multiple
relationships and types of interaction between teacher and students.

There are, however, debates as to how much the visual actually adds to
the learning and teaching situation, particularly with respect to the lecturer
him or herself. Mason (1994) argues that video contributes to a more social
and facilitative learning environment. Taylor and Swannell (1997), on the
other hand, criticize the idea of video-conferencing that simply reproduces
the lecture in its transmission mode as 'the tyranny of futility'. The debate,
of course, raises the important issue of the human/social dimension in the
use of new technology.

While access to the Internet is still limited for significant parts of the
population, particularly in the less developed parts of the world, every
passing day sees more and more people connecting up to its broad services. It is also still somewhat limited in terms of the quality and magnitude

of video and audio segments that it is easily able to deliver. Again, these are technical issues which are continuously being addressed and improved. The ability to download software programs as well as material from the Internet will permit students access to whatever range of course materials in whatever format higher education institutions wish and are able to provide.

Assessing learning

While an online environment can easily support summative assessments, such as traditional exams, virtual tools and techniques can do much to assess student learning more formatively (Rocco, 2007). Indeed, many of the assessments described in Chapter 8 can be readily modified to an online environment to gauge learning as well as the acquisition of key concepts and skills.

Online quizzes and polls

Surveys, polls, quizzes and short classroom assessments can all be administered online, either through a course management system or by web-based survey software (Ko and Rossen, 2004). While traditional paper-and-pencil quizzes can also assess learning, there are benefits to asking students to submit responses electronically, including the immediate tabulation of responses for administrative purposes, as well as offering immediate feedback that allows the student and the instructor to gauge comprehension and to predict the responses of the class.

Online intergroup peer evaluation

This method is helpful for assessing students in groups. In an online literature class, for example, students are divided into groups and then asked to comment on an element of a Shakespeare play. Each group can then post critical responses to two other groups, in a round-robin fashion (Rocco, 2007) (see Chapter 8 for more details on this type of method). Both the critiques and the responses can serve to help all the groups identify and learn from their collective strengths and weaknesses.

Electronic portfolios

Through web-based software or course management systems, students can use electronic portfolios as a virtual space to compile their course or practical work. These materials might include critical reflections, practice pieces, peer and self-feedback, revised and final drafts or reports. Students and the instructor can follow the student's progress and development as a learner (Jones and Harmon, 2002).

Simulation

In medical and health-related fields, it is increasingly common to use computer-generated simulations to assess student performance, knowledge and decision-making. In highly sophisticated simulation settings, for example, computer sensors can track a med student's movements and register appropriate pain responses, making it clear whether the patient has been caused undue pain or suffering, without having had to practise on real patients. And, in a meta-analysis of 32 studies, McGaghie et al. (2006) found a strong association between time spent on high-fidelity medical simulations and the achievement of learning outcomes.

Synchronous and asynchronous learning

Most scholarship and research on the use of technology in learning and teaching make a widespread distinction with respect to time. If technology provides a more flexible approach to space in its ability to transcend distance within learning and teaching, it also provides a more flexible approach to time. The main distinction here revolves around synchronous interactions in teaching/learning and asynchronous interactions.

In synchronous interactions, teacher and students are present at the same time in the learning environment. The advantages of this kind of interaction are usually described in terms of social and human 'presence'. The fact that the situation is actually 'happening' in 'real time' focuses group energy, cohesion, feelings of community and decision-making. It permits more 'authentic' dialogue, including issues of tone, nuance and emotion, and allows for immediate comments and 'feedback'. It also provides support, discipline and the motivation for students to keep up with the course and the group pace.

Asynchronous interactions, on the other hand, are often seen in terms of students' more personal learning. It provides students with flexibility as to when they access the course materials. It allows them opportunities for going back over and working on the materials both at their own pace and at their own convenience. It also provides time for reflection on the material and for integrating it within their working and/or home environment.

The synchronous–asynchronous division is, of course, not unique to the use of new technology. It has always existed. Contrast, for example, the immediacy of lectures and seminars with the asynchronous reading and study which students have traditionally done outside the classroom. For all its advanced paraphernalia and wizardry, new technology does not extend the basic types of human and social interactions through which teachers and students have traditionally engaged (Table 7.1). It does, however,

Table 7.1   *Types of human and social interactions in teaching and learning*

Types of Interactions	Traditional	New technology
Teacher–learner	Tutorials	Email, voicemail
Teacher–learners	Lectures, seminars	Course management system, video-conferencing, personal responses system seminars
Learner–learner	Projects/lab work	Discussion boards, wikis, blogs, chat rooms
Learner–material	Books, journals, etc.	Websites, CDs, DVDs, podcasts
Learner–others	Open/public lectures	Internet, podcasting, social networking

extend and enhance the potential of those interactions for addressing the 'learning matrix'.

EXTENDING THE MATRIX

In terms of the learning matrix, the development and use of new technology are most commonly characterized by an *independence* context of learning and teaching. It involves, as we mentioned earlier, the delegation of responsibility to learners and is highly reliant upon their ability to work autonomously and independently from teachers. While it provides opportunities for developing *interpersonal* contexts, it is probably least effective at present for students requiring highly *support*-oriented contexts. A significant number of students who take courses that are primarily self-paced and asynchronous end up contributing rarely, and quickly falling behind with exercises and tutorials.

The optimum student profile for *independence*-structured courses employing large degrees of new technology will be those who are highly motivated independent learners, good at self-pacing, employment focused, computer literate and interested in technology-mediated environments (Conceição, 2007). This should not exclude other students who do not match this profile from profiting from new technology. It does suggest that teachers designing courses offered to students who require more support will need to recognize the potential pitfalls when developing their designs. One of the chief challenges to the future expansion of the use of technology in learning and teaching will focus precisely on this issue – devising more clearly developed systems for supporting students online (see below).

Before we look at some of the issues involved in the design, it is worth looking at the role which new technology might play with respect to the four main dimensions of our learning matrix: intellectual, practical, personal and social. Table 7.2 summarizes some of the positive and negative attributes with respect to these dimensions.

Table 7.2 *Positive and negative effects of new technology on four learning dimensions*

Dimension	Positive	Negative
Intellectual	Promotion of interactive learning Increased written output Access to a wider range of material Opportunity for reflection/revision before contributing Access to multiple frameworks/discourses/ perspectives	Slowness in decision-making Less reading Reduced feedback Loss of impetus to reply
Practical	Acquisition of computer skills Opportunities for 'learning by doing' Management of multiple perspectives Language skills enhanced through activity in the new technical and disciplinary 'literacies'	Over-focus on computer and keyboard skills at the expense of others
Personal	Removal of time and space constraints to learning Opportunity to take control of one's learning Empowerment of learner Opportunity to develop self-skills: self-discipline, self-motivation, self-confidence, self-disclosure	Contextual deprivation Information overload Techno-stress Dehumanization of learning Aloneness factor
Social	Opportunity for dialogue with wider groups Increased collaboration between teachers and learners and between learners Increased participation by minority groups Opportunity to develop multiple 'voices' within rapidly changing discourses	Need for a skilled moderator to facilitate (or control) dialogue 'Flaming' Lack of accountability Reinforcement of existing inequalities

Source: Adapted from Peterson, 1997

Many of the negative effects associated in Table 7.2 with the use of new technology are concerned in some way with losses related to face-to-face human contact. Thus 'flaming', or expressions of rage and the use of inappropriate language, linked to feelings of anonymity, isolation, 'techno-stress' and information overload, are less likely to occur in face-to-face situations. The human aspect of communication needs to be emphasized.

On the other hand, this technology offers positive learning experiences for students along all four learning dimensions. It is also worth stressing the potential it offers students for developing capacities to engage with and manage rapidly changing multiple frameworks. This includes both different ways of thinking about a discipline or subject, or even multiple subjects, and developing diverse ways of handling the varied 'knowledge' and 'understanding' associated with these range of frameworks. The comprehensive access to a wide range of frameworks afforded by new technology (including its own developing discourses) provides a platform for teachers to challenge their students.

DESIGNING FLEXIBLE COURSES

In designing a flexible course, it is critical to explore beforehand the extent of the role which new technology might play in delivering a course's overall aims and objectives, including, where appropriate, the negotiation of those aims and objectives with students. Which aspects of the learning matrix will it focus on and which aspects are better left to other forms of teaching? And how will this be integrated with the rest of the programme? Will the use of technology play a relatively minor role, providing, for example, social support – e.g. social chat rooms for informal discussion between interested students – with a reduced role for delivering on intellectual and practical objectives? Or will it play a substantial role in delivering aims and objectives encouraging the intellectual, social and practical independence of students by integrating, for example, online seminar and project groups with video-conferencing, extended website materials and so on?

How elaborate such a programme should be will depend to a large degree on the institutional resources available (Hannan, 2005). More specifically, the evidence available from experienced practitioners suggests that online courses need to observe a number of indispensable principles:

- Staff and students are trained in the relevant technology.
- The course is clearly structured.
- The course provides access to collaborative activities.
- The course caters both to individual and group student needs.

Relevant skills training

While the first of these appears obvious, teachers and course designers often underestimate its importance. Basic skills are often assumed, as are skills in more than one technology. Students, themselves, are often not the best judges of their own abilities, frequently not realizing the complexity of either the technology or their own access to that technology. Many teachers and faculty members also mistakenly assume they have the requisite skills for a course to which they have agreed to contribute.

Many courses recognize that not all students will have the whole range of technological skills at the outset of a course, including, crucially, the collaborative and team-working skills associated with technology-mediated programmes. Therefore, many programmes now integrate training and development in the relevant educational technologies alongside the actual content of the course.

Course structure

Technology-mediated learning needs substantially more structure than was originally assumed. Mere access and arranged provision for discussion groups, for example, are not sufficient to develop a shared sense of community or substantially to engage all students. While some may actively thrive, other students lurk, remaining in the background, observing without actively contributing. In addition, unstructured or under-structured discussion groups without the 'presence' of the teacher often lack rigour, leading to a corresponding reduction in the quality of the learning.

Collaboration

Ways of providing structure centre primarily on the organization of online groups and might include:

- setting collaborative tasks for students in pairs or small groups;
- establishing discussion groups around specific topics, readings, activities;
- assigning a specified number of students to groups to prevent overloading;
- reviewing group composition and changing composition if necessary; and
- providing opportunities for peer leadership and facilitation.

Balance

In designing group work, teachers will always need to strike a balance between the level of structuring involved and the flexibility it provides for the student. In this, Pincas (1999) suggests that the main factors to take into consideration are as follows:

- There is a purpose and good reason for working as a group.
- The students understand a specified outcome at any stage.
- There is a facilitator (usually the tutor but occasionally a student).
- There are options (as far as course regulations allow) – e.g. the time in the week when they do their work, the length of required work, the number of contributions expected, the knowledge they bring and so on.

Guidelines

Finally, as with traditional courses, it is important to give students clear information and guidelines about the programme or course, especially the relationship between online and non-online elements:

- What, for example, are the overall aims and objectives of the programme?
- What are the primary methods of delivery and the methods of assessment and evaluation?
- What is the credit rating of the programme?
- What provision is there for student support, advice and counselling?
- What access to technical support and help-lines will be available?
- Are there any hidden costs associated with provision?

Two key areas unique to online provision which will need to be specifically spelt out concern guidelines for:

- face-to-face contact that students might expect and/or be entitled to; and
- encouraging students to consider fully, in the light of a full programme description, how they will organize and adjust their study and approaches to study to the requirements of the course.

Are they fully prepared to engage with the course intellectually, practically, personally and socially, given its particular parameters?

CONCLUSIONS

Many commentators exploring developments in technology to enhance learning and teaching in higher education have focused on three essential features it offers. These include its potential for developing learner-focused approaches to teaching; its capacity for promoting collaboration and team-work; and its central role in encouraging autonomous, independent learners. These features are not unique to new technology but, rather, powerful outcomes of its imaginative and innovative use.

Innovation, here, does not therefore simply rest in the new technology, nor does it arise through its educational application. It consists, rather, in the new and creative ways in which technology can be used to develop, support and extend student learning in the myriad ways described by the 'learning matrix' described in Chapter 2. Innovation embraces a wide and diverse range of inventive and resourceful 'flexible' strategies for integrating traditional and new methods of educational delivery. It appreciates the intrinsically 'human' character of technology as being essentially concerned with the development of 'dialogue' and community.

Finally, however, it recognizes that new technology is not another way of extending educational delivery, but is itself a defining cultural and social feature of our increasingly unpredictable, changeable and contestable world. Its very application is now a necessary part of higher education's role in preparing students for the culture and challenges of the future, as it rapidly becomes the present. In this way, innovation, itself, becomes 'knowledge content' in the higher education curriculum – its very use a model for students critically and creatively to reconstruct for themselves through their own learning.

Final questions: While thinking about integrating technology into their teaching at the broad level, teachers might ask themselves: how do the different tensions surrounding the use of technology play out in my teaching context? How may I seek to resolve or reconcile these tensions? What types of technology, for example, might best meet the learning goals of the course? But, more specifically, they may want to reflect: why am I opting to use this innovation? How do I ensure that I am not just adding 'bells and whistles', which may look stunning but have no impact on learning? Is the innovation actually hindering or helping learning?

chapter 8

ASSESSING: STUDENT ASSESSMENT

If we wish to discover the truth about an educational system we must look into its assessment procedure. (Rowntree, 1987: 1)

As we develop through the markers, the examiners are expecting more of you, to show that you've understood the material. They're not just wanting the facts regurgitated. ... We can't go on preparing for exams the way we have been. (engineering student cited in Thomson and Falchikov, 1998: 382)

In this chapter we explore assessment, beginning by looking at its critical relationship to learning. We then review a number of key aspects of assessment, including issues of reliability and validity, differences between formative and summative assessment and contrasting systems of assessment, such as norm-referenced and criterion-referenced. A wide range of assessment methods is discussed in relationship to the different dimensions of the critical matrix.

INTRODUCTION

Assessing students is perhaps the most emotionally sensitive part of teaching. It is intellectually demanding for teachers and can be socially disturbing and divisive for students. Students may easily feel that it is not just their learning being assessed, but also their developing identity as people. Associations with right and wrong can trigger the more primitive associations with good and bad, creating fear and a loss of confidence. This may be particularly palpable in subjects such as mathematics, where being wrong can be painfully obvious.

Thus, whether assessment appears to be valid is no trivial issue. Students must feel that they have received the best opportunity to demonstrate their ability in a course, and that they have had the chance to convey something of themselves and what the subject means to them. Otherwise, students may associate assessment and marking with a system of control. With some students this may produce either conformity or alienation, while other students may see it as a rejection of what they have to offer as mature adults. For these reasons, the whole experience of assessment must be matched with what the course is trying to achieve and the culture it is trying to create. Certainly, assessment and course design must be integrated with the key issues of student learning.

In this chapter, we first address a number of general concepts and issues pertaining to assessment. We then explore assessment as it relates to the intellectual, personal, social and practical dimensions of learning within the critical matrix. Throughout, we discuss a wide range of methods designed to aid in the development of a balanced assessment strategy for effectively gauging student achievement and enhancing learning.

DEFINITIONS

While there is some variation in the common use of the term 'assessment', particularly in conjunction with the term 'evaluation', in this book we understand assessment to mean the gathering of information about student learning, which may be qualitative or quantitative in nature and used for some purpose. These purposes include providing feedback to students about their progress and development, assigning grades and making instructional or pedagogical choices (Brookhart, 2004). As such, assessment includes, but also transcends, the simple measurement of student achievement.

We distinguish assessment from 'evaluation', which forms the substance of the next chapter. We reserve the term 'evaluation' for making informed judgements on the value or quality of an educational entity – including such things as programmes, courses, sessions, teachers, books, etc. – aimed at fostering student learning. Assessment of student learning thus plays a key role in evaluation, but they are distinct.

Table 8.1 *SOLO and assessment*

Level	Pre-structural	Uni-structural	Multi-structural	Relational	Extended abstract
Associated verbs	Misses the point	Identify, do a simple procedure	Enumerate; describe, list, combine, do algorithms	Compare/contrast, explain, analyse, relate, apply	Theorize, generalize, reflect, hypothesize
Example of question in each level	Question will be irrelevant or nonsensical	'What is the capital of France?'	'Identify the major powers in the First World War and outline the key foreign policy associated with each'	'Explain how the government's nutritional requirements concerning food groups have changed over time and discuss how different social groups have been affected by these changes'	'Design an outreach programme that will help educate a diverse community about the government's new nutritional guidelines'
Example of response	Misses the point and/or is irrelevant	Focuses on only one relevant conceptual issue in a complex case	Focuses on more than one issue but they may be a disorganized collection of items; may reproduce a 'shopping list'	Shows understanding, applies or uses a concept(s) which integrates a collection of data, issues, etc.	Goes beyond existing principles; higher-order principles are used to bring in a new broader set of issues

Source: Adapted from Biggs, 2003

THE CENTRALITY OF LEARNING OUTCOMES

Learning is a critical aspect of assessment. For assessment to be effective and meaningful, it must be clearly aligned with the learning objectives and teaching methods and activities employed in the learning context. As we discussed in Chapter 3, Biggs's SOLO taxonomy provides a useful framework for designing both learning outcomes and assessments (Biggs, 2003). With five stages of rising complexity (pre-structural, uni-structural, multi-structural, relational and extended abstract), SOLO also offers a systematic way to demonstrate how a learner's performance grows as tasks grow more complex (see Table 8.1).

To a large degree, Biggs's SOLO maps on to Bloom's taxonomy, with the movement from lower-order to higher-order thinking, in complexity and level of skill. Unlike Bloom's taxonomy, however, Biggs's SOLO also offers a means to assess learning outcomes, exploring the breadth and depth of learning. SOLO can be used by instructors to elicit the critical thinking and learning they want from their students.

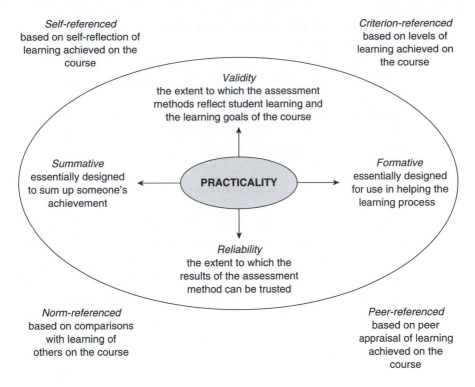

Figure 8.1   *Aspects of assessment of student learning*

KEY ASPECTS OF ASSESSMENT

There are several key aspects of assessment, each with its own set of tensions (see Figure 8.1). Whether the assessment is intended to be formative or summative, where the point of reference is (instructor-referenced or peer or self-referenced) and how valid and reliable the assessment is (or perceived to be) are all crucial in assessing learning. Practicality is at the heart of all tensions as there are usually significant practical implications limiting the full achievement of these aspects.

Formative and summative assessment

The first tension focuses on the overall purpose of assessment. Two general purposes of assessment – enhancing learning and measuring student achievement – are often referred to as formative and summative assessment, respectively. Simply, formative assessment concerns development, improvement and learning, while summative assessment concerns accountability and performance. Formative assessment, for example, can be used to:

- provide feedback to improve learning;
- motivate students;
- diagnose a student's strengths and weaknesses; or
- help students reflect critically on their own learning.

Summative assessment may be used to:

- pass or fail a student;
- grade or rank a student; or
- predict a student's success in other courses or employment.

Although different methods of assessment may fulfil one or the other of these two purposes – an exam may be summative, while a first draft of an essay is formative – almost all methods can be applied to either of these two purposes. For example, Wininger (2005) describes how he teaches his students to study their graded (summative) exams to improve their learning and methods of studying in a formative way. Neither should the two purposes be regarded as mutually exclusive. 'Enhancing learning', as we saw in Chapter 2, could mean either deep (transforming ideas of learning) or surface (reproducing ideas of learning). Similarly 'measuring achievement' could suggest a measurement of either deep or surface learning. 'What' we assess becomes more important that 'why' we are assessing.

This distinction is important, particularly if we agree with Rowntree (1987: 1) that 'to discover the truth about an education system we must look to its assessment procedures'. Working purely for marks or grades can indicate a cynical and purely strategic approach to assessment. Traditional finals, for example, have often elicited surface or strategic approaches, especially in terms of course content, enabling students to evade the harder or deeper demands of their courses and still pass.

If, however, assessment goes beyond basic information and techniques to include higher-level intellectual demands and reflects a commitment and enthusiasm for education and the deeper values of the discipline, then 'high grades' will reflect the deeper issues that the course may really be about. In this respect, 'high grades' might reflect the students' appreciation of alternative perspectives, their recognition of the need to change and to reconceptualize and construct knowledge, and their capacity to cope with unexpected and new complexities. In addition, college offers many valuable experiences that should neither be incorporated into grades nor marginalized by them, experiences which are more appropriate to formative assessment.

Classroom assessment

Classroom assessment provides a relatively simple form of formative assessment for teachers. It is a process of critical inquiry and analysis that instructors use to assess student learning with an eye on the impact of their teaching. It is, moreover, learner-centred, teacher-directed, mutually beneficial, formative, context-specific, ongoing and rooted in good teaching practice (Angelo and Cross, 1993). As such, more instructors than ever have begun to use classroom assessment better to understand the learning that transpires in their classrooms.

Rather than simply assuming that students are learning what they are teaching, instructors can use classroom assessment to assess their students closely as they learn, collecting frequent feedback and asking critical questions to gauge student comprehension, skill acquisition, application of materials and knowledge construction. Several common classroom assessment techniques (CATs) are discussed more fully throughout the chapter in terms of the critical matrix.

Reliability and validity

The second tension considers the nature of reliability and validity. Reliability refers to the extent to which the results of the assessment method can be trusted, whereas validity refers to the meaning and value of the assessment, and the extent to which the assessment methods reflect student learning and the learning goals of the course. Lack of reliability or consistency of marking and grading, both perceived and real, has contributed to students' lack of confidence in marking systems, particularly as wide discrepancies can occur in individual cases (Montero et al., 2006). Indeed, as Pieron observed in the early 1960s, 'assessment by different examiners produces marks with considerable variability such that in the determination of these marks the part played by the examiner can be greater than that of the performance of the examinee' (1963: 140). Even today, academics may still discuss marks as if they were accurate and absolute.

Although marking can sometimes be reasonably reliable, accuracy depends on the hypothetical mark that might be obtained if the marks given by a large number of markers were averaged. This does not mean that there is an absolute, true and accurate mark; rather, that the mean of one large group of examiners will tend to agree with the mean of another large group of examiners.

There are similar problems associated with a lack of validity, particularly if students cannot clearly see or understand the connection to the rest of the course or if the learning objectives and teaching approaches are not clearly and constructively aligned. Improving reliability and validity, then, is crucial. Both may be improved by encouraging teachers to reflect more fully on their approaches and interpretations of marking, developing thoughtful criteria based on intended learning outcomes; using appropriate teaching activities to meet those outcomes; and communicating those criteria to students ahead of time (Brookhart, 2004). A few methods follow.

Double marking

In this activity, two examiners rate the same work, without knowing the other's mark. Each marker is, in effect, blind. In one variation, the two marks are simply pooled and averaged, which may contribute a partial solution to the above problem. However, the real use of double marking is to encourage the discussion of issues that the discrepancies raise, and to encourage a clarification of the criteria and their interpretation. Real improvement will only occur when these issues are resolved through the development of a genuine community of assessors with a shared culture of standards. While such approaches to marking are undermined by the increasing modularization of courses and pressures on time, examiners' meetings need to focus on developing shared contexts and criteria for marking as well as determining the actual marks.

Rubrics

A criterion assessment grid, commonly called a rubric, is a scale or set of scales designed to evaluate student work, by identifying different degrees of quality for individual criteria. There are two common types of rubrics:

- *Analytical,* in which several scales are applied to the same work, with each criterion examined separately (see Table 8.2).
- *Holistic,* in which only one overall judgement is made, with all the criteria considered together (Brookhart, 2004).

There are, however, advantages and disadvantages to each rubric type. For example, an analytic rubric provides more specific feedback but may be less practical as it generally takes longer for the instructor to use, with more criteria to consider. Conversely, a holistic rubric may not provide the student with much information about how to improve, but may speed the grading process for the instructor. As such, holistic rubrics, unlike analytic rubrics, tend to be more summative than formative in nature (Brookhart, 2004).

Table 8.2 *Sample rubric*

	1) *Weak* Little or no evidence of outcome	2) *Developing* Initial or developing evidence of outcome	3) *Accomplished* Thorough evidence of outcome	4) *Strong* Highly developed, creative outcome
Criterion 1 Thesis	Ideas are confused or incoherent; based on personal opinion; poorly structured	Ideas supported by some evidence; structure works at a basic level	Ideas are well structured and supported by logic and evidence	Ideas are sophisticated thoughtful, and persuasive; strong structure
Criterion 2 Use of sources	Minimal or no use of appropriate sources	Some use of appropriate sources, little integration or analysis	Sources effectively integrated and analyzed	Sources smoothly and critically integrated and analyzed
Criterion 3 Writing Quality	Choppy; many grammar problems; poorly organized	Some grammar problems; shows some organization	Minor proofreading errors; generally well organized	Error-free and smooth; highly organized

Exemplars

Offering examples of student work that can represent or 'anchor' each level of performance quality may also enhance validity (Brookhart, 2004). By comparing the model with each level, the instructor will maintain consistency. This is also helpful when working with multiple graders or examiners.

Norm, criterion and peer/self-referenced assessment

The third tension concerns the point of reference for the assessment: whether it is instructor-referenced or peer or self-referenced. There are two main types of instructor-referenced assessment: norm and criterion-based. Marks and grades are, of course, essentially norms by which to judge the difference between students. This kind of assessment, often referred to as 'norm-referenced' assessment, aims to enable effective and reliable discrimination among students. While students often seek information about these differences, this does not necessarily tell them much about the quality of their thinking or what they are able to do.

The issue is not so much about what they achieve but more about what their status is in relation to other students. If too many students achieve the required outcome, then the norm-referenced assessment has been a failure since it will not discriminate. Assessments which grade against sets of predetermined criteria, on the other hand, are 'criterion-referenced'. With criterion-referenced assessment, every student can realize the levels established by the set criteria. In this respect, criterion-referenced achievement helps students to understand how far their thinking and their performance have progressed.

Finally, while assessments are often instructor-referenced (generated by the instructor), they may also be generated by individual students (*self-referenced*) or by their classmates (*peer-referenced*). In so far as they offer different perspectives on a student's growth and development, they also tend to be more criteria-referenced than norm-referenced in structure.

Issues arising from traditional assessment

Although there have been more recent moves towards a diversity of assessments, traditional assessments are still pervasive and automatic, often still weighted heavily in many classes. Despite the intentions of faculty, and even students, traditional timed, in-class, cumulative or partially cumulative exams do not give an adequate picture of the many and varied abilities which are developed in higher education. Distortions are frequently encouraged by exaggerated and stereotyped perceptions that students have of traditional exams. They are sustained by the idea that exam results provide a grand verdict on a student's academic worth.

This verdict, however, is rarely based on evidence accumulated from a variety of settings that resemble the sort of tasks and situations they will face in later life. Instead, under the traditional system, it is based on a situation – typically several hours of writing with very tight time constraints and a heavy memory load – that they will probably never face again. Criticisms of how such a traditional assessment can disadvantage a student will be familiar to many teachers in higher education. These critiques include:

- too much emphasis on memory;
- too much stress on factual knowledge;
- too great a reliance on speed of writing and thinking;
- too great an element of luck;
- too much pressure of a kind seldom found in later life;
- too little scope for originality and sustained writing; and
- too little opportunity for constructive feedback.

A major difficulty with the traditional exam system is that it gives teachers so few leads on how to learn more about a student's experience of learning in their course. A great deal can be done to diversify our assessments so that different desired outcomes are evaluated separately. While the administrative functions of assessments may be simplified by overall one-dimensional grading, they are not necessarily effective predictors of a student's future work, even as predictions for graduate work (Kuncel et al., 2001). Overall assessments may differentiate students reasonably consistently, but the purpose of this particular way of categorizing students is too general. What is needed is a range of information about the very different abilities of students that can be used in different ways, depending upon why that particular selection is being made.

Formative assessment is also not well served within the traditional system, primarily because of this lack of differentiation of abilities, but for other important reasons as well. The timing of traditional assessments is usually too late for early feedback and information is often regarded for some reason as confidential, but perhaps even more important are the attitudes of faculty and students. Few students regard their exam performance as an accurate indication of their ability, and faculty may not encourage a discussion with students who do not seem to want it.

Traditional exams can be used to direct students' efforts to important areas of the course, but they are generally not good at directing students' efforts towards developing a higher level of intellectual abilities to be used in these areas. The general purpose of providing an incentive to work is often successful, but extrinsic motivation is an unconvincing part of higher education. Indeed, it conflicts with the often stated aims of education which rank love of learning and intellectual development above all else. This distinction may not always be very clear, but intrinsic motivation is generally considered more valuable. It can certainly make a greater contribution to the important question of student identity mentioned earlier.

Ultimately, how we assess students affects the way they learn and develop. Yet, any system of assessment must be practical and acceptable to faculty and not unduly increase their workload. As assessment becomes more closely integrated with learning and teaching, the time spent on it is not just concerned with grading but is an integral part of teaching. The acceptance, moreover, of peer and self-assessment methods can save faculty time, as well as contribute to students becoming more independent professionals. It can counter, for example, some of the unfortunate consequences of objective, machine-scored exams which, while time saving, can encourage routine low-level learning and dependency. Indeed, we might heed the warning put forth by the Senate Committee on Examinations at the University of Edinburgh in the nineteenth century: 'The excessive employment of selective examinations is gradually subverting all that is best in the education of our youth and a reaction is threatened which may bring the use of examinations altogether into discredit if remedies be not found for the worst abuses of the system'.

Student views on traditional assessment

Although many students may take a strategic attitude towards traditional assessment, and do what they need to do to get high marks, they are not necessarily naïve about the nature of academic work. Early work on face (perceived) validity (Jones et al., 1973) suggested that students were very concerned about what was being assessed within traditional examinations. Two thirds of students in a wide range of disciplines agreed with the statement that 'in planning my work I frequently found my real intellectual interest had to take second place in the need to get good marks'. A high proportion felt that the intellectual qualities that the lecturers valued were not tested in the examination. Despite claiming to know what lecturers wanted, almost two thirds of students felt that they were not given a clear idea of the academic qualities faculty expected in their work.

Moreover, students often found their experience of assessment contradicted their own personal and educational aspirations. Over thirty years ago, a student answering an interview question about his experience with traditional assessment observed: 'Writing four questions in a three hour exam paper is a total contradiction of what you've been training yourself to do throughout the year'. Answering the same question, another commented: 'It's a great mistake to be over sophisticated in exams: its part of the technique not to be: one has to limit oneself' (Cox, 1975). Both these comments suggest the students' realization of, and possibly frustration with, an assessment system that asked them to take a strategic approach to studying, rather than a deep, perhaps more satisfying, approach to learning.

In a more recent study, students revealed similar attitudes towards traditional assessments (Thomson and Falchikov, 1998). One student remarked on the futility of delving into course content deeply: 'You skim over the surface ... it's just a rush job all the time'. Another student, agreeing, added: 'You get the situation where people are not learning anything, they're just doing the assessments ... and doing enough work to get through the exam' (Thomson and Falchikov, 1998).

Assessment, the dominating instrument of control in higher education, gets bound up with the struggle for independence. Conformist students may lose out in this battle and become passive learners whose view of education is dominated by memorizing. Other students can become rebellious and find their energies are dissipated in hostility or may withdraw in apathy from a system they disagree with. Only the more independent students can cope with the system and yet maintain a sense of integrity.

For an increasing number of students, however, integrity dissolves into simply coping and/or the quest to attain higher grades. And as students so respond, ensuing pressures build within the assessment system towards the giving of even higher grades. Indeed, in recent years, as issues like 'grade inflation' have become a more pronounced concern across academia, higher education's very marking practices have been called into question (Hu, 2005).

Faculty conceptions of assessment

It is not surprising, perhaps, that the differences in students approaches to study and assessment, is somewhat reflected by contrasts in how teachers understand the role and meaning of assessment in their courses. Watkins et al (2005 [DK1]) found that faculty members conceptions of assessment fall within three basic types. For teachers with the least sophisticated type of conception, assessment is seen as a separate process, external to teaching and learning, which conveys to the instructor the basic knowledge and skills students have learned. In contrast, while teachers holding the second conceptions are aware of an internal relationship between assessment and teaching, they still see assessment as essentially measuring students acquisition of basic knowledge. At the most sophisticated level, assessment is viewed as internal to teaching and focused on developing deep learners. Assessment for these teachers is understood as helping students develop sophisticated strategies for learning, e.g., reflecting, analyzing, interpreting (Watkins et. al 2005). To some degree, the contrast between these conceptions of assessment reflect potential tensions inherent in the aspects of assessment depicted in Figure 8.1. Less sophisticated teachers conceptions often focus on the summative, reliability and norm-referenced aspects of the figure which are more external to the teaching, while the more sophisticated tend toward the more formative, validity and criteria-referenced aspects of the figure which are more internal to teaching (see Figure 8.2).

THE INTELLECTUAL DIMENSION

Communicating assessment expectations

This section focuses on how we can support student learning through assessment. It provides a rationale for the way we assess students that will:

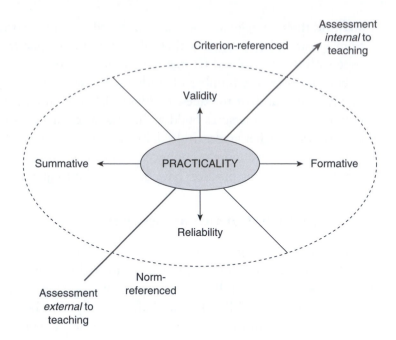

Figure 8.2 *Faculty conceptions of assessment by aspects of assessment*

- enable them to achieve a clearer understanding of the criteria and standards;
- give them more confidence in the reliability, validity and fairness of the system; and
- provide better feedback and reporting.

Often, students derive more understanding of a course from the demands of its assessments in the course than from their teachers and course hand-books. If we want students to understand what their courses are meant to achieve, we need to offer more than course descriptions and objectives. We need to convey clearly the 'real' demands of how they are being assessed in the course.

Making criteria readily understandable and transparent is an important component in helping students understand what is expected of them in a course. But merely telling students may have little effect if they do not share with their teachers the same assumptions and understanding of the criteria used to assess their exams and assignments (O'Donovan et al., 2004; Hounsell, 2005). They interpret the written criteria and feedback comments in a way that fits their assumptions rather than the teacher's intentions.

Helping students develop a deeper understanding of the course by looking at the demands of the assessments is challenging and involves a gradual development of skills that require practice. One of the most pressing challenges in this respect, and one which incites the ire of most teachers more than any other, is the issue of plagiarism.

Avoiding plagiarism

Despite dour warnings and strict punishments, student plagiarism still remains prevalent in higher education (Lieberg, 2008). Technology may have exacerbated the problem as well: with a few clicks, students can cut and paste online text into a paper or simply access an essay or report readily available on the Internet (Scanlon, 2003; Martin, 2005; Purdy, 2005).

But there are several layers underpinning the practice of plagiarism that need to be sorted out. On one level, the teacher might consider whether the student truly intends to steal the words of others and pass them off as his or her own. In some cases, plagiarism may have been an act of:

- deliberate treachery ('this is the easiest way to a high mark', 'I won't get caught because my professor isn't likely to look at this book or at this website', 'I know my friend wrote this for a different class');
- laziness ('I don't feel like doing this assignment; this person expresses everything much better than I ever could anyway'); or
- desperation ('I can't cope with the expectations of this assignment').

Other students may have committed plagiarism unwittingly, for a variety of reasons. They may erroneously believe that simply changing a few words or reordering a list, for example, is sufficient to avoid the charge of plagiarism. Plagiarism may also be culturally conditioned: meaning what is understood to be academic theft or the unwarranted borrowing of words and ideas may vary across cultures (Sowden, 2005; Gu and Brooks, 2008). Lastly, what constitutes plagiarism may differ widely across disciplines. For example, it may be common for students in the sciences to work together on lab reports, but the point where they must work independently may vary.

On a different level, teachers will want to consider the overall course design in deciding the strategies and methods they can take to minimize plagiarism, whether deliberately or unwittingly committed (Lieberg, 2008). They will want to define and discuss their expectations for their students and to explain clearly what constitutes plagiarism in the course and for specific assignments. They shouldn't assume, either, that students will enter university knowing what plagiarism entails or that they should have learnt it on a specific course (e.g. English composition) at some point in their undergraduate career.

To minimize plagiarism, teachers will want to tailor assignments in a way that allows for specificity of topic (to avoid the easy replication of general ideas) and which requires students to show independent creative thinking. If students are asked to apply principles or concepts to something specific and unique, engaging their own experience, there is less likelihood that someone has already written on the exact same subject. Giving students autonomy and choice – by allowing them to pick topics, materials and methods that are meaningful to them, or which allow them to relate material to new contexts (as appropriate) – will also help motivate them and spur deeper learning.

Engaging students in assessment

Marking exercises and criteria

Engaging students in marking exercises is an important way to improve their confidence in their understanding of the criteria and demands of the course. For example, an instructor may ask her students to mark or comment on an essay or assignment written by a former student, rather than completing the assignment themselves. She could then lead a discussion about what sort of criteria should be used in their own assignments, rather than simply offering an official line on criteria and marking standards. They are likely to learn a great deal more about marking if they attempt to formulate the criteria themselves. By comparing and discussing the marks with the teacher, they can begin to revise and develop their criteria in ways that might improve their own work. Gibbs (1981) provides an interesting exercise where students mark two contrasting approaches to the same essay question that brings out interesting points related to the issues of deep and surface learning.

Comparison of rankings

Another way to increase students' understanding and ability to operate with varied criteria is to give them a range of essays on a particular topic which have already been graded by faculty. Their task is to rank them and compare their rankings with those of the faculty. The instructor can assess their performance on this task by comparing how close their rankings correspond to the faculty ranking. This has two very practical advantages: it enables students to see and consider a range of alternative responses to a set question and it enables faculty to mark large numbers very quickly.

This type of activity can be a useful preliminary to more serious attempts to develop self- and peer assessment. It can enable students to move from a quantitative view of the value of their work, expressed in terms of more and more detailed information, to a more qualitative approach based on differences that reflect different levels of intellectual understanding.

Objective testing

When factual information must be assessed, objective testing – such as those employing true–false and multiple-choice questions – can contribute to the overall assessment of student learning. Easily graded and time-saving, objective tests are a staple in many fields, especially in the sciences and health professions. In one sense, they can be very reliable: answers are right or wrong and frequently are machine graded. In another sense, however, the choice of right answer and the nearness of the 'distracters' to this right answer can create areas of ambiguity and uncertainty that diminish this 'objectivity'. In addition, such assessment methods frequently appear artificial and detached from any meaningful context.

While generally used to measure knowledge, comprehension and application, when well designed, objective tests can also gauge higher-level areas of learning, including a student's ability to hypothesize, predict, analyse and generate new ideas. Indeed, it is now becoming common to insert factual questions within a narrative where the questions are linked to a specific, concrete context, argument or diagnosis (Case and Swanson, 2001).

Certainly, objective tests are in danger of being overused, particularly as faculty get more pressed for time. They may find that their advanced students have to unlearn years of study practices – such as memorization and rote-learning – developed from too much emphasis being put on objective tests. Since the more important challenges of assessment are essentially holistic, demanding the demonstration of understanding and the construction of meaning, objective tests may be best used alongside other forms of assessment that do not require the reproduction of excessive factual information. Such abilities are difficult to assess within an objective format, although more objective kinds of questions can be successfully integrated into complex texts that require a more holistic approach from the student (Brown et al., 1997). Asking students to explain or annotate their objective testing responses, even if they selected the wrong choice, may help students address their misconceptions and clarify their thinking to the instructor (McKeachie, 2006).

Feedback to students

One of the key findings which Light (2001) reports in his study of what students felt helped them the most during university was receiving timely feedback from their teachers. Feedback serves several important purposes, including:

- helping students understand the mistakes they have made, as well as the underlying causes of those mistakes;
- suggesting ways students can keep tabs on their own learning;
- helping students find ways to help themselves;
- identifying areas of achievement (Hattie and Timperley, 2007); and
- enhancing a learner's professional and personal growth (Bhattarai, 2007).

Frequent feedback to students can be particularly supportive, especially for those who are rather anxious. It is important for students to have a sense of their own progression through the course and how they are coping with its requirements. Feedback from summative assessments in the form of grades or marks alone might provide students with a general sense of where they stand in the course and among their peers, but might not contribute much to their sense of intellectual growth. These, of course, can be supplemented with constructive comments where appropriate and possible.

Criterion-referenced assessments at least provide students with the opportunity to reflect upon and understand how far their thinking and their performance have progressed. Summative feedback from norm-referenced assessments provides little more than a sense of peer positioning which might, depending on that position, develop or undermine a student's confidence in their progress. Support for students through formative assessment is generally criterion-referenced, helping students to achieve the learning outcomes of the course in accordance with its established criteria and standards.

Feedback can, however, be given in different ways with different objectives. In a study of feedback given to Cambridge students in the UK and MIT students in the USA, Cox (2007) mapped out four ways in which faculty approached the giving of formative feedback on assignments. These approaches to feedback are contrasted with respect to the ways in which they may be classified – closed and open – and the ways in which they are pedagogically framed – controlling and non-controlling (Table 8.3).

The four approaches presented in Table 8.3 are described in terms of their respective frame and classification, and they are illustrated by examples of the kind of comments which might be given to students by teachers providing the feedback. Closed-boundary approaches to feedback restrict the feedback to the specific assignment. Comments from open-boundary feedback, on the

Table 8.3 *Approaches to feedback*

Classification: focus on boundaries	Framing: focus on pedagogy	
	Controlling: didactic teaching style	Non-controlling: facilitative teaching style
Closed boundaries Restricted feedback Focus on assignment or topic	Closed directive: Narrow orientation – feedback is focused on generating excellent assignment Teacher-centred – feedback is directive and focused on providing clear directions to meet clear criteria with clear grading	Closed explorative: Narrow orientation – feedback is focused within the narrow boundaries of generating an excellent assignment Learner-centred – feedback focused on engaging the student and eliciting student-centred responses. Informal
	Illustrative comment: 'Your discussion of … is not relevant' 'You need to give examples in section two'	Illustrative comment: 'How could you improve this assignment?', 'What would be another approach to this problem?' 'What did you mean by…?'
Open boundaries Developmental feedback Focus on wider educational context	Open directive: Wider orientation – feedback is on the assignment but open to crossing the specific assignment boundaries to looking at the wider educational context and issues Teacher-centred – feedback is focused on the wider context of the assignment but in a direction and on material controlled by the teacher	Open explorative: Wider orientation – feedback on assignment is used as a stimulus for educational development: critical reasoning, writing and creative skills Learner-centred – feedback is open, informal and less directive – focused on eliciting student-centred responses
	Illustrative comment: 'What do you think Bernstein would say about your point of view?', 'You need to review more about the history of this problem', 'You should read his last two books'	Illustrative comment: 'How do you go about writing assignments?' 'What have you learnt about structuring arguments?' 'Can you think of other areas where this applies?' 'Do you think all your assumptions are appropriate?'

Source: Cox, 2007: 110

other hand, direct a student's attention outside the assignment boundaries to the wider educational context and issues of the topic.

Comments provided in controlling pedagogical frames are essentially teacher-focused, directing a student's attention to the solutions and material the teacher feels will achieve the goal of the assignment most effectively. Non-controlling frames, in contrast, are focused on engaging a student in a more reflective, learning-focused activity for which the assignment is essentially the catalyst. Faculty may, indeed, provide comments which span these categories.

The dangers of feedback are that students can become over-dependent on this support. The less controlling approaches are a step in the direction of moving them away from such dependence, encouraging students to internalize critical feedback processes of their own work. The ultimate aim in students becoming professionals is, of course, that they are no longer highly dependent on others for judgements about the quality of their work. As Bruner comments: 'the tutor must correct a learner in a fashion that eventually makes it possible for the learner to take over the correcting function himself, otherwise the result of instruction is to create a form of mastery that is contingent on the perpetual presence of the teacher' (1966: 53). This is where the self and peer-assessment techniques (see below) and the necessary training for doing this can play a useful role. It can aid students in developing the skills to reflect upon and assess their own work and progress.

Encouraging creativity, choice and self-critique

If we are too supportive, as we have suggested above, students may become dependent and avoid the more challenging demands that would enable them to become independent learners and professionals. In this section, we consider what methods of assessment might be most appropriate in encouraging intellectual independence and helping students achieve higher-level objectives: creativity, choice and self-critique.

To encourage independent thinking, however, it is necessary to make it clear to students that their work needs to reflect those deeper, higher-level processes. These include the processes of analysis, synthesis and evaluation described, for example, by Bloom's Revised Taxonomy and in the higher-level outcomes expressed in the SOLO taxonomy mentioned above.

Operating at these levels is not easy and a major obstacle to doing so is a lack of time. Overloaded courses are notorious for encouraging surface-level approaches to learning and assignments. Examinations with high time constraints can give little opportunity for reflection, considering alternatives, appreciating different contexts and integration. The tasks set on many courses, especially on foundation or survey-level courses, are very often short term, to be completed in a single session. Work which requires extended concentration over weeks or months is usually restricted to the final year of a programme, but the quality of the thinking that is generated out of a long-term commitment can be very important for encouraging independence.

Table 8.4 *Student experiences of projects*

Advantages	Student experiences
Enable the student to explore deeply a field or topic	'It's the only time you do your own work'
Develop initiative and resourcefulness	'It's not just an exercise, it's good that you have to do it all on your own and fit it into a theoretical framework'
Enhance time and project management skills	'The best opportunity we had – other work is other people's thoughts'
Provide personal ownership of learning	'Very much me, my biases and beliefs,' 'It's something you can get your teeth into, something you choose yourself'
Foster independence and creative problem-solving	'Some original thinking is required, essays are more regurgitatory [sic] of other people's opinions'

Sources: Adapted from Cox, 1975; Brown et al., 1997

Projects

Projects have long been recognized as perhaps the most important area for self-expression and commitment (Cox, 1975). For many students, the first years of college may be spent memorizing other people's work and only in the final years are they able to begin seriously to engage with the discipline and subject matter. Table 8.4 provides a list of the educational advantages suggested by Brown et al. (1997), augmented by comments from students on project work from seminal research by Cox (1975).

Project work also provides a good opportunity for students to engage in divergent – as opposed to convergent – thinking (Rowntree, 1987). Although this will vary among students and disciplines, the undergraduate in particular is frequently not provided with a substantial opportunity to engage with coursework which permits them to diverge across a range of possible answers, concepts, meanings, solutions, approaches and so on. Yet, this is an essential feature of any creative work or in-depth inquiry or research. Many, if not most, of our methods of assessment encourage convergent thinking, asking students to converge upon a right or best answer. While project work, like any coursework, can be derivative, poorly planned, badly referenced, tedious, etc., it does also offer students opportunities for choice, creativity and divergent thinking – indeed, it can be written into the criteria for project assessment.

The disadvantages of project work include concerns that it is time-consuming to set up, monitor and provide feedback on, and that it is difficult to assess failure fairly. Wide variations in the help sought by students and the fear of plagiarism – the latter enhanced by access to the

Internet – are also obstacles to consider. None of these disadvantages is, however, insurmountable, and Brown et al. (1997) regard problems in assessing projects as no more than those involved in assessing coursework, essays or written papers.

Portfolios

Portfolios are another form of assessment that allow students a wider range of choice than more traditional methods, and may be a more accurate reflection of student learning (White, 2004). Students may be asked to provide a portfolio of evidence of achievement in terms both of outcomes specified by the course and a wider range of abilities and achievements which are more personal to the individual students and their particular interests.

Research on the personal development and motivation of students often stresses the importance of them having a sense of control over their own environment, and this may increase the students' sense of responsibility in the learning process (White, 2004). This is typically expressed in terms of how many choices they are able to make in regard to what they learn and how they learn (Cox, 1996). They can show a respect for individual differences and the varied contexts in which people work.

Portfolios are becoming a widespread way of assessing professional and continuing development – now including the accreditation of teaching in higher education. Nevertheless, their use is usually accompanied by guidelines as to what should be included and how they should be structured. They have similarities with records of achievement and are quite often used for assessing prior learning and prior experiential learning.

Open-book exams

Most assessment that is concerned with encouraging independence is much more open than traditional assessments. Allowing textbooks into examination rooms may encourage independence to an extent, but it depends on how a student uses that textbook. It may assess an ability to locate information quickly rather than the ability to use it in more independent, creative ways. Open-book exams usually specify the texts and resources that may be consulted, but with the expansion of coursework as opposed to examinations, it becomes more difficult to justify making these types of assessment within an examination hall.

Prior-notice exams

A more useful method of assessing the ability to produce work under time pressures and in a more secure environment is via examinations where the topics or the actual questions are given out in advance. Students can carry out research and develop their understanding in libraries beforehand. Cox (1975) found that sociology students reacted differently to the change in constraints. While prior-notice exams relieved the constraint on memory, many students feared that the standards expected would be correspondingly higher. However, they provided the more independent students with the opportunity to explore issues in depth and to take risks and express what they had themselves thought about issues rather than reproducing textbook answers. They had the chance to justify their ideas in a way in which they felt they had never had in traditional exams. For some dependent students this form of assessment provoked anxiety and they found it difficult to stop preparing for it. The majority, however, found it quite liberating.

Problem-based learning

Problem-based learning (PBL) and inquiry-based learning (IBL) are an important development for encouraging independence in students (Sadlo and Richardson, 2003; Lee, 2004). PBL courses are designed around real-life problems, whereas in IBL they may focus on a specific lecture or assignment. The more abstract and, sometimes, less engaging aspects of the course are learnt in relation to a close involvement with problems which are highly relevant to students' more concrete ideas of what the course is about and what competence would mean within it.

Although PBL and IBL courses use examinations, they are generally less important than in courses that are more traditional. The actual solving and understanding of problems is the most prevalent form of assessment. This more contextualized and naturalistic assessment enables students to feel that assessment is not a control mechanism, but is a natural feature of learning.

Self-assessment

The development and increasing use of methods of self-assessment is, perhaps, the most important innovation in assessment for the development of intellectual independence. In contrast to the vast majority of assessment methods, it directly addresses the paradox of a highly dependent education leading to the independent responsible status of a professional person. Indeed, self-assessment is a critical aspect of a student's growth and development as a scholar (Cassidy, 2007).

Introducing self-assessment is not without challenge, however, particularly in academic cultures unused to innovation, or where students are unduly competitive. To thrive requires a culture of mutual trust among students and faculty. Teachers have also frequently resisted the development of self-assessment methods, suggesting that students can be overgenerous in their marking. In fact, there is evidence to suggest the opposite. Generally, student reactions are very positive. Five times as many students found it a worthwhile experience as those who did not, and a similar ratio found the exercise helped them to pinpoint their strengths and weaknesses (Boud, 1995).

A critical issue in the development of self-assessment concerns strategies for generating criteria against which the student will assess his or her work. It is important that teachers do not simply issue criteria from above but rather provide students with a role in formulating and refining them together with teaching faculty. Exercises in peer marking can be helpful in this respect. Although learning from mistakes has its benefits, there can be serious problems in introducing self-assessment into an unprepared environment. Early bad experiences can easily make it extremely difficult to try to introduce it later.

It is important to establish clear rationales for involving students in developing the criteria. In the process they will also learn to make qualitative judgements, including justifications for the assessments they make. Boud (1995) also stresses that self-assessment practices should permeate the total course. They should make an identifiable contribution to formal decision-making and be part of a profiling process in which students are actively involved.

Self-assessment can be viewed, not as a distinct element of teaching and learning, but in relation to reflection, critical reflection and meta-cognitive practices. It is part of that set of activities which encourage students to take responsibility for their own learning, monitor their learning plans and activities, process their studying and assess their effectiveness. Self-assessment would then become something which is embedded in courses designed from the very start to assist students with their learning (Cassidy, 2007).

Interpersonal (peer and group) assessment

Historically, higher education has been primarily focused on the individual, encouraging the student to 'think for himself [sic] and work on his own' (Hale, 1964: iii). Collaboration with respect to assessment was highly suspect. The development of interpersonal skills, co-operation and abilities to work in teams is, however, increasingly valued. In this section, we look briefly at the widening of the scope of our assessment systems to engage with interpersonal skills.

Peer assessment

The discussion of self-assessment inevitably raises questions of peer assessment since the ability to become an effective self-assessor is often enhanced by assessing and being assessed by peers. It is an important issue in assessment generally to be able to appreciate different perspectives and points of view. Attempting to assess a range of different student assignments can be extremely interesting for students, enabling them to see a wider range of perspectives and solutions. Of course, in seminars, students will be exposed to different views, but this is a very different experience from assessing and analysing them critically for their different strengths and weaknesses.

These skills are also critical in a multicultural society that expects people to understand and tolerate multiple views and perspectives, which values the intellectual virtues of parallel thinking (De Bono, 1994) rather than patterns of critical thinking which encourage the rejection and substitution of intellectual positions. Employers value interpersonal skills and communication in a way they have never done before. Modern companies are less hierarchical and their employees are more likely to work collaboratively on projects rather than simply follow instructions.

Issues of co-operation and competition permeate all levels and activities in society, a point well understood by millennial students long used to working collaboratively in groups and teams (Howe and Strauss, 2003). We think less in terms of single dimensional intelligence (IQ) and more in terms of 'multiple intelligences' (Gardner, 1999), which include the interpersonal which can be enhanced by peer assessment as well as the intrapersonal intelligence which can be enhanced by self-assessment.

Being able to discuss assignments with faculty has long been an invaluable part of higher education. Written comments on assignments followed by discussion can be one of the most effective learning activities in academic life. While still an essential aspect of graduate supervision, it is growing harder at the undergraduate level, given the larger faculty–student ratios. Peer assessment can provide students with new perspectives in a way that teacher assessment now seldom can.

As with self-assessment, peer assessment is not something that can be effectively introduced without considerable practice and reflection. This development, however, may be done in larger groups and the investment of considerable time in extending the skills of giving and taking criticism can be an extremely valuable learning activity. It is important to see this as a skill that is developed over the whole range of teaching and learning in higher education.

Traditional student-led seminars, for example, are often painful experiences, either in the sense that criticism is badly given or badly taken, or in the sense that serious discussion and criticism are difficult to initiate and sustain. Process-oriented time in seminars – conducted in an atmosphere of mutual trust – can be a useful occasion for developing the interpersonal skills that are essential in peer assessment. Equally, what is learnt in peer assessment may enable group work to function in a more constructive and helpful way. Certainly, research has shown that peer assessment can support the goals of group learning, particularly collaborative learning and co-operation, and can allow a group to assess individual contributions holistically (Lejk and Wyvill, 2002).

Consultants and assessors exercise

An interesting way to combine group work with peer assessment is the simulation exercise of consultants and assessors. This very useful teaching exercise consists of setting up consultant teams to address a specific problem in the particular subject area.

Briefly, the class is divided into consultant teams of about four to six members. Each team prepares a report on the problem for a group of assessors drawn from each team. The assessors' group formulates criteria by which to judge the several consultant team presentations. The exercise can take anything from an hour and a half to several days and may involve purely thinking and discussing in the groups or consulting various resources. Questioning by the assessors can draw out many issues in assessment, as can the judgements themselves.

As important, however, is a debriefing session when the consultants assess the assessors on the criteria they devised and applied. The way in which they are applied can come under very active scrutiny by both the student consultants and the teacher. The debriefing can also be a further time for co-operation both in terms of the intellectual task set and understanding the process.

Group projects

Group projects provide a further opportunity for intellectual and interpersonal development with respect to assessment (McKeachie, 2006). Their increasing use in higher education parallels the growth of project-orientation approaches developed in industry. The traditional focus on assessing the individual is one reason why group projects have not been used as often as they might. How do you 'fairly' allocate marks? Do you give all members of the group the same grade despite the fact you may know that some have actually played very little part in it? Many teachers feel that competition for marks within the group may not facilitate effective problem-solving, co-operation and learning. Answers to this question are very much dependent on the nature of the projects and the aims which they are designed to achieve. There are at least three different approaches.

In the first approach, the instructor or the group divides the tasks into sections, which are then completed individually and marked separately. Some parts, such as the introduction and the conclusions, might need to be considered by the whole group. In this context, each individual might receive two marks: a common group grade given for the overall quality of the project, and a grade for the each member's individual contribution. This may be an effective approach if the project can be divided into equally challenging sections.

A second approach might be taken if dividing the project into separate sections is too difficult or artificial. Here, each member receives the same group grade, but also writes a reflective commentary on the process, describing their own specific contributions as well as different levels of commitment and understanding within the group. This approach has the added advantage of encouraging and rewarding reflective practice.

The last approach involves aspects of peer assessment and asks the group to allocate a proportion of the total mark to each of the participants. Conducted badly, such an approach can be a recipe for antagonism within the group. As with other forms of peer assessment, it needs to be carefully discussed and planned with the students before they actually begin to work on the project (McKeachie, 2006). Students will need to agree beforehand how decisions will be made and the criteria for dividing the joint mark. In any group work, of course, the issues are not purely intellectual. There will be many personal issues raised and the social composition and practical functioning of the group will be crucially important and will materially affect the outcome.

THE PERSONAL DIMENSION

Supporting personal development

In this section, we stress the importance of assessment in providing support for personal development and suggest some ways of doing this by encouraging choice, learning contracts or agreements and reflective commentaries.

Encouraging choice

We have suggested in earlier chapters that higher education is not just about transmitting information and developing particular competencies and skills. It is a time for self-understanding and personal development, both in the sense of coming to know ourselves better and coming to know what sort of professionals we may be. In professional courses, the match between a student's understanding of what it means to be an engineer or a doctor and what the course seems to be providing can be crucial both for motivation and for intellectual development.

Higher education is often less about learning specific topics and more about developing constructive ways of approaching them. Our own identities are very much an expression of the successive choices we make in life. This is extremely important for students beginning to know themselves (Weinstein, 2003). If there is little choice in the courses and the assessments they have to cope with, then they can easily feel they are being shaped and moulded by others. In extreme cases, students might rebel against what they perceive and experience as external control and the lack of choice, even to the extent of failing. Indeed, failing in such cases – where narrowly constructed parental and academic expectations are experienced as oppressive – is often seen as the only way for some students to exert choice and develop themselves personally. 'Success' simply acknowledges the pressure to succeed and conforming to it. Choice and opportunities for self-direction might alleviate this desire to frustrate the aims of others by failing.

Learning contracts or agreements

Providing students with the opportunity for informed choice and the time to take that seriously is an important part of a teacher's role. As noted above, project work provides one way to do this, but many other assignments can also offer choice among alternatives. The development of both informal and formal learning contracts – where teacher and student agree procedures and areas of inquiry – can also encourage students to feel they have a more personal role in their education. These can also provide an important platform for personal reflection. In arts subjects and, to some extent, the social sciences the expression of personal perspectives has always been valued but, in the sciences and medical sciences, this has been difficult. With the decline of positivism and a willingness to take more open positions in many areas, the possibility of developing personal views is increasing.

Reflective commentaries

Supporting students to reflect on their choices and judgements enables them to feel they are developing personally while in higher education. In some disciplines, it may appear difficult to find areas of personal expression. Even in very technical projects, however, asking students to write a section in reports on their personal response to the experience can be a useful way of encouraging them to understand and extend their own responses and experiences of learning.

Encouraging identity exploration

Many of the issues discussed under personal support are designed to enable students to have a more secure sense of personal identity. This is also, of course, an essential aspect of developing independence. Changes in the nature of higher education in the past three or four decades have, however, emphasized 'independence' aspects of a student's identity more acutely than was once the case. In the earlier more homogeneous and restricted 'elite' system of higher education, students could expect to develop their identity through 'identification' – stressing an apprentice role. In the radical changes in the latter part of the twentieth century and the development of mass higher education (Trow, 2001; Thelin, 2004), the focus of student 'identity' shifted towards exploration, gaining self-knowledge and intellectual autonomy.

The traditional examination system corresponds to the 'apprentice' role and the more modern, open and diverse forms of assessment corresponded to the 'exploration' route (Cox, 1973). This distinction matched the parallel changes in society in relation to conceptions of the structure of knowledge, occupational structure, teaching, participation, adolescent development and cultural and social life. The 'traditional' cultural life involved fewer boundaries and expectations, identity was more prescribed, there was more consensus of values and duties, and clearer artistic styles and conventions. The more 'modern' social life – with its blurred boundaries and expectations, lack of prescriptions about identity, lack of consensus upon values and duties and lack of conventions in artistic expression – is even more prevalent in the new millennium's 'supercomplex' world.

Ironically, academic pressures – the lack of resources and rising faculty–student ratios – threaten to return faculty and students to some of the more formal, traditional approaches to assessment of the past (Hu, 2005). We still find within some of the more formal subjects, fears that under the pressure of overloaded curricula there is no scope for individuality and creativity, only for learning the right answers and reproducing them. On the other hand, PhD guidelines may recommend reflective commentaries on the experience of writing a PhD and conclusions about what they have learnt from doing it (Sloboda and Newstead, 1995). Even the personal pronoun 'I' is not automatically rejected, and contextualizing writing in terms of particular personal responses is seen as more academically respectable.

Encouraging this generally within assignments might weaken the tendencies towards bureaucratization and the commodification of higher education and assessment.

Enhancing self-knowledge in groups

Encouraging the interpersonal within the personal dimension is very close to considering the interpersonal within the social dimension. An important distinction to recognize is the aspects of self-knowledge – crucial to working within groups – which group work and assessments/reports on group work can emphasize. We learn a great deal from reflecting on our own behaviour; this is particularly the case when we reflect on it in terms of the responses, reactions and interactions of other people.

While it is still somewhat unusual for courses to emphasize self-knowledge and interpersonal skills in their assessments, recent interest in key skills and transferable skills has, as we noted above, raised their profile. At present, this might be more in theory than in practice but assessment, even formative assessment, may help to make it a more important aspect of education.

Accurate and reliable assessment in this area is still problematic. Nevertheless, the development of reflective commentaries which, for example, ask students to look at how far they have changed in response to a course and what they have learnt about their own participation and reactions to various events and activities during the course can be invaluable. Careful programmes in peer-tutoring and peer-mentoring might also provide a valuable interpersonal role in assessing self-knowledge. Encouraging students to look at their own strengths and weaknesses and their own ways of benefiting from a range of different relationships can contribute to their overall formative assessment.

THE SOCIAL DIMENSION

Fostering informal peer interaction

Traditionally, there has long been an emphasis upon the value of college life at university and the importance of participating actively in social life and student societies. Seminars and group work, however, do not have a reputation as valuable social experiences. More recently, however, there has been more emphasis upon syndicate learning, peer-managed groups and group projects. The development of more reflective study has often focused upon peer support but, generally, there has been little emphasis on the assessment of the social dimension of learning.

Assessment has always generated emotional problems for students, and even with less emphasis placed on finals, considerable anxiety is still felt by many students undertaking and completing assignments. Isolation can be a serious problem for foreign students and for those who feel less able and may be liable to fail. Frequently this is simply not true but it is usually difficult for teachers to convince students of this. The opportunity to discuss drafts and problems and the way they are approaching their work with fellow students, however, can be very useful in allaying the anxieties that can make their pessimistic predictions self-fulfilling.

Many students provide each other with support in informal 'learning communities', usually without assistance from faculty. Unfortunately, the students who most need such support often cannot do this. The formalization of such 'learning communities', while not simply focused on assessment, can play an important role in supporting and fostering student approaches to assessment.

Innovative approaches with new technology, for example – particularly through the use of online chat rooms and discussion groups – have been valuable in helping courses become more robust learning communities rather than merely a collection of individuals. Such groups, for example, might engage in the kinds of formal marking exercises and/or activities setting up the criteria for self- and peer assessment, discussed above. The social dimension of coming together, however, extends its broader pragmatic and utilitarian reasons. The enjoyment of social interaction can often provide an important context enabling students to discuss their problems and worries.

Fostering independence within groups

Encouraging independence within a social dimension seems rather paradoxical. Nevertheless, developing students' interpersonal skills might merge the somewhat incongruous aims of encouraging independence and providing students with emotional and intellectual support. Working in teams or groups – attempting to solve problems, develop knowledge or design new objects and processes – requires mutual group support and encouragement within a strong emotional and intellectual climate. At the same time, students also need to make independent contributions and not simply reflect the prevailing opinions and ways of working. They need to learn to preserve their sense of individual identity while, at the same time, working in harmony with the group.

Contributing to the working climate of the group demands accepting support and making contributions which others cannot or are less able to make. Assessment can be an important aspect in achieving this. Higgins et al. (1989) report on an initiative in a department of chemical engineering to encourage problem-solving skills. They developed a two-week programme for the early weeks of the first term as an introduction to university life with respect to both the problem-solving and the social perspectives. Teams of about six worked on general problems and then problems in chemical engineering. At the end of the programme they presented two kinds of written and oral reports, the first concerned with solving the problem and the other on how the group functioned as a group. From the beginning, assessment was used to indicate the value of the social dimension of learning and students were encouraged to reflect upon the nature of their interpersonal contribution to the group and its ways of interacting to solve problems.

Students' commentaries on their group participation need not be formally assessed. In some universities, while it is a condition of assessment, the commentary is not itself assessed. Group work, of course, is generally designed to encourage openness and risk-taking, and assessment can be an inhibiting factor to such social interaction, especially if the criteria are left vague. Nevertheless, assessing a student's actual contributions to a group can be managed effectively although it is very different from encouraging students to write about their experience and simply assessing their writing. If, for example, reflective commentaries are an integral part of the learning on a course, the task can be less threatening and criteria can be developed which are more attuned to individual variations within a group and the context in which they work.

THE PRACTICAL DIMENSION

Supporting practical skill development

There have been many changes in practical assessment over the past few years and there are many disciplinary differences. We begin each section, therefore, with some general characteristics. Essential aspects of giving support in practical work include providing:

- clear detailed instructions/briefs/checklists;
- close tutor/technician supervision;
- clear support documents/materials/equipment supplied and specified;
- clear criteria for correct methods and solutions; and
- faculty assessment for both process and product.

Objective, structured clinical examinations

While traditional practical examinations are rare now, variants of the objective, structured clinical examinations are common in the health disciplines (Hounsell et al., 2007). The exams consist of about 20 short, clearly defined practical tasks that represent the key objectives of the course. Students move from one problem/task to another at specific 'assessment stations' every five minutes. These might require taking the history of a patient and diagnosing a problem, interpreting test results, interpreting radiographs or slides of tissues, setting up or using equipment, making dissections or putting in stitches in simulated wounds. Each task can be assessed in a variety of ways and might involve simulated patients and/or the completion of short-answer questions. Generally a trained observer or a trained interviewer conducts the assessment. Although setting up the tasks can be time-consuming, the system can be very efficient – in two hours 20 students can be assessed on 20 different tasks. Careful attention will need to be paid to security issues – particularly for summative assessment – although the tasks can be varied for subsequent groups of students.

Objective, structured clinical examinations are mainly effective in assessing the specific goals of practical work. They can improve individual technical skills and even develop problem-solving skills. How far such exams can improve understanding of scientific inquiry, reinforce good practice and/or nurture professional attitudes is more problematic, but may be lessened with the developing trend towards competency-based evaluation in the medical and health fields (Carraccio and Englander, 2000).

Performance evaluation guidelines

Another way to introduce highly structured and supportive practical assessment is to document activities with comprehensive report sheets. Brown et al. (1997) describe details of performance evaluation guides and a self-assessment manual of standards developed for practical work in dentistry. Levels of practical competence are defined very closely for failing, passing and excellent grades. A failure, for example, is defined as: 'unacceptable outcomes as a result of treatment or lack of treatment which has already caused irreversible damage to the patient's aural environment, or will cause severe damage in the future' (1997: 107). Further criteria employed in the assessment include both the 'aesthetics' and the 'structural and biological integrity' of the task.

Such comprehensive reports can be made for observing groups of students who are doing such things as setting up apparatus, with such headings as reads instructions, checks layout of apparatus, checks instructions in relation to apparatus, seeks advice from the demonstrator. Each can be given an estimate of the proportion of time spent on each activity. Box 8.1 illustrates how creative work can be assessed in terms of acquired skills and overall aesthetic.

Box 8.1 *Case study: assessing creative work*

When Cameron, a professor of fine art specializing in sculpture, first started to teach at the university he struggled with assigning final marks to his students. How can one assess creativity and originality, he wondered, since art is so subjective and personal? Previously, he had taught in a selective art school, where most of the students were highly motivated and very talented and where very little attention had been paid to marks. In his current teaching context, most of his students did not major in art and very few expected to be professional artists.

He decided that, rather than trying to assess his students' work in terms of pure creativity, he would break down the assessments by considering his learning objectives. He wanted his students 1) to learn to appreciate art within its larger social, cultural and political context; 2) to acquire basic sculpting skills and techniques; 3) to create a sculpture incorporating different techniques; and 4) to be able to articulate their artistic vision of the sculpture.

To support their learning in class, he demonstrated specific techniques during class, and then let his students practise, sharing their progress as they worked. Outside class, he promoted their independence by requiring them to visit different sculptures and analyse the vision of different artists. At the end of the course, the students all showed their work to the rest of the class and an assortment of other faculty and students, enhancing the interpersonal. The final grade, which had so worried Cameron, was no longer based on a single project but, rather, on his students' participation (including feedback on each other's work), critical reflections, their level of technical skills and their written and oral explanations of their artistic vision. In the end, he still reserved a small part of the mark for each student's imagination and creativity, but a student did not need to be a 'genius' to get a high mark.

Reports on laboratory work, of course, are common forms of assessment now. While they may be concerned with more open forms of assessment, they can be very closely structured according to rigorous guidelines. Such detailed and rigorous guidelines and criteria are often obligatory – particularly with respect to health and safety procedures – and have the added benefit of improving the overall reliability of the assessment.

There are disadvantages, however. While such guidelines need not restrict independent activity, in general the more detailed and prescriptive, the less scope there is for individual and independent response and expression. Students can end up reproducing practical techniques without understanding the principles behind them. Detailed criteria and guidelines may not be sensible if used to the exclusion of more open forms of assessment.

Practice tests

Another method to support practical assessment is to allow students to complete sample exams or practice tests that are similar to the types of exams used in the course. Snooks (2004) offers a method in which students take short tests based on the required reading, which they then compare and discuss answers with a partner, and then the rest of the class. The process is designed to enhance critical thinking, question analysis and test-taking skills; to reduce student anxiety; and to imitate a real-world professional context in which colleagues share and discuss written work.

Recorded skills

In some fields, especially in medicine and other professional areas, students might benefit from having their skills recorded electronically as they perform a task or skill in a real or simulated environment, to review their strengths and weaknesses later (Silvestone, 2004). These can be very effectively combined with peer and self-assessment approaches informed by detailed discussion with respect to the development and use of the assessment criteria.

Encouraging independent engagement

As in the other dimensions, encouraging practical independence involves a higher degree of student involvement in the assessment process. Generally it will include:

- a wide choice of practical tasks or problems;
- student involvement in planning and decision-making;
- student responsibility for finding and providing support materials;
- student involvement in the criteria for success;
- student self-assessment;
- time for development; and
- risk-taking and creative responses.

All these characteristics take time but they should be seen as contributing not only to the assessment and development of practical work but also to the general development of students. Such characteristics can apply to many different forms of practical work as well as straightforward work in laboratories.

The development and use of portfolios (see above) can be a useful way of enabling students to work independently, permitting them to assemble evidence of their practical achievements and skills – including their laboratory work. Broad practical outcomes can be negotiated and established with students regarding both what would be included and what criteria would be used for assessing them.

The types of problems and tasks considered appropriate are important in widening the scope for independent work. Brown and Knight (1994) report a range of alternative possibilities for practical work including the production or generation of artefacts and products, designs, drawings and plans, design and build, games and simulations, and IT-based work. Wherever design and production are involved there is also considerable scope for creativity or at least for significant differences between the various student products which highlight the possibilities for more independent and engaging practical work. Broadening the scope of this work can also contribute to overcoming some of the dull routine that can characterize work in laboratories and other practical settings.

Fostering interpersonal practice

Developing interpersonal skills through the conduct and assessment of practical work requires, again, a substantial focus on students as operating in 'learning communities' or, at least, within active groups. General aims here would be to:

- establish a reasonable proportion of group practical work and projects;
- focus on the group process and development as well as group tasks;
- emphasize group negotiation in executing and completing tasks;
- include the group in the setting of assessment criteria; and
- involve the group in actual assessment.

These aims or characteristics are similar to those we have discussed for other areas of assessment but they take on an added significance in practical work, particularly when it involves a more emotional engagement. Such real-world assessment is often called 'authentic assessment'. Here, the assessment reflects how the skills would be used in the real world: the problems are unstructured and may require students to make an informed decision from several options and may allow for feedback and second chances (Svinicki, 2004).

The actual concrete experiences of practical work can engage people as whole people rather than simply intellects. Experiential learning (as we saw in Chapter 2) involves observing, feeling and acting as well as thinking – areas in which the development of interpersonal skills can be particularly powerful. Of course, these skills can be developed through reading, discussing and watching videotapes, but the more realistic the setting, the greater the possibility for deeper learning. Real-life settings can be the most effective but can often be difficult to arrange. Partial versions of actual experience, however, can be effectively developed. Brown and Knight give an interesting example of a practical assessment using real people in real situations:

> Surveying students are assessed on how they undertake negotiations between a client and a housing association for the lease of premises. Local professionals are involved in the setting of the assignment, using actual local properties and, when possible, role play themselves, before contributing to the student's assessment. (1994: 85)

Similarly, how a student performs before an audience in a creative field, such as music, might offer another real-world assessment (Stanley et al., 2001). Such activities are not restricted by discipline and provide a useful and valuable compromise between students actually operating in the 'real' world – as in practice placements and fieldwork – and in the more formal environment of the seminar room. Interpersonal issues can easily be lost in such activities unless care is taken to ensure particular concern that students do reflect upon the nature of the interactions and begin to develop a more sophisticated understanding and responses. As with seminar work in general, the topic or task can completely take over from the development of interpersonal understanding and the ability to respond to the demands of the process.

CONCLUSIONS

The approach we have taken towards the issue of assessment in this chapter has been to offer information and arguments from which readers will draw their own conclusions and make their own professional judgements. There are no ultimate prescriptions or rules for the practice of assessing students in higher education. It is, rather, a developing genre of the language of learning and teaching. It needs, as we have indicated, to be reconsidered and reflectively practised within the context of both our changing understanding of higher education generally and of learning in particular. In this respect, it is a multifaceted and multidimensional phenomenon positioned at the heart of learning and teaching and its scope for innovation and the improvement of student learning should not be underestimated.

For intellectual and academic reasons, assessment needs to be carefully and accurately balanced and to emphasize the key elements of a course. For a student personally, and for the development of his or her sense of identity, the control and certification functions of assessment need to match the intellectual, personal, social and practical demands of a course. In this respect, assessment needs to be less a rite of passage and more a significant and relevant personal achievement.

This relevance needs to be apparent not just in terms of today's needs, reinforcing the status quo, but also in terms of the demands of tomorrow's increasingly complex and indeterminate challenges. Graduation must promise a stake in the future, not just the past; its rituals need to take students beyond traditional culture to a world of change and uncertainty. A forward-looking quotation from the past might be a useful way of ending: 'Only when the students become competent evaluators of their own goals, experiences and accomplishments do they become truly educated (liberally educated, one might say) and capable of engaging in the individual fundamental processes essential in a democratic society' (Dressel, 1976: x).

Final questions: As the last quotation suggests, assessment need not be simply an assessment of student learning, but it can model a critical student learning experience in itself – self-assessment. In designing and constructing their assessments, teachers might carefully reflect on the learning experience as well as the learning assessed. Do my assessments match, or constructively align with, the deeper learning objectives I have identified for my students? Do the assessments provide the kind of evidence which allows me to determine whether they are achieving the kind of learning outcomes I expect? Are my students engaged with the assessment process? Does success on the assessment provide them with a meaningfully sense of accomplishment?

chapter 9

EVALUATING: TEACHING AND COURSE EVALUATION

Happy are they that hear their detractions and can put them to mending.
(Benedict in Shakespeare's Much Ado About Nothing, Act 2, Scene 3)

In this chapter we extend the notion of evaluation beyond collecting information for the accountability and improvement of courses and teaching to include the development of reflective practitioners, self-knowledge and the nature of learning for the future. We introduce a wide variety of ways of evaluating educational processes, which we relate to the context of more sophisticated conceptions of quality assessment, appraisal and accreditation, together with research on learning and assessment. We suggest that a closer integration of learning with evaluation can make the process less an imposed distraction and more an opportunity for linking research and teaching and making educating our students a field for lively, shared inquiry and development.

INTRODUCTION

Evaluation can make all of us feel anxious and defensive, whether it is through examinations, appraisals, reviews, observations, student ratings or even friendly critics. As academics, we can even feel anxious when we are just being judged by ourselves. But as Shakespeare suggests, anxiety

| 237

can change to pleasure provided we can put our detractions to mending. This suggests that we should link the critical process with a constructive one, just as we would link feedback with student work, as discussed in Chapter 8. To do this, evaluation needs to be well balanced. To achieve balance, evaluation must derive from many complementary sources, since none is adequate in itself.

Good evaluation requires a thoughtful rationale and, as such, will be time-consuming. Of course, there are external incentives. For example, the Quality Assurance Agency (QAA) in the UK and the European Association for Quality Assurance in Higher Education (ENQA) both use a careful process of subject review to evaluate programmes by monitoring the curriculum and examining core skills. While there is no such parallel national agency in the USA, in many colleges and universities, the evaluation of teaching is linked to reaccreditation by such entities as the Higher Learning Commission (HLC) and to promotion, tenure, salary and retention decisions. The professionalization of teaching in higher education is also beginning to require reflective commentaries and portfolios for achieving accredited teacher status. But are these incentives and the traditional need to improve our courses enough?

In the Introduction to this book, we stressed that there have been two important developments in higher education: the emphasis upon generic skills – especially learning to learn – and the change of focus from teaching to learning. What has been seriously underestimated is the role of evaluation activities in enabling students to understand more about the way they learn from the different styles of teaching and the different environments and learning resources they encounter. This can help students become more effective lifelong learners when the constraints and supports of formal courses are behind them and they take full control of their own learning.

Hurried completions of brief institutional questionnaires may contribute little by themselves, but many of the evaluation methods we discuss in this chapter have much to offer in helping students to understand themselves and their responses to different ways of learning. Reflective exercises in evaluation can become important features of courses rather than a conformity to institutional demands but, like the development of study skills and writing skills, they need to be regularly integrated activities.

As in the previous chapters, we consider evaluation to be a particular 'genre' of teaching in higher education with respect to the matrix of learning. Evaluation needs to reflect all aspects of a course and, at the same time, to draw on the distinctive contributions of a very wide range of methods and approaches. While some evaluation methods may be more appropriate to certain contexts or dimensions of this matrix, we highlight a handful which relate to several aspects of the critical matrix and, as such, illustrate how evaluation can achieve balance.

We are not attempting a comprehensive review of all the issues and possible methods of evaluating teaching. In this discussion, we draw primarily on those categories of evaluation which are concerned with the effectiveness of teaching, including doing small-scale studies of the courses or teaching with which the reader may be chiefly concerned. Before we consider the particular methods, however, a brief overview of some of the key aspects of evaluation research might be helpful.

Aspects of evaluation

Figure 9.1 gives an idea of the complexity of the issues and dimensions of evaluation that would need to be considered in any major research study and suggests some which would be important in more local evaluation reports. The arrows are meant to indicate the variety and range of factors that influence and shape the sort of approaches that might be taken towards evaluation research.

One especially important aspect is the educational ideology or values associated with different approaches. The technology of evaluation has often been described as ideology in disguise and it is worth considering whether the recent emphasis on the behavioural and market-driven approaches is at odds with major developments in social research which have tended to moved away from a more positivist paradigm towards a more qualitative anthropological paradigm.

Illuminative evaluation, pioneered by Parlett and Hamilton in the 1970s, is an approach where the investigator studies a programme or course by examining how it operates, focusing on describing and interpreting, rather than measuring and predicting – essentially taking a case-study approach to evaluation (Gray, 2004; Russell et al., 2004). Qualitative inquiry delves into a deeper impression of the experience of an educational programme, allowing us to appreciate the more complex context of education: we learn not just about the achievement of specific objectives, but the unintended outcomes as well.

We have become more aware of the importance of perceptions and of the motivational effects of programmes. Courses that might appear to be very efficient in one way may be very inefficient in another and liable to generate alienation and the distortion of deeper, more holistic learning. If, for example, we look at the impact of problem-based learning, purely

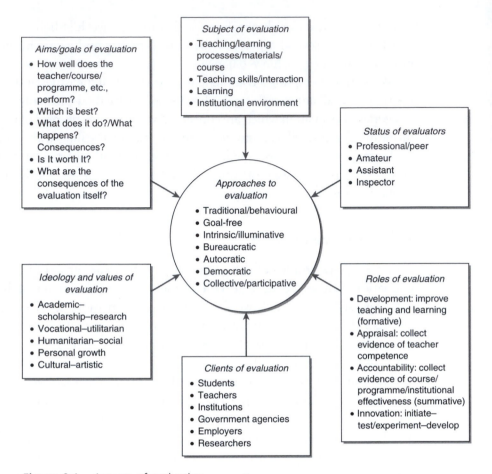

Figure 9.1 *Aspects of evaluation*

through the perspective of formal test examination results, we may feel that it is not worth the effort. On the other hand, if we focus on the nature of the discipline and professional values and commitment, we may feel otherwise. This is not to suggest that measurement should not be made in these more diffuse areas but the difficulties involved may dissuade researchers from trying to give an intellectually respectable account of it.

Much educational research now gives qualitative accounts of the experience of learning and teaching, using the actual words of the faculty and students involved. This has led to a deeper appreciation of the different ways in which students learn and value their different experiences. Faculty may be less inclined to generalize about students now, and may perhaps be more aware that average ratings often conceal differences which are important in developing better courses and teaching methods.

The emphasis with illuminative approaches to evaluation is very much on the educational processes – what it is like actually to participate as a teacher or a student. It is not simply employing a different set of methods or methodology. The starting point is different. We now appreciate that evaluators may not take the formalized plans or descriptions of the courses or other instructional systems seriously, since actual practice often diverges significantly from what has been officially proscribed. A central preoccupation is the learning milieu, and how complex social, cultural, institutional and psychological variables interact in multiple ways, creating unique and intricate patterns within different teaching and learning contexts (Parlett and Hamilton, 1977; Gray, 2004).

Since measures of accountability will affect the financing of programmes as well as issues such as hiring, promotion, tenure and salary decisions, it is important that we do not allow simplistic scores and ratings to dominate our understanding of what we are doing. We may need to show evaluations of our teaching – not only with respect to individual performance reviews and, in the UK, institutional audit by the Quality Assurance Agency, but also for the formal accreditation of our teaching through, for example, formal courses and programmes accredited by the Higher Education Academy (HEA) in the UK, and the increasing number of certificate programmes for graduate students in the USA (Aravamudan et al., 2008). Hopefully, such bureaucratic pressure will not drive us to take the line of least resistance, providing the simplest data that we can manage. In this chapter, we explore a range of other methods that might be taken. In emphasizing the need for multiple perspectives of evaluation, we hope to contribute to providing a richer account of the value of what we are doing, not only to those to whom we are directly accountable but also to ourselves.

TEACHING AND COURSES: METHODS OF EVALUATION

To get at these multiple perspectives, instructors can draw on a great variety of evaluation methods. Table 9.1 offers a summary of the strengths and weaknesses associated with some of the most common types of methods. Full descriptions of each follow in the sections below.

Student questionnaires and course ratings

Typically administered at the end of a term, standardized course questionnaires or surveys – also called student questionnaires, student ratings,

Table 9.1   Relative strengths and weaknesses of common evaluations

	Questionnaires	Interactive teaching	Group discussion	Informal feedback	Focus groups	Peer Observation	Student work
Relative strengths	Broad coverage of opinion	Integration of teaching and evaluation	Flexible, explore issues as they arise	Explore issues at a personal level	Students identify aspects of personal interest	Faculty perspective may complement or clarify students' perspective	Close integration of work with evaluation
	Quantifiable for comparison	Frequent, immediate link with remedial action	Can set tone to encourage criticism	Explore significance of the course as a whole for individual students	Individuals feel they can contribute without being influenced (silent majority have their say)	May be less inhibited in certain respects	Links with areas of high concern
	Easy to administer	Specific learning problems identified, linked to specific teaching	More time and encouragement to think, less 'off-the-cuff' responses	Get to know students better	Letting off steam, without raising emotional temperature	Can be reciprocal learning experience	Enables students to learn self-evaluation
	Close link to particular teaching – immediate	Not explicit teaching evaluation so less inhibition	More responsive to students' perceptions and perspective	Help students to understand their own response to the course	Provides teachers with rich information with minimal time, effort	General opportunity to share ideas about teaching	Enables students to critique their own learning
	Easily confidential or anonymous	Students learn about own learning in concrete situation	Can focus on really important themes	Check on data from other sources	Identifies the group's priorities		Enables students to explore own interests and motivations
	Systematic coverage of themes	Students share problems	Can discuss faculty views more easily		Can identify learning progress towards ability to adapt to and engage in change		
	Longer time perspective		Develop a dialogue				
	Opportunity to explore links between different aspects of course						

Table 9.1   (Continued)

	Questionnaires	Interactive teaching	Group discussion	Informal feedback	Focus groups	Peer Observation	Student work
Relative weaknesses	Frequency use may alienate students May be too simple or too complex Ambiguity difficult to eliminate Encourages 'off-the-cuff' responses rather than serious reflection Can encourage complacency Time limited Even with open questions teacher perspective dominant Needs skill in questionnaire design and analysis	Students may feel over-controlled Exclusively concerned with teacher's learning objectives Too specific, not linked with general review Tendency to avoid teaching process	Dominant personalities can be over-influential Initial tone of discussion can make it difficult to change to a different point of view Coverage of issues may be limited by time available Difficult to assess distribution of opinion Lack of anonymity may be inhibiting Skill in group discussion may be needed	Can be biased by personal impact Coverage of students poor or very time-consuming, biased sample unless careful	Aspects of interest to teachers may be omitted May not provide causative information More time-consuming for students	May be intimidating, especially if status difference May lead to under-emphasis of student viewpoint May be mutual support for undesirable or restricted view of teaching	Can encourage too much introspection May emphasize work as learning exercise rather than 'real-life production'

course evaluations and teaching evaluations – are the most traditional and pervasive type of teaching evaluation in higher education. First used in the USA in the late 1920s (Ory, 2000), they have been increasingly implemented as part of the general move towards accountability in Britain and other countries. These questionnaires are what faculty typically think of as traditional evaluations and may be used for diverse units, including whole courses, individual teaching sessions and specific projects. They may be primarily quantitative or qualitative, or a hybrid of each.

Course evaluations, whether they are simple surveys or more complex questionnaires, often concentrate on the 'intellectual support' aspect of the learning matrix, to the detriment of other aspects of the matrix. Teachers interested in doing more – who wish, for example, for their students to think critically, to relate the course to other problems in the field or students' own experience or to question assumptions or conceptions – may suffer if the questionnaire has no way of evaluating whether these aims are being achieved. To get more comprehensive, richer feedback about the course and their instruction, teachers must carefully consider the questions they ask their students.

General questionnaire

Table 9.2 gives an overview of one of the most common and traditional types of general teaching evaluations used widely in Australian universities: the Course Experience Questionnaire (CEQ). The CEQ has been used for several decades to measure the quality of teaching and serves here as an example of what individual teachers might wish to consider in their own questionnaires (Ramsden, 1992/2003). It currently uses scales that measure good teaching, generic skills, clear goals, appropriate workload and appropriate assessment, although new scales have been developed to measure student support, learning resources, learning communities, graduate qualities and intellectual motivation (Griffin et al., 2003). Their potential applications are included in Table 9.2 and discussed more fully below.

Of the original five main categories, the first three – as in many questionnaires – are mainly concerned with providing support. Scoring well on these three scales suggests faculty are both aware of student concerns and generally supportive of their students. The fourth category, however, begins to address wider issues of understanding – although not exclusively – and the fifth category addresses the issue of

Table 9.2 *Categories and examples of questions in the expanded Course Experience Questionnaire*

Scale	Examples of questions
Good teaching	The [professor] made a real effort to understand the difficulties I might be having with my work
	The [professor] normally gave me helpful feedback on how I was doing
Clear goals and standards	It was always easy to know the standard of work expected
	I usually had a clear idea of where I was going and what was expected of me in this course
Appropriate workload	The sheer volume of work to be got through in this course means that you can't comprehend it all thoroughly (negatively scored)
	I was generally given enough time to understand the things I had to learn
Appropriate assessment	To do well in this course all you really needed was a good memory
	The [professor] seemed more interested in testing what I had memorized than in what I had understood (negatively scored)
General skills	The course developed my problem-solving skills (variations include analytic, written communication, team-building skills)
	As a result of my course, I feel confident about tackling unfamiliar problems
Student support	Relevant learning resources were accessible when I needed them
Learning resources	Where it was used, the information technology in teaching and learning was effective
	Course materials were relevant and up to date
Course organization	The course was well organized
	There was sufficient flexibility in my course to suit my needs
Learning community	Students' ideas and suggestions were used during the course
	I learnt to explore ideas confidently with other people
Graduate qualities	I learnt to apply principles from this course to new situations
	The course developed my confidence to investigate new ideas
	I consider that what I learnt was valuable for my future
Intellectual motivation	The course has stimulated my interest in the field of study
	I found my studies intellectually stimulating

Sources: Adapted from Griffin et al., 2003; Murdoch University, 2008 (http://www.tlc.murdoch.edu.au/eddev/evaluation/ceq/questions.html)

encouraging independence. As a general questionnaire designed for widespread use, it does not, however, address the range of learning issues particular to individual learning and teaching situations. In this respect, teachers should feel free to extend the design of their questionnaires to an even wider range of learning issues focused on what is appropriate for students on their particular courses or parts of a course.

In relation to intellectual support, for example, instructors might want to know more about student experiences of the resources available through the course or the intellectual level of the work or, indeed, the extent to which students are able to gain a sense of achievement. In relation to intellectual independence, teachers might wish to augment

CEQ-type questions with those about whether there is an opportunity to identify medium- and long-term tasks, or become involved in creative work or design and/or how far students have been able to increase their confidence.

Similarly, when considering the personal dimension of learning, if we are trying to evaluate how supportive our courses are, we might use questions that delve into students' sense of security, their enjoyment of class work or their interpersonal relationships with faculty. Questions that emphasize independence might also be extended to explore the more personal aspects of choice, including students' perceptions about their own responsibilities and independence. Students might feel, for example, that their personal identity was undermined by having to conform to more surface ways of learning simply to deal with a heavy course load. Simply coping with course requirements may preclude students from feeling they can work in a way that contributes to their sense of developing a personal identity or even an occupational identity. Questionnaires may not include such terms, even though they are clearly important for motivation and for enabling students to become independent professionals later in life.

In considering the social dimension, questionnaires might address the development of peer learning communities and the general academic and departmental culture they are learning within. To what extent are there opportunities for supportive peer-working groups and those that run independent of the faculty? Teachers, with some reason, often feel they are not responsible for students' social life or their accommodation, yet these can be vital to student learning. Many students, moreover, are clearly concerned about the social relevance of their courses but this again is usually not considered.

In relation to the 'interpersonal', peer assessment activities, learning from alternative perspectives and peer teaching sessions which focus on understanding, self-knowledge or communication skills can all be important aspects of student life which evaluation questionnaires might help us to understand. Group projects, peer-managed learning or problem-based learning often focus upon interpersonal skills and processes. These are much more valued than they used to be but they seldom appear in evaluation questionnaires. Such issues might, as we shall see, be better addressed through different forms of evaluation but quite often the 'hard' data of questionnaires carry more weight than that from less formal methods.

Questionnaires for particular sessions or projects

Faculty might opt to administer short questionnaires or surveys during the term, which can help gauge:

- student understanding of difficult sections of the course;
- whether the course is being taught at the right intellectual level;
- whether there is an overload of material;
- whether the lecturer is going too fast or slow; and
- whether more general student perceptions are related to particular sessions rather than averaged over a course.

Questionnaires can be helpful in exploring some of the problems of group work as well, although often the most important source of feedback is time out on discussing some of the problems. Questionnaires about group work can also be particularly helpful as a basis for assisting a group to reflect upon its own processes (Jaques, 2000; Jaques and Salmon, 2007).

With both group work and lecture sessions, the ratings quite reasonably focus upon judgements about the quality of teaching but it can be helpful to ask more descriptive questions about the structures and purposes of the session. If, for example, a teacher is intending to focus a session around a particular problem – clarifying the problem, presenting particular forms of analysis and evaluating different solutions – it is essential to know whether students perceive the session as such. Often it simply appears to them as an ordered presentation of data or information. Similarly, if a lecturer is focusing on a comparison of different interpretations or approaches or theories, it would be important to know whether the session was being interpreted in this way. A mismatch between student perceptions of a session and the teacher's intentions is an essential issue which questionnaires can disclose.

Faculty perceptions of traditional evaluation

Traditional evaluations – particularly the course questionnaire and student ratings – have long caused anxiety, concern and resentment, particularly when faculty believe they are used unfairly or are too heavily weighted in issues concerning promotion, retention, tenure and salary decisions (Johnson, 2000; Ory, 2000). All too frequently, questionnaires are used for administrators (who wish to maintain accountability) or for students (who wish to communicate their opinions of an instructor or the instruction to their peers), and not for faculty. Not surprisingly, many faculty are suspicious of questionnaires and have sought to attack their validity and reliability (Calkins and Micari, 2008).

On the one hand, research on student ratings has disclosed – and mostly dispelled – at least 16 myths related to student evaluation. These include the beliefs that:

- students cannot make consistent judgements about the instructor or course because they lack the necessary experience or maturity;
- only faculty colleagues with strong publication records can evaluate their peers' teaching;
- students' ratings are just a popularity contest, favouring the friendliest professors;
- questionnaires generally lack reliability and validity;
- students' ratings correspond with their real or expected marks in the course; and, finally,
- students' ratings are primarily summative and not useful for improving instruction (Aleamoni, 1999).

On the other hand, there are factors that have been shown to influence traditional evaluations, including:

- the instructor's age and student perception of teaching experience and expertise in the subject area;
- specific instructor personality traits;
- student achievement level; and
- students' approaches to learning (Entwistle and Tait, 1990; Shevlin et al., 2000; Bosshardt and Watts, 2001; Wolfer and Johnson, 2003; Sprague and Massoni, 2005).

Indeed, research has found that some of the biggest disparities in ratings are found between different disciplines. Ramsden (2003) reports research from the CEQ which indicates that the visual and performing arts are the most highly rated subjects, with the health sciences and engineering rated the worst. Social sciences come in the middle, rated higher than the natural sciences but below the humanities.

Gender, too, may have an impact on student ratings. Early on, Martin (1984) found that sexist stereotypes negatively impacted on evaluations of the effectiveness of female teachers, while Baker and Copp (1997) have suggested that an instructor's pregnancy and gender may have had an adverse impact on students' ratings even in a feminist studies class. More recently, Miller and Chamberlain (2000) contend that students' misattributions of their female professors' educational attainment and university rank may subtly bias course evaluations.

Despite their potential limitations, however, faculty can certainly use course questionnaires in a formative way, in order to improve their teaching. To provide meaningful feedback, questionnaires must be both well designed and carefully interpreted.

Designing course questionnaires

The design of questionnaires is, as Oppenheim has suggested, an intellectual exercise in which we are constantly trying to understand our goals (2000). Unfortunately, questionnaires and scales are not always constructed in accordance with normal psychometric processes (e.g. establishing validity and reliability). All too often, questionnaires are simply a collection of isolated *ad hoc* items that can be reported in terms of particular questions or as overall scores, both of which are dubious if we are trying to diagnose problems and 'put them to mending'.

Questionnaires can be constructed in terms of scales or major themes, such as the themes suggested in Table 9.2, and tested to see whether these themes are a reality. In general, questionnaires vary a great deal in how much background information is collected. It may be important to know, for example, whether high ratings or a particular category of responses are restricted to certain types of student: for instance, women, non-traditional students or those in danger of failing the course.

To help diagnose problems, a questionnaire might offer a range of course objectives and ask students to comment on whether those objectives were reflected in the course. This works best when they do not assume the teachers want all the objectives rated highly. Matching teachers' ratings and students' ratings on these can be particularly interesting. Students and teachers often have different perceptions, and where discrepancies are seen it is useful to clarify them early in the course. Other questionnaires have asked students to compare one course or one lecturer with another and comparisons are often more useful than attempts at absolute measures. Other useful variants can include asking students how important they think certain characteristics of the course are, again perhaps comparing them with the teacher's views. Assuming that all the characteristics are equally important can often make interpretation very suspect.

Table 9.3 *Contrasting responses to a supervision course*

Question	First student ('Sunil')	Second student ('Pilar')
What were the most successful parts of the course?	'The two rather formal lectures'	'I enjoyed all of the course. I found the whole course helpful'
What were the least successful parts of the course?	'Working in small groups and reflective triads'	'None, it ran very smoothly, the frequent changes in teaching, learning style maintained interest. I have learnt a lot'
What was the most surprising element of the course?	'How much time was wasted, just as much if not more can be got by reading the book'	'That supervision at so many different levels can have so many similarities'
What changes would you suggest?	'Replace the "games" with solid, sound lectures and whole-group discussion'	'None! I expected more guidelines in the beginning but accepted my role in deciding my responsibilities and negotiating other people's'
What is your overall impression of the course?	'Not a fruitful use of [course time], uninspired and uninspiring'	'Excellent. I will recommend it to colleagues. I now feel much more confident about supervision and supporting colleagues'

Interpreting written remarks

One of the most challenging and frustrating things for teachers is to interpret student written comments, especially when students seem to have had widely disparate experiences of a course. Without a thematic framework, student remarks can seem random, unconnected, contradictory and lacking discrimination, leaving faculty feeling frustrated, annoyed or simply dismissive of the students' ability to judge the course or their instruction (Lewis, 2001). Table 9.3 offers a typical set of such disparate remarks, in this case found in a course on supervision, which reflect the extreme contrasts many teachers often experience.

Although the course referred to in Table 9.3 had been advertised as interactive and hands-on, the first student ('Sunil') came to the class with quite fixed ideas about what courses should be about, expecting the teaching to be mainly about the transmission of information. He viewed acquiring a quantity of information in a short period of time to be a key criterion for success in the class. The second student ('Pilar'), on the other hand, came with an open mind and was keen to make the class as useful and

Table 9.4   *Study orientations and evaluation*

Reproduction orientation	Meaning orientation
1. *Focus on efficiency*	**3.** *Focus on communication*
Basic lecturing skills	Quality of explanations provided
Provision of clear goals and standards	Use of real-life illustrations
Systematic organization of course	Use of humour and enthusiasm
Workload and level of difficulty	Empathy for students
2. *Focus on organization*	**4.** *Focus on independent learning*
Interesting and relevant content	Assignments providing choice, resources
Level at which material is pitched	Full explanations in feedback
Pace at which topics are covered	Assessment related to course aims
Clear structure within lectures	Advice on study skills and strategies

Note:
Categories 1 and 2 are endorsed more strongly by students with reproducing orientations.
Categories 3 and 4 appeal more strongly, on the whole, to those with meaning orientations.
Source: Adapted from Entwistle and Tait, 1990

enjoyable a learning experience as possible. Individual discussion can assist both in identifying such mismatches between expectation and what is happening on a course, as well as helping students to adjust their expectations appropriately. Alternatively, it may enable students to choose courses which more closely match their expectations.

Approaching a set of students' written comments as a process of qualitative inquiry can help make the process of interpretation not only more palatable, but also useful for assessing the strengths and weaknesses of the course and instruction, and for learning from one's instruction. Lewis (2001), for example, suggests that instructors categorize the responses either by simply comparing the responses directly with course ratings (e.g. 'What were the specific comments of students who numerically rated the class above average?') or by using a more complex matrix which compares individual course ratings with specific teaching areas or learning objectives ('What did students who rated the class highly say about their critical engagement with the course material?').

Considering the approaches to study that students take may also help understand the approaches students take to evaluation. Table 9.4 shows one way that remarks can be categorized.

Students taking different approaches to their learning in a course will tend to focus on different sets of evaluations items (Entwistle and Tait, 1990; Entwistle et al., 2000). Students taking more surface types of approaches to study, with reproducing orientations towards their learning, will tend to focus on items assessing the efficiency and organization of the teacher's teaching. These are areas which could help or hinder students' ability to memorize and reproduce the content which the teacher is teaching.

Students taking deeper approaches to their study, with an interest in constructing their own meanings from what the teacher is teaching, while still interested in the issues of categories 1 and 2, will, nevertheless, tend to focus more on the teacher's ability to communicate in a way which stimulates and offers the potential to make meaning from the content being taught (category 3), and on the teacher's provision of opportunities for students to develop the capacity to learn independently on the course (category 4).

Interactive teaching

We all learn a great deal from our experience of teaching, but some learn more than others. Similarly, some use ways of teaching that offer more in terms of understanding student responses than others. Even with traditional, non-interactive 'transmission' lectures, we can observe certain features in our students that tell us whether or not learning is occurring. We may see signs of attention and non-attention, for example, although the actual quality of learning may be difficult to discern from the expressions of faces or the activities of pens, or the use of laptop computers. Reflecting on our lecturing, even keeping reflective diaries – an activity encouraged by many accreditation programmes – can make us more aware of our own activities and be useful for many lecturers, but it may not tell us very much about learning.

Background knowledge check

One of the best ways for learning about learning is through interactive lecturing (see Chapter 4). As a method of teaching, it improves learning by enabling students to consolidate their thinking and relate it to their own experience and their knowledge of the field (Bain, 2004). It can also function as a good method of evaluation, helping lecturers see whether the way they are teaching is appropriate to the level and interest of the students.

While focusing upon the learning of specific content of the session, it can also enable a lecturer to understand where students are coming from and the sorts of expectations, assumptions and even hang-ups they might have about the topic of the session (Lieberg, 2008). Beginning a lecture with a quick exploration of what students already know will not only convey the sense that the lecturer cares about and values their experience, but also serves as a valuable method of 'evaluation-in-action', indicating whether the lecture is appropriate for their current development. We all make assumptions about what our students already know, but rarely do we test out those assumptions.

Buzz groups

Sometimes, rather than posing open questions to a group, a quick brainstorming session may be appropriate, eliciting and outlining some of the students' major concerns and preoccupations regarding the course. It can contribute to creating a shared agenda that can be an excellent basis for understanding whether our teaching is producing effective learning. During the session short buzz groups, with or without setting specific tasks or problems, can also provide a concrete basis for evaluating how much and what sort of learning is occurring (McKeachie, 2006).

Open tasks, such as asking students to 'discuss what we have talked about so far and raise any problems or other issues you would like to share', are also useful at getting at more unexpected problems. And specific tasks calling for the application or interpretation of some of the content can be useful for checking on what sort of learning is occurring and how far students are changing. This kind of evaluation is excellent for adding to our understanding without contributing to our workload. Teachers and students may, however, feel they are covering less content if used too frequently. On the other hand, evaluation feedback from this source may indicate that the course is going too slowly, or that the content is not being pitched appropriately.

Clarifying conceptual knowledge

This type of evaluation is mainly concerned with issues of intellectual support, helping to clarify problems and explore misconceptions. Engaging students with their responses can, for example, lead to a clarification of what is expected and the criteria for making progress. A study of engineering students (Cox, 1987) found that a major problem of comprehension was not the difficulty of the material but the speed of lectures. They did not allow students to consolidate their learning. The opportunity to reflect when you feel you understand is not widely appreciated in the rush to cover enough ground. Rushing on can create a sense of 'retroactive inhibition' blurring earlier learning by passing on before the 'ink has dried', so to speak.

Asking the group as a whole to explain or discuss a diagram or graph or perhaps even a quotation, again, might enable the lecturer to understand where the students are coming from and some of the conceptual problems they might be having. It provides the lecturer with time out from their monologue as well, valuable time to evaluate-in-action. Such strategies can also emphasize intellectual independence, but we might also ask for more creative responses and applications. Students often talk of taking down notes which they do not understand and which often undermine their confidence. Providing students with the time and opportunity to explore and express their own ideas and ways of understanding can help them to become more independent learners (McKeachie, 2006). It also enables teachers to understand how far they are assisting their students to become more independent as opposed to conformist learners.

Other CATs

Classroom assessment techniques, discussed in reference to the assessment of student learning described in Chapter 8, can also be useful for evaluation. Often quick and easy to create and implement, CATs can help evaluate aspects of particular sessions (Angelo and Cross, 1993). The 'minute paper' is a good example of a simple but effective evaluation (McKeachie, 2006; Lieberg, 2008). Here, students are asked to answer just two questions at the end of the session:

- 'What is the most important thing you learnt during the session?'
- 'What is uppermost now in your mind at the end of the session?'

Not only can teachers (and possibly students) get a grasp on the students' knowledge, comprehension or ability, but they can also reflect on their teaching or instruction, to gauge whether they may need to rethink their explanations, assignments or activities if their students do not seem to be learning as they would like.

Generally, then, within the *personal dimension*, if the questions and the problems are not too difficult or posed too aggressively, such exploration can enable students to feel a closer personal relationship with the staff. It helps develop a sense of security and even enjoyment. Interactive teaching generally encourages students to behave and feel more as engaged people and not simply passive recipients. In addition their sense of 'personal independence' may be strengthened by a sense of participation in exploring their own relationship to the subject. Interactive teaching can contribute to deeper learning by encouraging students to relate a topic to their own experience and interests.

Interactive teaching can also address the social dimension of learning, helping to generate an atmosphere in which staff and students work together. Teaching is not that of a remote teacher doing their own thing with a group of unrelated others, but rather a mutual exploration which facilitates participation. It can assist in reducing the impersonality of higher education which many students experience. Where periods of group work are interspersed with more formal teaching, this can also help to develop 'interpersonal' skills. Students often learn from each other things that it is difficult for the lecturer to help them learn. As one student said: 'when another student speaks you prick up your ears, it's something different.'

Group discussion

Very often questionnaires raise more problems than they solve, especially in relation to divisions between those who rate the course highly and those who rate it poorly. Background questions can sometimes help solve this problem, but may become too cumbersome or numerous to manage efficiently. In these areas, group discussions can be an effective form of evaluation. They not only help focus on the background data, but also analyse certain likes and dislikes. They can be very formal with pre-specified agendas and topics or can arise more informally.

Less formal open questions, for example, can explore more fully the issues behind good and poor ratings and the disparity between students. The responses are frequently very enlightening but, unfortunately, they are also often ignored. Although spontaneous meetings are helpful, it is useful to prepare students with an idea of what you would like to hear from them. Questionnaire responses provide a basis for discussion but may also be too restrictive. Discussion that is cursory or unreflective may repeat some of the 'off-the-cuff' likes and dislikes often obtained from questionnaires.

Table 9.1 lists several advantages of group discussion, particularly where flexibility and the development of a genuine dialogue are essential. In such situations, teachers can encourage deeper criticism and work through the nature and implications of these criticisms. It also provides an opportunity to focus on the essential themes and to be more responsive to student perceptions and perspectives. A few dominant personalities, however, can unduly influence that discussion, making it difficult to hear diverse points of view and discern more subtle differences. For some, the lack of anonymity is also inhibiting, often making it difficult to assess the distribution of opinions.

Reflective triads

In this activity, groups of three students reflect together on their learning at the end of a session, which offers a useful way to stimulate evaluation through discussion. They not only remind students what has happened but they also encourage deeper thinking about the nature of the session and their own learning. In large classes, reflective triads can help students think through their ideas and what they wish to say without too much interference (unless, of course, they happen to be with the one or two dominant personalities in the group). It is often helpful to begin the discussion with a review of the course (McKeachie, 2006). It is important that the discussion is not seen as just a collection of views and opinions but, rather, puts those opinions to test. Ideally, the reflection session should provide time to work through criticisms and help students to understand intellectually what the course is doing and what it is not doing.

The timing of evaluative discussions is also very important *vis-à-vis* student learning. Discussing aims and objectives after the experience of a course is very different from discussing them at the beginning or during the course. Provided some discussions are held halfway through the course or at other times before the end, discussion can be very supportive for students who may have concerns, anxieties or misconceptions about what the course is doing.

Independence can be encouraged by not treating students as passive consumers for whom evaluation is conducted simply to improve the quality of the product. Students need to believe they are active participants in the evaluation and its role in course development. As such they will be expected to respond intelligently to the positive features of the course as well as its faults and problems. As in the example of the general medical practitioners (see Chapter 3), responsive discussion after a poor start can be extremely useful in encouraging a strong sense of commitment to making the course develop in a way that both the students and teachers feel is useful. More formal courses may not have the opportunity to restructure substantially but there is always some flexibility. Students should not feel the only point of them being engaged in evaluation is to improve future courses.

In the personal dimension, discussion can be very supportive in providing students with a sense that faculty value their views and priorities and encourage them to express these. Appreciating the alternative perspectives within the group will also contribute to developing student independence. Without the opportunity to hear about these, students often feel their own opinions are what everyone else thinks. Discussion should be an opportunity for them to learn more about their own responses to the constraints and opportunities of the course. Finally, as in any group process, if the discussion goes well, it can be experienced as an enjoyable social event contributing to the interpersonal context of learning. It can help generate a genuine dialogue among students and teachers in which each learns to share and appreciate other points of view and learning.

Student-generated statements combined with group discussion

This method usefully combines some of the characteristics of questionnaires with that of group discussions. In this case, the questionnaire elements are statements generated by students that may concern various elements of the design, content, methods and environment. Individual students are asked to write four to six statements and three recommendations related to some or all these areas on separate slips of paper. Pairs of students then look at each other's statements, discuss them and select the four or six most interesting statements and three most appropriate recommendations. These pairs then join another pair and do the same selection in a group of four.

Teachers can also introduce and test out their own concerns in statements that are then rated by the class in conjunction with the student statements. Asking the group to rate the statements and recommendations as to how far they agree with them can also produce useful numerical data. If there is time, rated collections can be circulated to the total group for more general discussion. Especially important themes or issues for the course can also be taken up in subsequent sessions, pursued in small groups and/or integrated with student presentations.

Students are not only introduced to the variety of each other's alternative perceptions but they also have to engage with this in making decisions as to which they should select for the next move. In our experience they frequently enjoy the process and find it provides the basis for moving beyond 'off-the-cuff' comments and perfunctory general discussion. It enables them to think more deeply than they do when filling in questionnaires and is often very effective in generating engaged discussion about learning across the intellectual, personal, social and practical dimensions in a very interactive way. It also produces a wide range of interesting issues that may not have been reflected in teacher-designed questionnaires. Time can be a consideration here but, as with some of the other methods mentioned in this chapter, it can also be an effective learning and teaching activity (in contrast to a bureaucratic task) and is worth spending the occasional half an hour pursuing. The details of this process can be varied to suit the particular situation, discipline or institution as is appropriate.

Student work

Ironically, evaluations of teaching and the teacher drawing upon student work (and its assessment) offer valuable opportunities for teacher evaluation. Assessment provides a mutual object for engaging students about problems or issues in their learning and from which teachers may gain valuable insights about their course. As Ory (2000) reminds us, the original Latin root of 'assessment', *assidere*, literally means 'to sit beside'. Thus:

> Assessment as 'sitting beside' promotes a developmental perspective. It is not a single snapshot but rather a continuous view. It facilitates development rather than classifying and ranking the faculty by some predetermined measurement such as a student rating item or number of publications. It encourages breaking away from the winner-loser mind-set, comparing one person to another. Instead the focus is on understanding the colleague's perspective and achievements, which means the focus is on real-world performance.

Certainly, examination results do not typically provide good opportunities for extended insights, but will often indicate gaps in course content or difficulties with understanding specific concepts. Reports, essays and projects will generally provide more in-depth opportunities: the feedback given to students – whether written or oral – should alert teachers to student problems which may need to be dealt with more comprehensively. This feedback also frequently provides the basis for discussion through which teachers might understand their students' problems on the course more fully.

This method allows a closer integration of student work with evaluation and can provide an opportunity to explore areas of high concern. There is often a tendency, however, for students to want to be told what to do to improve their assignments. If teachers do this in a rather prescriptive way, then, as Hounsell et al. (2007) suggest, the student may not understand – as they bring different assumptions about learning – and it may make very little difference. If, however, the teacher explores alternatives with the students, getting them to suggest possibilities, then they may enable students to take more responsibility for the improvement.

It is a process that can enable teachers to understand better student problems and why they have them. Simply telling them what to do to improve may add little to the teacher's understanding of student learning. Although such discussions usually fall within the intellectual dimension, they are also an opportunity for addressing personal issues: for developing a better understanding of why students fail and how personal motivation and/or social issues might be more responsible than purely intellectual failings. Several processes of assessment that may help the evaluation of teaching emphasize the formative over the summative.

Portfolios and reflective commentaries

There are a number of less traditional forms of student assessment that deserve a separate mention with respect to evaluation. They display many of the benefits described above but, in addition, provide scope for evaluation over a longer period of time, comparing, for example, recent written feedback with earlier feedback. They also enable the development of a much broader perspective of student learning on a course (McKeachie, 2006).

One of the most useful assessment methods which teachers might use for evaluation purposes is the reflective commentary, which frequently draws upon material collected in private reflective diaries as well as from the course itself. Students are increasingly submitting such commentaries either as assessment or as part of assessment, often as part of extended portfolios (see Chapter 10). They usually comment on a wider set of issues of student experience and learning than simply course content (White, 2004). At different times they may focus upon all the aspects of the matrix but perhaps are most useful in enabling students to develop towards more independent reflective practitioners. They involve many personal choices and are designed to encourage independent reflection on responses. Their very breadth and depth mean they can be extremely valuable documents for teachers wishing to learn more about the impact of their courses and teaching on their students.

Journals and session reports

The use of journals or diaries and session reports can be related to and even provide the basis for much of what is written in more public reflective commentaries and portfolios (McKeachie, 2006). They are, however, not methods of assessment so much as group and class-learning activities providing extensive scope for evaluation. Students might, for example, be encouraged to keep reflective journals over the period of a course, describing their learning experiences – including concerns, delights, responses to particular sessions – across all four intellectual, personal, social and practical dimensions.

Despite good intentions, such diaries are rarely put into practice. Linking them with specific activities and responsibilities on the course helps maintain a commitment to them. Providing time for diaries in class and even – as was done very effectively on a course for general medical practitioners – asking for individual students in pairs to report back to the class in turn on previous sessions has wide-ranging benefits. It extends and consolidates learning, generates interest among the students in the different ways in which different students experience and learn on the course and provides the teacher with substantial evaluative data.

The rich information that journals contain and the reports generated from them will frequently become part of further diary sessions. Time permitting, these reports and diary reflections can be developed as part of group projects on which groups can be asked to report back both halfway through a course and at the end of it. Reports may be written or oral or both, and can be integrated with more elaborate student presentations. It is worth emphasizing, however, that the quality of the material generated – both for individual learning purposes and for course evaluation purposes – is dependent on students being given the choice to retain those reflections they wish to remain as private and/or to report material anonymously to the course.

One-on-one discussion

As with group evaluation through discussion, individual discussion with students may provide important feedback. Such approaches may range between formal approaches, such as interviews, and informal discussion as the opportunity arises. Such discussion helps to explore both particular issues and the significance of the course as a whole at a more individual and personal level (McKeachie, 2006). It can also be a good chance to get to know students rather better as some can be very inhibited within groups. On the other hand, personal impressions might bias evaluation if generalized to the course as a whole.

Teachers cannot expect to have long discussions about the course with all students, so the sample and the lessons learnt need to be carefully judged. Individual discussions are also useful for exploring and understanding differences in individual perceptions and responses to the course. Substantial differences in preconceptions of what a course consists of, or should consist of, can make the role of evaluation extremely problematic if not more clearly understood by the teacher.

Student focus groups

There may be times, however, when teachers would rather have an outside facilitator discuss the strengths and weaknesses of their teaching and the course. Student focus groups, also referred to as small-group instructional diagnosis (SGID) or small-group analysis (SGA), are a form of nominal group process which offers a means for collecting early and substantial feedback directly from students using a whole-class interviewing technique (Diamond, 2002).

Simply, the professor leaves the room and a trained facilitator breaks the class into small groups, and asks them to respond to a series of questions about aspects of the course that enhance or challenge their learning. The facilitator asks the groups to share their responses with the rest of the class, and then asks the class to determine as a whole which items are most important. The facilitator may also ask students to consider their role in the learning process, by asking them to identify what they can do as students to enhance their learning in the class.

While there are many variations to this process, the facilitator may also ask the students to rate the importance of the top-three items individually, to help determine if the comments or concerns are shared broadly by most of the students in the course, or if just the ideas of the most outspoken students in the class. During the session, the facilitator can address apparent contradictions in student opinions, peeling the layers off a problem to get at the source of discrepancy. Later, in a confidential consultation, the facilitator will report the students' feedback, categorizing the comments thematically and discussing what, if anything, the teacher needs to do in the course to facilitate student learning (Lewis, 2002) (see Box 9.1).

Box 9.1 *Case study: small-group analysis*

Halfway through the term, 'Alexander' requested an SGA be conducted in his class on 'Political decision-making' – an upper-level seminar in political science. After the outside facilitator divided the class into five groups of four, the students identified three key aspects of the course that they believed enhanced their learning: 1) the experience Alexander brings to the classroom (relevant stories, anecdotes, etc.); 2) his easy conversational, informal classroom style; and 3) the overall organization and structure of the course (particularly, the sequencing and progression of topics and readings). When surveyed individually, nearly all the students agreed with the class consensus on these points.

(Continued)

(Continued)

The students were then asked to explain how the course could be improved to enhance their learning. While individual responses varied somewhat, as a group the class generally agreed that it would help 1) if the individual sessions had more structure and focus (he apparently frequently meandered off-topic); 2) if the readings could be less complex and lengthy; and 3) if he could intersperse his lecture with more small-group discussion activities.

Finally, when asked what the students believed they could do themselves to enhance their learning in the class, they agreed they could 1) read the assigned texts more thoroughly; 2) bring extra materials from outside the class into discussions; and 3) come to class prepared with questions.

In the follow-up consultation, the facilitator clarified for Alexander the students' two uses of the term 'structure' which, without explanation, would seem to contradict each other ('class structure helpful', 'class lacks structure'). The facilitator suggested ways to make his lectures more interactive by interspersing some common classroom assessment techniques to engage students more meaningfully. She also suggested that Alexander consider a 'lecture script' to keep him more organized and on track during individual class sessions, or at least to provide clear segues between topics. Lastly, she suggested he reflect on the readings, not necessarily to reduce content but perhaps their density. At the next class session, Alexander spoke to the class and clarified a few additional points with them directly. While he did not change the readings right away, over the second half of the term he worked several minute papers, 'think-pair-shares' and more small-group work into his lectures.

Although the process requires some planning and explanation, the student feedback provides teachers with a wealth of information without taking up too much teacher time. The process helps identify the group's priorities and with appropriate follow-up can be a useful stimulus to change and provide students with the opportunity to participate in change. In addition, it can provide an opportunity for both personal expression and group interaction, enhancing a sense of social participation and enjoyment. It may even provide an opportunity for students to let off steam. On the downside, the teacher's interest in the learning and teaching encounter may not be well represented and the activity may not provide any in-depth account of why these opinions and priorities exist.

Teaching observation

Observers drawn from peers and colleagues provide a very valuable alternative perspective to those obtained from students. They will likely have the benefits of:

- having relevant subject expertise;
- having personal experience of teaching;
- experiencing the course over a longer time perspective;
- having knowledge of related courses; and
- understanding the constraints under which the course is operating.

While aspects of observation may elicit additional anxieties and concerns about one's teaching abilities, in some respects the process can also be less inhibited, particularly if the arrangement is handled sensitively and is reciprocal, with each person learning from being a critic as well as receiving criticism.

There are, of course, other problems that may need to be addressed. The process might be especially intimidating if there is a power and/or status difference between observer and observed. Observers with their own 'agenda' and/or a different conception of teaching from that of the observed could seriously undermine the observed teacher's development. They might also de-emphasize the student perspective, leading to mutual support for undesirable or restrictive views of teaching. Ideally, issues such as these should be discussed prior to the observation. (See Appendix for an example of a detailed observation protocol and guidelines.)

The activity of observation, including prior and post-observation discussion and/or reports, should be supportive and challenging. It should – especially if participants are able to share some of their fears and inhibitions – also encourage independence in the teacher's learning about their teaching. 'Co-counselling' is another valuable way of enabling teachers to work through some of their teaching concerns and problems, although it entails the development of skills that have a wider application than evaluation.

Under the impact of programme and quality reviews, observers are increasingly coming in to assess directly the quality of individual departments. Observations are becoming a much more common feature of these reviews, but the 'accountability' purpose behind them is likely to restrict significant mutual learning. Peer observation has the added benefit of preparing colleagues for these visits. Observations may either be very structured or more informal, depending on the purpose and nature of the observation.

Structured observation

In this type of observation, the observer – whether a peer, a new colleague, graduate student or trained outside facilitator – focuses on specific teaching areas during the session. Taking an anthropological approach to observation, the observer carefully logs the events and activities that occur during the session, keeping track of how long each aspect of the session takes. Leaving interpretation until *after* the session is complete, the observer simply records what she sees, considering key teaching areas:

- sharing learning objectives/rationale for activities;
- promoting critical thinking, engaging students, effectiveness of teaching methods, organization and clarity of session;
- familiarity with material; and
- effective use of course materials and technology.

After the session, the observer will write up her notes more concisely and offer suggestions or comments thematically (see the Appendix for an example).

Combined observation and focus group

Here, the observer will first conduct a structured observation and, when the teacher has left the room, will then talk to the students directly about his observations in a focus-group format. The observation thus serves to enhance and clarify the student remarks, and helps explain ambiguities, discrepancies and points of confusion, as well as adding a richness to the overall observation.

Teaching squares

Other teachers might opt for a less formal observation method. Here, four teachers take turns observing and reflecting on one another's teaching sessions. The process is meant to be mutually beneficial, self-referencing ('How can what I observed improve my teaching?' not 'Here's how you can improve your teaching'), and appreciative and respectful of one another's teaching methods and style (Hafer et al., 2002).

Digital recording, playback and discussion

Video-recording (now digital recording) has long been a very important part of educational development workshops designed to improve skills in lecturing and small-group work. Telling teachers what is wrong with their teaching is not, as we have seen, always the best way of achieving significant change. It is particularly true where there is a strong emotional element in what we are doing, and certainly teaching styles are quite closely bound up with a sense of personal identity.

This is not to say that comments from others cannot be extremely helpful but they are likely to raise far fewer defensive responses when the teacher can plainly see what the observer is talking about. Even viewing a recording by yourself can enable you to take a more objective stance and a greater sense of responsibility for what is happening and how you might improve. The tape or DVD can be stopped and time given to thinking why mistakes were being made and how they could be avoided in future. Simple reflection after a teaching event can, of course, be very helpful but it is easy to forget the more worrying parts.

There is more likelihood for change if this activity is seen in a positive light. It is useful to have agreement on the kinds of areas of teaching performance and their relationship to learning. It is also usually better to begin reviewing a performance from the point of view of what was successful. If the recording is watched in the company of students, peers or educational developers a positive attitude may, indeed, be reinforced by their comments if the positive side is explored before suggestions are made for what can be changed.

In approaching the areas needing improvement, it is often better to begin with critical comments from the observed teacher rather than from the observers. We are far more likely actually to change our behaviour or attitudes in response to criticisms we have made of ourselves than we are from those of others. Nevertheless, we all have our blind spots and, given the right atmosphere, critical comments can be taken on board and acted upon, especially within the context of a revealing tape and discussion within a supportive atmosphere.

There is considerable scope within such reviews, particularly if students are involved, to explore the performance with respect to the various dimensions and contexts of the learning matrix which the recorded session is addressing:

- What aspects of learning are being addressed?
- What are the teacher's intentions in this respect?
- Are they appropriate?
- Are they shared with the students?

It is worth mentioning that the critical matrix (Chapter 2) also informs the teacher's learning in such situations. Intellectual support and challenge are essential when working with students, but perhaps the most important area is development within the personal dimension. Achieving the right support–independence–interpersonal balance in an atmosphere of mutual respect and shared responsibility is a necessary ingredient of good (and enjoyable) professional development.

Less conventional methods

There is clearly a wide range of other ways of learning about the effectiveness of our teaching – even if using 53 of them (Gibbs et al., 1993b) is asking a lot of teachers! Teachers should feel free to explore (with colleagues and students) other, less conventional approaches to evaluation that may address specific issues important to their course or enhance learning in an innovative way. Indeed, they may regard it as part of their professional role.

One example of such an unconventional method might be using role-plays of various kinds. In this category of method the student and/or teacher steps outside their normal roles and assumes other roles, and even 'persona', to examine complex issues of the course, or even to instigate development of it. Participants in role-play are permitted to express things which are very difficult to express when they are constrained within their normal roles. Students (and/or teachers) may take on the role of, for example, a 'traditionalist' or 'radical' teacher (and/or student), interpreting that in ways which can be instructive to developing a shared understanding of what the course is about and the different ways it is being perceived. As with most role-play, debriefing about the experience afterwards is particularly important, not only to look at the reality behind the roles but also to reconcile and come to terms with some of the things expressed, some of which may have been more emotional than expected.

The widespread use of communication and information technology also provides opportunities to engage in more unusual approaches to evaluation. Establishing an online course 'chat room' or discussion room for students to exchange their views on the course can be a useful way of eliciting information on a course. This may be left entirely up to the students to operate with the teacher simply 'eavesdropping' in on the conversation, or it may be one in which the teacher plays an active role in the discussion.

Similarly, the rules of the discussion may be very open to 'whatever happens' or they might be set up more formally with guidelines and specific themes preset by the teacher and/or negotiated with the students. It needs to be handled with care and the limitations of IT-based systems taken into consideration (see Chapter 7), but can be an instructive and rich supplement to more traditional methods.

Collecting concrete critical incidents of good and bad experiences is another less conventional method which can make evaluation more interesting and help to reveal the unexpected. Such methods generally may meet with traditional resistance to change and there can be difficulties in interpretation as well as finding the time actually to make them happen. On the other hand, developed and used creatively, they can be very useful for addressing issues that are unseen and/or ignored by more customary forms of evaluation.

EVALUATION OF ACADEMIC OUTCOMES AND CHANGE

Ultimately the success or failure of a course depends on whether or not students change in the way desired by them or their teachers. In addition to the direct measures of student learning and their work (discussed above and in Chapter 8), there are several indirect measures which are frequently collected and used by institutions for evaluating their impact on students. These indirect measures include:

- alumni, employer, student surveys;
- exit interviews of graduates;
- focus groups;
- graduate follow-up studies;
- retention and transfer studies;
- length of time to degree;
- standardized achievement scores;
- graduation rates;
- transfer rates; and
- job placements.

Of course, the relationship between the type of change suggested in these measures and the quality of teaching is highly problematic. Notoriously, large- and small-scale studies of teaching methods and teaching resources often fail to show the relationship to academic performance as measured by traditional measures, let alone indirect measures. This is likely mainly due to the restricted nature of assessment systems, but compensation for inadequate teaching must be another important factor – the course succeeds in spite of the teaching rather than because of it.

An added difficulty in most normal teaching situations is that there is very little pre-testing so that assumptions have to be made in order to credit students with actual gains in academic achievement. In general, it would seem that pass rates, graduation rates, job placements and academic standards are relevant to the evaluation of teaching but the relationship is a difficult one to interpret. At present they are mainly useful as warning signals when there are large fluctuations over time or between similar courses.

An important limitation on their use that deserves more attention is the infrequency of follow-up assessments of past students. When done this is usually very restricted. Ideally, it should address:

- how what was learnt on the course was or is being used;
- how efficiently it is being used; and
- whether it was relevant and effective.

While such an approach is not essential for all types of courses and pro-grammes, it would be a strange course that did not expect to have some positive intellectual, personal, social or practical impact on the future lives of students.

We suggested earlier that problem-based learning, for example, may not lead to a greater improvement in a student's actual knowledge or compe-tence in specific skills and techniques than traditional courses, but it does seem to have a significant effect upon their attitudes and their desire to go on learning. Despite a long history in psychology of attitude measurement, it is still not common within academic courses, despite the fact that employers are increasingly interested in many of the attitudes towards learning and lifelong learning which students will bring to their future work. In the long run, these may be more important than knowledge and the development of specific skills. While maintaining a degree of scepti-cism about the accuracy of our attempts to measure these attitudes, the actual attempt to do so may, nevertheless, be a useful way more fully to understand the sort of attitudes we are attempting to encourage.

It is important not to regard the assessment of attitude change as com-pletely separate from academic assessment. Less highly formalized methods of student assessment – such as diaries and portfolios (see Chapter 8) – can reveal a great deal about the more emotional and personal changes in students' attitudes brought about by their educational experience. They have an important role to play in enabling students to become more aware of the relationship between their education and their developing sense of identity, and enabling teachers to become clearer about the way in which teaching relates to the personal and social concerns of their students.

CONCLUSIONS

Despite social pressures transforming accountability into a system of accounting that favours quantitative evaluation methods over qualitative ones, there is a clear need for a wide variety of complementary methods. No single method is likely to have the necessary range or depth for evaluating the complex processes and outcomes of university teaching. The emphasis on institutional audits and programme review, plus the explosion of 'league tables' and ranking systems both national and international (Liu and

Cheng, 2005; Usher and Savino, 2006), has raised the profile of evaluation in recent years, but it is also an essential feature in the appointment and promotion of individual staff. It is essential that its processes and methods live up to high standards of academic work expected elsewhere in the academy and that they contribute to the maintenance of the academic values which place learning and knowledge at the centre of higher education. Critically reviewing our evaluation methods with respect to the extensive and complex wealth of that learning is at the heart of both future educational development and the practices of the reflective professional.

An essential part of that review, however, will take the reflective professional beyond simply an examination of which methods most comprehensively address which aspects of student learning. It will (as much of the above discussion suggests) transform the conception of evaluation (found in most of the literature) from its focus on assessing teachers and teaching quality in terms of student learning to an engaged process which itself facilitates student learning.

The most significant developments in the evaluation of teaching will come not from teachers thinking about their own courses as delivering quality or from students as consumers expressing their judgements about the quality of the courses provided for them, but by an integration of evaluation into the learning process. In this conception, evaluation is, itself, an important part of a student's learning and self-knowledge, helping them to explore the strengths, weaknesses, inhibitions and styles of their thinking and working in relation to the constraints and opportunities of the course. Just as the assessment of students' academic attainment has become increasingly integrated into actual learning activities, so the evaluation of teaching may develop away from retrospective and external judgements towards the constant reflection upon the significance of the educational experience and the transition to becoming genuine reflective professionals.

Final questions: Dressel's (1976) comment at the conclusion of the previous chapter that 'only when the students become competent evaluators of their own goals, experiences and accomplishments do they become truly educated' is equally applicable to teachers. Indeed, the two are mutually interdependent. This raises questions for the reflective professional. What does this mean in practice? How can I integrate evaluation into the learning process? What methods of evaluation work best for my teaching context? Will the methods I use allow me to judge clearly my teaching and its impact on student learning? And finally, and most simply of all, how can I learn from my teaching and seek to improve?

PART 3

PERFORMANCE STRATEGY

chapter 10

REALIZING THE REFLECTIVE PROFESSIONAL

In this chapter we consider the role of teaching within the overall academic context. We explore key issues surrounding the relationship with other academic practices (research, management/service). We suggest that while research, teaching and management/service have traditionally been regarded as conflicting duties and practices (often heightened by institutional and funding practices), a more productive perspective would be to focus on the shared aims/purposes of these practices: the discovery, extension, construction and dissemination of knowledge. In this, we focus on questions of teaching within a research culture, working with colleagues and so on.

INTRODUCTION: DEVELOPING A STRATEGY

In this chapter we address the third component of the language of the reflective professional that we introduced at the beginning of this book. We draw upon the foregoing discussion to propose and describe a general strategy of professional realization – a strategy to engage and master the language of reflective practice.

In a climate of escalating interest in opportunities for the development of teaching and learning for teachers across the global higher education sector (e.g. UK (HEA) and USA (US Department of Education, 2006)), the realization of such a professional language is of increasing importance. The realization of such a language, moreover, draws upon substantive research developments in our understanding of both teaching (Prosser and Trigwell, 1999; Samulelowicz and Bain, 2001; Ramsden, 2003; Bain, 2004; Light and Calkins, 2008) and the academic or professional development of teaching (Mckenzie, 2003; Gibbs and Coffey, 2004; Booth and Annenberg, 2005; Dall'Alba, 2005; Akerlind, 2005, 2007, 2008; Light and Calkins, 2008).

While the specific models and suggestions for academic development arising from these research projects are rich in diversity and difference, the cumulative thrust of this research is aimed at moving the teaching and learning culture beyond the impoverished paradigms of academic development (Light, 2000) still prevalent in higher education. Teachers working within the *ad hoc paradigm* (paradigm 1, see Introduction) primarily rely on a combination of their own experiences as a student and/or on what they observe as good practice from their colleagues. They cobble together an impoverished language, used more or less skilfully as personal and situational factors permit. And academics working in a *skills paradigm* (paradigm 2) have tended to perceive the development of teaching in terms of the accretion of 'handy' performance, communication and associated technical skills. The realization of practice is essentially additive, mechanical and decontextualized, and resides within a rather limited language of skills.

The aim of this chapter is to describe a *professional* (paradigm 3) strategy for the realization of the practice of learning and teaching. We draw evidence from the literature, describing the reflective and critical use of practical skills with the appropriate professional knowledge, an understanding of relevant conceptual frameworks and a command of the central genres of practice. This professional strategy locates the development of learning and teaching within the concrete teaching situation of one's discipline, department, students and institution. The intention of this strategy is to offer a critical approach for the development of a reflective, evidence-based approach to realizing and improving teaching and learning.

Three descriptive features frame the general structure of this strategy, which we hope we may be forgiven for expressing as *space*, *time* and *matter* (Figure 10.1). The first feature describes the concrete spatial location of the realization. It is not a neutral space – as suggested by generic skill-based programmes – but, rather, is situated within the teacher's discipline, department and institution. Ideally, it depicts a space in which engagement with students, colleagues and the disciplinary knowledge-base is critical to a full and complete realization of the language.

The second feature reflects the idea that the overall strategy is not simply a one-off programme set within bounded temporal limits but,

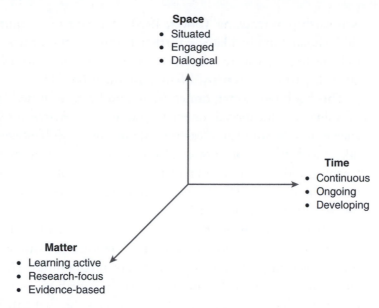

Space
- Situated
- Engaged
- Dialogical

Time
- Continuous
- Ongoing
- Developing

Matter
- Learning active
- Research-focus
- Evidence-based

Figure 10.1

rather, draws on past experience and looks forward to ongoing experience and development. The third feature focuses on the nature and character of the matter within the space and time of practice and constitutes the main focus of our discussion. It encompasses the wide range of material, experience, practices, situations, relationships and values with which the academic engages. It suggests that teachers be informed in their relationships with that matter by the conceptual framework of engaged-dialogical learning, and guided by the critical learning matrix, which have been the central themes of this book. It emphasizes learning as the underlying concept integrating the worlds of teacher, researcher and student (see Chapter 1). Research and teaching were characterized as the same practice, providing exemplars and models of learning for one another and, notably, for the student. The third feature of our strategy, then, describes an active, research-focused, evidence-based, theory-informed approach to realizing practice within the space–time parameters described above.

This strategy is entirely consistent with the 'spirit of inquiry' which defines academic life and practice. In this, it is not new. It is new in helping to bring about a rapprochement between the methods of inquiry which faculty engage in while doing research/scholarship and those methods of inquiry which they are developing with their students. It does so by transforming the process of teaching into a 'process of inquiry', into the 'scholarship of teaching' (Boyer, 1990). The spirit of inquiry envisaged in this scholarship elucidates a further feature of the professional language to be realized, a feature recalling the idea of language from Chapter 1: 'language is part of an activity' (Wittgenstein, 1968: 11).

This book has, so far, drawn upon and been informed by a wide range of valuable educational research and theory. Active research with colleagues into learning and teaching is, however, as Zuber-Skerrit reminds us, 'likely to have a more powerful effect on the improvement of learning, teaching and staff development than research (solely) produced by educational theorists' (1992b: 115). This chapter will look at how to initiate and implement such an approach.

In the first instance, it will explore a sequence of four critical ways to understand and develop actively the relationship between research and practice within professional development programmes. This sequence will culminate in a detailed examination of the fourth way – activity or action research – that draws upon and incorporates the first three. This form of action research offers 'ways of investigating professional experience which link practice and the analysis of practice into a single developing sequence and link researchers and research participants into a single community of interested colleagues' (Winter, 1996: 14). It provides us with the principal model and method for realizing the professional language of practice. The rest of the chapter will flesh out the essential aspects of this approach to professional realization.

INTEGRATING PRACTICE AND RESEARCH

In Chapter 1, we saw how the relationship between subject-based research and the practice of teaching in higher education is characterized by a problematic, often deeply uncomfortable relationship. Both research and teaching have traditionally focused on the distinctive nature of the particular subject or discipline, rather than their mutual aspirations in learning and their shared aims in the construction and extension of knowledge. The focus on the common goal of learning and the advancing of knowledge highlights the critical significance of this research–teaching relationship within disciplinary practice.

The following discussion employs the term research in a broad sense, including both quantitative and qualitative approaches, and incorporating a wide range of empirical, scholarly and creative perspectives drawn from across the range of disciplinary cultures. It also regards research as intrinsically fused with theory in so far as it informs theory, modifies theory, subverts theory, embodies theory and/or generates new theory. We can broadly group the research and theory regarding the practice of teaching explored in this book into four categories:

- The first concerns research looking at the practice of teaching. See, for example, the research looking at conceptions of teaching in higher education described in Chapter 1.
- The second category draws together the vast reservoir of research on adult and student learning discussed in Chapter 2.
- The third focuses on research of more specific relevance to the individual genres of practice (addressed in Chapters 3–9).
- The fourth category draws upon research concerned with the professional issues facing learning and teaching in higher education (see the Introduction and Chapter 1). It addresses the social and epistemological issues and values of the professional role of teaching within academic practice, higher education institutions and society in general. It challenges academics to reflect upon and think about their teaching in the changing wider social, political and economic contexts in which it is situated.

These categories offer a wide range of research that can be drawn upon in the development of the practice of learning and teaching. They do not describe a practical framework for understanding the different relationships between research and practice in the realization of professional practice.

In the following, we offer a schema for considering and managing these relationships. Again, it is not intended as an authoritative or prescriptive programme but, rather, as a conceptual tool for reflecting upon, developing and improving practice. Figure 10.2 illustrates four ways in which research and practice may be conceptualized in the realization of the professional practice: *practice defined by research*; *practice v. research*; *practice informed by research*; and *practice as research*.

These four ways of conceiving research and practice are four phases or movements in the realization of the reflective professional. They do not describe a necessary sequential order. Realization will always be a recursive process in which teachers will individually and collectively reflect upon and rethink their practice in the light of their various academic and personal experiences. Our discussion, here, will comment briefly on the first three phases. Other chapters in the book have considered the essential issues of these phases in some depth. In the following section, we shall address the fourth phase in some depth.

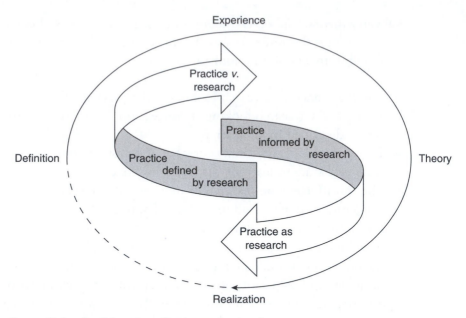

Figure 10.2   *Realising the reflective professional*

Teaching defined by research

The initial movement which may be referred to as the 'definitional phase' challenges practitioners to reflect critically upon their own implicit, often unspoken, definition or conception of teaching practice in respect of research and theory. In the first instance, this reflection will most likely consist of the relation of teaching to issues of learning and knowledge. Watkins and Mortimore, for example, define pedagogy or teaching as 'any conscious activity by one person to enhance learning in another' (1999: 3). But making the link between teaching and learning is not, of itself, sufficient. It does not take a huge critical leap to recognize such a relationship. What does demand a more critical approach is our personal examination of the nature of that relationship.

It is worth reiterating, however, that this phase challenges us to de-centre teaching and to re-centre learning within our personal definitions of practice. As discussed in Chapter 1, most if not all research on teachers' understanding of teaching has identified critical differences around this key structural issue – teaching as focused on transmitting information to students *v.* teaching focused on developing students' conceptual understanding (Akerlind, 2007). The former view of teaching tends to understand its relationship to learning as essentially linear, one in which teaching causes or produces learning. The definitional phase looks for a reversal of this perception in favour of one which views teaching as an outcome of learning, or as defined by learning.

As Freire (2000) had long maintained, the authenticity of teaching is authenticated only by the authenticity of the student's thinking (learning). If there is a genuine engagement with knowledge such that conceptual development and change are happening, the teacher can be said to be teaching. If, on the other hand, learning is not genuinely occurring, then irrespective of the teacher's efforts, one may legitimately question their right to the use of the term 'teaching'.

Re-centring the practice of teaching does not necessarily mean that teachers need to be schooled in the literature and research on student learning. In a study examining what the best teachers do, Bain (2004: 25–6) found that few had substantive awareness of this literature but all had 'conceptions of human learning that are remarkably similar to some ideas that have emerged in the research and theoretical literature on cognition, motivation and human development'.

There are numerous examples of excellent teaching by teachers who have not studied the literature. Nevertheless, they focused their teaching around the facilitation of student conceptual understanding. Akerlind (2007) and McKenzie (2003) have, moreover, demonstrated that a teacher's understanding of teaching is linked to their understanding of the development of their own teaching. Teacher-focused understandings of development (associated with the skills paradigm, for example) relate to teacher-focused understandings of teaching. Similarly student-learning-focused understandings of development (related to the professional paradigm) are related to similarly focused understandings of teaching.

This first phase, then, challenges both the faculty/academic developer and the not so excellent teacher to redefine teaching for themselves – to centre student learning in their practice – by engaging with the research and re-constructing it in their discipline for both themselves and their students.

Such a redefinition, of course, has implications, particularly with respect to our understanding of the nature and character of learning and knowing. This leads us to the next two phases or movements of the schema, which respectively address the practitioners' experiential and conceptual/theoretical understandings of learning.

Teaching *v.* research

The juxtaposition of the second and third phases is not a straightforward sequential matter. They do not occur separately or consecutively but are significantly interlocked in both development and ongoing improvement. The point of their separation here is to emphasize the commonality of learning at the heart of all our academic practices (see Chapter 1). Teachers in higher education bring their own rich experiences of learning to the learning and teaching situation. Through their own academic research and scholarship, they can also bring to the encounter with their students a shared experience of the struggle and exhilaration of learning. This includes considered and proficient exemplars or models of its achievement in an academic environment.

Unfortunately, all too often we leave the potential and richness of this common experience of research and teaching untapped and unexplored. More ominously within academic practice generally, teaching and research are frequently, even habitually, regarded as rivals: time and status pitting the 'learning' of one against the 'learning' of the other.

This phase or movement in realizing practice, then, is characterized by the challenge to examine critically this rivalry of 'learning *v*. learning' and the associated fragmentation of 'learning' more generally which this rivalry causes. The issue is not the academic role of researcher *v*. that of teacher but, rather, of developing practice beyond this partition and establishing an inclusive culture of learning – 'culture of inquiry' (Clark, 1997) – which encourages an active engagement in learning by all.

The model focuses, then, on the development of teaching within a broader conception of disciplinary research and scholarship. It includes a more thorough understanding of research as a deeply engaging learning activity with rich lessons for our understanding and practice of teaching. Teachers in higher education are, by definition, master learners in their disciplines and professions. That, probably more than anything else, is what makes them academics. They know how to learn deeply in their chosen field. The language of teaching does not, therefore, simply draw upon generic understandings of teaching/learning but, rather, on profound disciplinary experiences of research and learning:

> *How do I and my colleagues learn in this discipline? How do we collaborate? What does learning consist of in this subject? How can we improve this learning? What impedes it? How does this learning embrace, engage and extend the learning of our students? How can we collaborate with our students to improve learning? (Light, 2003: 158)*

Teaching, here, is characterized by the idea of an inclusive, critical language of practice and overcoming the rivalry of learning. Indeed, in a study of academics' understanding of learning across academic practice, Light and Calkins (2006) reported that some faculty maintained connected or integrated understandings with respect to both themselves in their research and scholarship, and their undergraduate students' learning in their teaching.

Unfortunately the study reported a much higher number of faculty with disconnected understandings of learning across these two aspects of their practice. The latter faculty had effectively internalized the rivalry of learning. The point of this aspect of the developmental model presented here is to assist faculty to become aware of the disconnection between the two understandings of learning which they hold in their different practices, with the goal of drawing their attention to different ways they may understand teaching (Akerlind, 2008), especially in terms of learning as conceptual development or change.

Teaching informed by research

The theory phase of integrating research and teaching has sometimes been referred to as scholarly teaching. Hutchings and Shulman (1999) distinguish it from excellent teaching, on the one hand, and the scholarship of teaching (Boyer, 1990), on the other. Excellent teaching is essentially best practice in which teachers focus on student learning but do not formally draw upon the literature on learning and teaching although, as Bain suggests above, they may have a deep but tacit understanding of learning. The scholarship of teaching suggests an inquiry into 'some or all of the full act of teaching ... in a manner susceptible to critical review by the teacher's professional peers and amenable to productive employment in future work by members of that same community' (Shulman, 1998: 6).

Scholarly teaching 'is informed not only by the latest ideas in the field but by current ideas about teaching the field' (Hutchings and Shulman, 1999: 48). The development of individual and collective practice is not limited to any one or two categories of research and theory. It will draw upon all the main categories we have been primarily concerned with in this book. It will also inquire into others, particularly those from other disciplines, other practices and other professions that are of special significance and relevance to the individual practitioner.

Teaching informed by relevant research, by theory, by specialized knowledge, by expert and critical ways of understanding is a vital ingredient of reflective and professional practice. It provides the knowledge and the conceptual frameworks for reflecting upon and 'critiquing' one's knowledge, practice and common experience as a learner. In this, it describes a movement of educational and professional *literacy*.

Such literacy, as we have attempted to show throughout this book, embodies the development and practice of a common and comprehensive *language* of learning and teaching. Characterized and informed by research, theory and scholarship, such a language offers opportunities for:

- sharing a common understanding with colleagues and students;
- moving beyond the mere acquisition of a series of communication and performance skills, tips or specialized teaching competencies;
- re-positioning teaching within a deeper and more critical understanding of professional life, practical engagement, reflective skill development, 'genre' refinement and continuing professional development, etc.;
- conducting personal micro-research – or even larger-scale collective research – as part of professional and academic development;
- reconciling academic practice, both through common experiences of learning and through a shared academic discourse of theory, evidence, argument and notions of rigour;
- managing uncertainty and change; and
- improving personal scholarship on practice.

TEACHING AS RESEARCH

The movement towards understanding teaching as research is not an end result so much as the bringing together of the cycle into a process/method of practical realization. It articulates a strategy for professional realization that incorporates and integrates the other three. In this, it describes a process of becoming critically engaged in practice through action research. It aims at professional realization by transforming academic practice as habitual or customary action into 'academic praxis' (Zuber-Skerrit, 1992a, 1992b, 1997), into informed, critical and committed academic action.

In its simplest formulation, 'action research is about promoting success-ful, sustainable and liberating change' (Greenwood, 2007). It differs from more traditional forms of educational research to the degree in which it involves issues such as critical practice, improvement, participation and the actual environment or situation of practice. Kember (2000: 24) describes the key features of action research as being:

- concerned with social practice;
- aimed towards improvement;
- a cyclical process;
- pursued by systematic inquiry;

- a reflective process;
- participative; and
- determined by the practitioners.

Action research has been employed as a method of developing learning and teaching across many regions of the world. Elton (2008), for example, notes professional development MA and certificate courses based on action research in London, Oxford, Dublin and Hong Kong. In the USA, several authors link the development of learning and teaching practices through the Scholarship of Teaching and Learning (SOTL) projects with action research (Raubenheimer and Myka, 2005; Hubball and Burt, 2006; Gray et al., 2007). The theoretical relationship to action research has, moreover, been discussed in some detail by Zuber-Skerrit (1992a, 1992b, 1997), Kember (2000) and Brew (2006).

Zuber-Skerrit (1992a, 1992b, 1997) emphasizes the power of action research to encourage the critical attitude we wish to foster in our students but also in ourselves – personally and as exemplars for students. It incorporates the integration of educational theory with personal *research into teaching*. It provides a rigorous research basis from which to understand and contribute to the debate concerning academic *accountability* to society, giving academic staff a professionally grounded voice with respect to academic policies, future curriculum decisions and so on. It offers practitioners a robust and critical method of *self-evaluation* for ongoing development. Finally, it sustains the capacity to contribute to the development of professionalism in higher education.

Carr and Kemmis (1983) describe three kinds of action research which address these issues, albeit at different levels of practitioner engagement. They are differentiated by the relationship between the educational researcher and the practitioner: by the degree to which practitioners are or become the principal researcher. In the first, *technical action research*, the researcher who facilitates the process establishes and judges the standards for improving the effectiveness of educational practice. The practitioner is mainly engaged in the process at a technical level. The second, *practical action research*, also aims to improve the effectiveness of practice but encourages the practitioner to engage more fully and self-reflectively in the research process to develop their practical understanding and professional development.

The third type, *emancipatory action research*, encourages the full participation of practitioner-as-researcher to explore critically the effectiveness of practice and its practical understanding within the social and organizational constraints that enclose practice. Improvement, here, encompasses

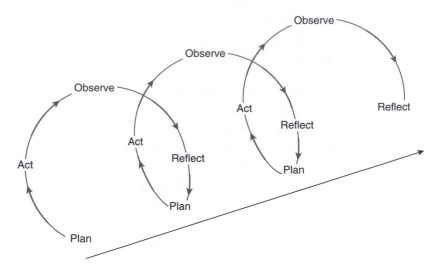

Figure 10.3 *The action research cycle*

organizational enlightenment. It is characterized by a more complete engagement and critical dialogue, essential to the full realization of practice (Reason and Bradbury, 2001).

Action research in this more inclusive guise is characterized by strategic action in its design, methods and realization. It consciously and deliberately sets out to improve, enhance and realize practice through actions informed, but not constrained, by research and theory. It is flexible, open to change necessitated by experience and circumstance, and it is subject to the practitioner's critical and rational practical judgements. Kemmis and McTaggart (1988: 7) describe the implementation of this strategic action as a continuous cycle of four moments:

- a plan of action to improve what is already happening;
- action to implement the plan;
- observation of the effects of the action in the context in which it is occurs; and
- reflection on these effects as a basis for further planning, subsequent action and so on, through a succession of cycles.

The implementation of action research is often presented in the form of a spiral composed of numerous iterations of this cycle (Figure 10.3). In the next section, we examine a practical way of reconstructing the ideas and methods of action research in professional realization.

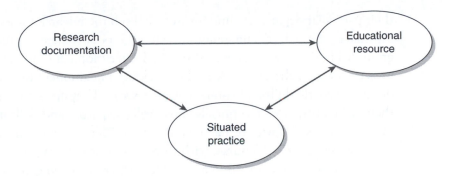

Figure 10.4 *Professional realisation: a research framework*

THE REFLECTIVE PROFESSIONAL THROUGH ACTION RESEARCH

The following discussion presents a tripartite framework for thinking about and engaging in action research with the aim of realizing professional practice. As a method of professional development, one of its essential outcomes is the degree to which it integrates the issues of learning apparent in research and scholarship with those of learning and teaching. It views professional development as moving beyond learning and teaching practice to embrace all academic practice (see Chapter 1) – one of the key aspects of our third paradigm of learning and teaching (see the Introduction). It is not a one-off event but, rather, an ongoing progression arising out of the unfolding developments in one's practice.

It is possible to use the general approach within a formal programme of training or to engage with it more informally. Categories of programmes might include:

- *institutional*: programme provided by an institution;
- *disciplinary*: programme provided by discipline associations;
- *peer*: programme established within parameters agreed with peers; and
- *individual*: programme individually constructed.

As the basis for action research, however, programmes require a systematic and strategically planned approach. Figure 10.4 illustrates three broad areas that such an approach would embrace: situated practice, educational resource and research documentation. We shall look at these features individually below, but it is worth briefly expanding on them here.

Teaching practice does not exist in a vacuum. It is *situated practice* and, in so far as the practitioner/researcher is researching their own practice within their particular department and institution, both the research project and the associated research documentation will also be concretely situated and grounded in their own academic discipline(s). Development programmes and projects are not, therefore, focused on helping practitioners to compile evidence of generic skills and competencies *in vacuo*. They are aimed at helping them to identify, examine critically and develop expertise and skills in relevant practices embedded within their own discipline, department and institution.

They shall do so, of course, with respect to a broad range of *educational resources*. While these are often associated and drawn from generic or cross-disciplinary aspects of a programme, they are not regarded here as answers to teaching and learning problems so much as tools for critically reflecting on situated practice.

Finally, the realization of practice will need to proceed towards the production of *research documentation*, for the provision of evidence of professional realization, for sharing with colleagues in the best tradition of peer review and for informing and developing ongoing development. The documentation most commonly associated with programmes for the development of learning and teaching practice has mainly consisted of a portfolio of evidence related to a number of carefully selected outcomes. In the UK, many of the programmes accredited by the Higher Education Academy (HEA) require such portfolios as providing evidence of achievement.

Such portfolios are, however, not generally explicitly regarded as a research document so much as a professional record of achievement. In the USA, Scholarship of Teaching and Learning (SOTL) projects often require a sharing of results through publication in peer-reviewed journals and/or presentations at peer-reviewed conferences. The approach taken here reinterprets the professional parameters of the portfolio – its outcomes, evidence, professional requirements, etc. – in research terms. In this way, the portfolio may be conceived as a research document or research report informed by situated practice and educational resource. It provides critical, practical evidence and theoretically informed analysis of those areas of teaching and learning relevant to the teacher's practice (see below for a more concrete discussion of portfolios).

Situated practice

The disciplinary situation of practice is at the heart of professional realization through action-research approaches. It provides the vital context of the practitioner's investigations and explorations. It is, ultimately, the space in which the research is embedded – where the plans are designed, interventions constructed, methods identified and developed. Within the situation, the multiplicity of the designs, interventions and methods available needs to be understood in terms of the overall realization of the objectives of the research. These will be dependent on the general parameters of the research (e.g. national professional requirements, institutional criteria, programme objectives) as well as the initial questions and the outcomes (e.g. improving learning, teaching development and improvement, evaluation of learning and teaching).

Action research of this sort is not aiming at wide-scale generalization or application but, rather, at individual development. Essentially it employs case-study methodology in which the case is related to the researcher's own practice within their own concrete academic situation. Such cases might range, for example, from exploring a single, specific teaching innovation or specific use of course material, to broader redesigns of an entire course or curriculum. In their project-based approach to faculty development, Calkins and Light (2008), for example, ask early career faculty to tackle a significant and professionally relevant teaching challenge, which they research and share with colleagues, and formally write up.

Case-situated action research will work with and draw from concrete categories of experience, evidence and activities, including:

- learning and teaching practices and resources, etc.;
- programme, course, module and session materials and documentation;
- relevant departmental and institutional documents;
- disciplinary and syllabus subject matter – texts, readings, techniques, etc.;
- disciplinary research and scholarship; and
- students, colleagues, mentors/advisers.

While not exhaustive categories, each offers significant research potential employing a broad range of methods and techniques of data collection and analysis. It is not possible to elaborate on the character and scope of these methods and techniques in any detail, but it is worth noting examples that might be effectively used (see also Chapter 9). These will include, for example, *document* or *textual analysis*: not only of the kind of institutional and programme/course documentation listed above but also, crucially, of student essays, papers, online discussion, project and lab reports (including drafts), etc. It may also include the systematic collection and analysis of both formative and summative written comments given to students.

Practitioners may also employ techniques and methods of observation, particularly with respect to classroom practice. This might include formal peer observation conducted with colleagues on your and/or on your colleagues' teaching practice. It could also include planned observation of student interactions between the students, with the teacher and so on.

Interviews with students also offer an invaluable source of data for analysis, reflection and further development. These might be structured and/or semi-structured. They might aim, for example, at coming to a better understanding of student experiences and/or conceptions of learning within the practitioner's particular teaching and learning situation. They might focus on a particular aspect of learning or be used across the learning matrix.

Strategic questionnaires and *surveys* of students, including but also extending beyond standard course evaluation and/or rating instruments, might also be effectively used. The use of interviews and surveys could also extend to other members of appropriate and relevant faculty and staff members. In addition, practitioners might wish to ask students – and colleagues for that matter – to participate in exercises utilizing a range of *focus-group* techniques.

Depending on permission, time and resources, practitioners might also find methods of cognitive experimentation valuable. The point here, however, is not to elaborate the diversity of methods, techniques or instruments that can be employed fully, but to suggest the scope of the research that can be strategically and creatively employed for the improvement of practice.

Educational resource

Realizing professional practice through action research and the development of research documentation will normally need to be grounded in the learning and teaching situation of the teacher's discipline, but also drawing upon material and resources from other disciplines concerned with understanding higher education. The tension between these two is often uneven and uncomfortable, and successfully managing it becomes an indispensable ingredient to realization. It is best managed if one accepts that professional realization is not generic but disciplinary. While it draws upon a range of different sorts of educational resources – which we shall look at in a moment – it takes place for the most part in the practitioner's discipline(s). The research is disciplinary research – albeit drawing on research approaches and methods from other disciplines as well as those of its own.

We shall not describe in detail the nature of the education resources available to practitioners in conducting action research. This book itself is intended as an essential resource. It is worth noting, however, the extent of the resources available for use. Three factors organize educational resource here: location, resource and activity (Table 10.1). They

Table 10.1 *Educational resources*

Location	Resource	Activity
International	Development programmes	Workshops/seminars
National	Sessions and workshops	Peer consultancy
Institutional	Educational literature	
Supervising/mentoring		
Departmental	Tutors/consultants	Appraisal
Programme	Fellow participants	Project groups
Course	Students	Evaluations

do not describe an exhaustive list of potential resources but, rather, constructive and useful dimensions for the design of development/improvement programmes and personal initiatives/projects undertaken within such programmes.

While sometimes located in disciplinary learning and teaching situations, the professional realization of practice frequently draws upon the support structures of institutional programmes of staff development. Such programmes normally expect participants to draw upon learning and teaching experiences and resources within the actual disciplinary teaching situation and require, for example, portfolios of evidence centred around such teaching. While the course–department–institution provide the main loci of action-research approaches to teaching development, educational resources from other locations can supplement it.

The expansion of national and international organizations for the support of learning and teaching can provide a wealth of information, materials and assistance. The HEA, for example, oversees 24 subject centres within the UK, which provide materials for practitioners focused on issues that are more discipline specific. And in the USA, the Carnegie Foundation for the Advancement of Teaching has provided disciplinary pedagogies related to the scholarship of teaching and learning (Huber and Morreale, 2002). In addition, most disciplinary societies and conferences have educational components with substantive resources available.

There are also a growing number of national and international courses, workshops and programmes focused on particular disciplines or on specific issues and/or genres of learning and teaching. They will normally provide access to the kind of educational literature and materials covered in this book as well as sessions and workshops for exploring this literature with respect to individual genres, sub-genres and/or combinations of genres. Such literature and materials will be available from a range of sources, including books, teaching materials, video, the Internet, academic and professional journals, conference papers and so on.

The provision of sessions – workshops, conferences and seminars – is not the preserve of integrated development programmes. An increasing number of organizations – regional, national and international – are providing valuable and specialized sessions outside institutional programmes. These are provided both in face-to-face modes and increasingly through distance and online education technologies. These sessions do not simply provide access to the expertise of the tutors and consultants facilitating them; they also provide invaluable access to the experience, knowledge and skills of the other participants.

The shared experience of fellow participants provides personal and social support as well as invaluable intellectual and practical help. They permit the scrutiny of one's knowledge and understanding of practical issues in a shared discipline and intellectual culture as well as the exploration of new possibilities across disciplines and other academic cultures.

Students are also a rich resource. Many will bring articulate and critically constructive accounts of their learning within and across disciplines. Practitioners will also have their own personal resources to tap into, not the least of which may be their own encounters with education through children, community groups, volunteer and charity work, etc.

We have noted some of the activities – workshops, seminars, lunchtime sessions, etc. – through which resources become available but the very processes of these activities are themselves often a significant resource (Sorcinelli, 2006). Other useful activities – many of which are becoming more widespread in university staff and management processes – include mentoring activities with senior or more experienced colleagues with regard to learning and teaching within the discipline and department (Mullen and Forbes, 2000; Levy et al., 2004; Calkins and Kelley, 2005). This can be extremely useful in contextualizing teaching as well as helping to develop effective communities of shared and constructive practice.

In the same vein, peer-mentoring and consultancy activities with colleagues exploring a range of learning and teaching genres can provide a useful resource for both personal and collective action research aimed at improvement. Peer observation has, for example, become a more widespread tool for examining practice – mainly focused on classroom performance but can be extended to considerations of activities central to other genres, such as supervision, assessment, evaluation, curriculum design.

Many institutions also provide appraisal schemes for faculty, which offer another potentially rich source of evidence and data for reflection and critical analysis. Informal support groups with colleagues sharing similar concerns and issues are also a promising resource upon which to draw. While many of these activities may be institutional or departmental, others have a much wider remit.

Finally, it should be restated that the staff development perspective emphasized here does not view these resources as ends in themselves but, rather, as means by which professional practice might be realized through strategically planned and implemented research initiatives.

Research documentation: portfolio of practice

Informed in part by Boyer's (1990) *Scholarship Reconsidered*, higher education in the UK and the USA has increasingly emphasized portfolios of assessment to show evidence of strong teaching practice. Such evidence might include descriptions of learning intentions and activities, detailed learning outcomes and critical reflections on the part of the teacher or the students (Brockbank and McGill, 1998). Collecting this information may become even easier with the use of electronic or digital portfolios – software programs that allow teachers to enter evidence (teaching activities, reflections, etc.) for continuing reflective development (Dornan et al., 2002).

Teaching portfolios, generally, also have the virtue of allowing teachers to work at their own pace and to control what they do and display as teachers. Thus, the teacher is the learner, meaning 'the learner is in control and feels more highly valued' (Tisani, 2008). Yet, while the mechanics of putting such a portfolio together are fairly well known and described in a variety of handbooks and how-to guides, the necessary critical reflection and knowledge of basic pedagogical theory may still be lacking (Tisani, 2008).

As suggested above, the portfolio as research document goes beyond such a reflective reportage of evidence to embody the idea of critical and strategic action. It will need to incorporate into its design a strategic plan related to and embedded in the situation in which the investigation(s) will be taking place and the educational resources on which it will be drawing.

In the case of professional accreditation programmes – such as those nationally accredited in the UK by the HEA – portfolio design will need to consider and incorporate strategically requirements to show a command of a range of 'genres of practice' (Chapters 3–9). These will need to be informed by the relevant educational literature (Chapter 2) and by academic values and principles (Chapter 1). In addition, portfolios may need to meet institutional requirements such as those for appointment and promotion. This does not preclude – indeed may entail – a critique of the parameters and criteria of such programmes.

Table 10.2 *Action research cycle: illustrative activities*

Illustrative activities	Diverse examples
Plan	
Determine relevant research question(s)	Do my teaching methods achieve the
Identify 'genres' of learning and	optimum balance of learning activities?
teaching for research	Lecturing, facilitating, innovating, assessing
Design a teaching innovation	Construct a method of peer assessment
Explore and establish research	Interviews with staff and students,
methods	follow-up questionnaires, etc.
Action	
Employ strategies and methods of evaluation	Conduct interviews with students,
Engage and/or test educational resources	focus groups with past students, etc.
Introduce changes, innovations	Attend a conference or workshop on
	methods for assessing students' practical skills
	Introduce 'group activities' into a lecture context
Observe	
Collect/interpret empirical evidence/data	Observe student classroom responses and interpret
Examine and interpret educational resources	survey of attitudes to using online materials in class
Map evidence to relevant areas of practice	Conduct a statistical analysis on student
	questionnaires concerning their motivation in a
	particular course
	Map research evidence on course design to a
	particular course in a subject discipline
Reflect	
Critically analyse outcomes	Critically analyse grade and exam data on the
Draw conclusions	impact of using problem-based curriculum
Develop new plans/strategies	design in a single course
	Draw conclusions and evaluate the implications of
	the survey data looking at the provision of
	feedback on student assignments online
	Modify and extend a new design for the
	evaluation of the impact of one's lecturing on
	learning to other courses

The portfolio is, nevertheless, a research document providing evidence of the process and results of personal scholarship and empirical research into teaching and learning practice. In this respect, it requires the identification of relevant research questions and methods, the appropriate discovery, development and generation of a variety of evidence of personal practice and the critical analysis, assessment and presentation of this evidence within a substantive theoretical context. It calls for the practical development of reflective skills of self-assessment and self-evaluation. It will, ideally, be characterized by a form of the action research cycle of plan–action–observe–reflect described above. Such a cycle might include the kinds of activities as given in Table 10.2.

The presentation of portfolios will require a scholarly format, including an appropriate table of contents, referencing, bibliography, relevant appendices, accuracy of presentation and so on. Indeed, the overlap of research and teaching practices might, as noted above, extend to academic publication.

The results of the action research supporting professional development may also be written up for publication in appropriate academic and professional journals. As well as contributing to the research and scholarship of teaching, it may have the added benefit, in some cases, of furthering professional careers. The general publication of personal or collective action research on issues of learning and teaching in one's discipline(s) as a commonplace activity for faculty would go some distance towards integrating academic practices.

On the other hand, we must sound a note of caution. Publication confining itself to research results can distort the professional developmental nature of that research. As Donald Kennedy, the past president of Stanford suggests, writing 'in a portfolio devoted to forms of scholarship related to teaching [is] ... scholarship beyond that reported in peer reviewed journals' (1997: 65).

CONCLUSION

It is important to recall at this point that the main idea that has been driving this book forward is that of a 'professional language of practice'. The realization of this language is critically inter-related with the two other aspects of the language that we have been examining throughout the book: its overall conceptual framework (Chapters 1 and 2) and its main genres (Chapters 3–9). Fluency in the language and practice is characterized by a reflective use of practical skills, informed by an appropriate professional knowledge, a critical understanding of the relevant conceptual frameworks and a command of the key teaching genres.

In many ways, however, the themes and content of this chapter must remain incomplete. This is due, in great part, to the critical 'openness' that must inevitably characterize realization. Realization must sustain this 'openness' with respect to its creative potential but also with respect to the diversity, multiplicity, complexity and uncertainty of the students, the university and the future with which it must continually and fully engage. It is also due to the prevailing way in which the university is primarily understood: as contrasting practices, research and teaching, and not as a unifying goal, knowledge and learning (Chapter 1).

Ultimately, the realization of reflective practice is grounded in the realization of student learning. The goal of 'teaching-as-research' is legitimated only in so far as that research explores and documents theoretical, empirical and methodological advances in the development of student learning at the 'cutting edge' (Chapter 1) and/or documents the actual results of a development of student learning at the 'cutting edge'. The former describes 'teaching-as-research' in terms of more traditional forms of faculty learning, research and scholarship (SOTL), while the latter characterizes teaching-as-research in terms of building research capacity through the learning of one's students. In the latter formulation, the teacher's research resides in the research capacities developed by their students and is, or should be recognized as, a critical part of an academic's contribution to a university's research mission. Such recognition requires new forms of documentation for which the kinds of portfolio of evidence described above provide a solid foundation. The implications of the latter formulation, however, are even more radical, raising the opportunity for a thorough rethinking and integration of research and teaching through the central idea of learning.

appendix

STRUCTURED OBSERVATION OF TEACHING: GUIDELINES

There are no hard and fast rules to be observed when observing teaching since individual differences on both sides are extremely important. The following points, however, may be worth considering when planning how to make the process an interesting and useful experience for both. The guidelines and the accompanying observation form are designed to help focus the teacher and the observer on the following:

- The learning objectives of the teaching session.
- The relationship of different kinds of structures available for teaching to those learning objectives.
- The relationship of teaching to the student experience of the session.

PART 1: PRE-OBSERVATION SESSION

Before the observation, the teacher and observer should meet to clarify their expectations about the process. The first part of the form will help both to understand the expectations of the session.

1. Agree on the aims and structure of the observation

- Do the instructor and observer both agree on the purpose of the observation?

- What role, if any, will the observer play during the observation process?
- Will the observer be able to talk to the students directly at any point?

2. Identify the instructor's learning and teaching objectives for the teaching session

Intention
- What is the instructor trying to achieve (generally in the course; specifically in the session)?
- What type of student learning outcomes are being encouraged?

Strategy
- What are the instructor's primary teaching methods for the class?
- Why has the instructor opted for a particular approach or format?
- How does the instructor inspire or motivate the students to learn?
- What is the observer's role, if any, in planning or structuring the session?

3. Understand the observation context

- Who are the students?
- What are the instructor's perceptions of the students in the class (diversity of learners, disciplinary mix, perception of class characteristics, etc.)?
- What expectations, attitudes, assumptions or skills do the students bring?
- Have there been any recent changes in the programme/course/student outcomes?
- Are there any special problems or constraints in the course/classroom, etc., to be aware of?

4. Agree on the post-observation discussion

- Will the observer debrief each session, or set of sessions?
- What type of style should be used (formal, serious, relaxed, challenging, developmental)?
- Format? Should there be a definite structure to the discussion?
- Are there any particular areas the instructor would like feedback on?
- Will the observer provide verbal or written feedback/reflections on the teaching?

PART II: OBSERVATION ACTIVITY

This part of the form is intended to provide both the teacher and observer with a way of looking at the teacher's general teaching practice in the session, particularly with respect to the session's learning objectives and the students' potential experience. The observer is encouraged to write comments within each area, but to defer deeper interpretation until reflecting on the session later, when preparing for the follow-up discussion.

PART III: POST-OBSERVATION DISCUSSION

The post-observation phase has been structured around a form designed to provide information for the debrief session and discussion with the teacher about specific areas of their teaching practice. The form consists of a combination of quantitative scores and qualitative comments. The quantitative scores are mainly intended to provide the observer with a useful way of quickly developing an overall sense of the session to provide the teacher with additional information from which to reflect and consider their teaching practice further and to help identify those areas where improvement and further development may be appropriate.

The assessment for the general skills is on a four-point Likert scale of agreement (or not), with statements about the skills:

- *Strongly disagree (SD)*: suggests that the skill has neither been integrated into practice nor has it shown substantial signs of being developed.
- *Disagree (D)*: suggests there are signs that the skill has been developed but it can be taken much further in practice.
- *Agree (A)*: suggests the skill has been acceptably developed but it can be taken further in practice.
- *Strongly agree (SA)*: suggests the skill has been very effectively integrated into practice.
- *N/A*: not appropriate to the session.

Scores are calculated by assigning a number from 1 to 4 on the level of agreement with the 12 'teaching skills' items (1 = Strongly disagree; 4 = Strongly agree). The higher scores suggest more ability in the particular teaching skill. Scores for the three different dimensions – providing support, encouraging independence and developing the interpersonal – can be scored separately here to help in the identification of issues concerning the balance between the three areas. (*Note*: to compare support, independence and interpersonal scores, an average for items in the specific category should be used.) An overall score can be calculated, although some criteria may be less appropriate to some forms of session. This needs to be considered if scores are aggregated.

Written comments related to the scores given to the 12 items are particularly helpful in facilitating the discussion between the observer and the instructor. Such comments help specify particular issues under each skill area. Table A.1 provides a range of statements which characterize the issues addressed by each of the 12 items. The observer may wish to draw upon these descriptions in constructing their written comments. They should only be seen as a guideline, however. In addition to comments, the observer may also wish to write down suggestions which the instructor might want to think about in developing and changing particular aspects of his or her teaching. These may also be useful for the instructor during the post-observation discussion.

Table A.1 *Descriptions of items by critical matrix categories*

Providing support skills			
1. Maintains students' curiosity and interest to end of the session	**2. Makes material and content clear and accessible to students**	**3. Acknowledges and clarifies students' role(s) during session**	**4. Communicates effectively**
Sets the scene for the session, relevance of the material Links the session to the overall course, to wider contexts, to students' personal interests, etc. Captures students' interest at the beginning (with problems, questions, key ideas, etc.) Varies presentation styles Ends the session in a stimulating and interesting way (leaves students with interesting questions, problems, etc.) Encourages the students to enjoy the session	Makes the purpose of the session clear Offers clear and accessible explanations Uses effective examples, illustrations and quotations Uses technology and visual aids effectively to interpret material Stresses important concepts and ideas Provides alternative explanations/descriptions of difficult concepts, issues or ideas	Clarifies the role or value of note-taking during the session Clarifies expectations about student participation Obtains feedback about students understanding of the material Clarifies work expected from the students after the session	Modulates voice effectively; speaks to (not at) the students Uses gestures and body movements effectively Maintains regular eye contact with the students Uses the space and resources (technology, multimedia, etc.) effectively Demonstrates energy; is lively and stimulating Paces the session appropriately Displays a strong rapport with students; seeks to engage students

Encouraging independence skills			
5. Chooses and organizes material well	**6. Encourages students to think critically during the class**	**7. Encourages students to relate their experience to class content**	**8. Encourages students to offer their own knowledge, ideas or opinions**
Chooses material relevant to course topic and objectives Organizes and offers material in a form appropriate to the students' ability and level Uses material that animates student interest and makes them curious to explore more	Provides time for reflection on problems, concepts, ideas Provides time for students to test positions, ideas, concepts with respect to content presented (in groups or with a fellow student or in the class as a whole) Encourages the consideration of alternative views	Provides time for students to reflect on their experience Provides time for sharing experience in groups or with peers Encourages active participation within the class as a whole Ensures access for a wide range of student experience	Provides opportunities and a 'safe' environment to contribute Allows time for students to answer key problems or questions raised Recognizes and permits a range of ways of expressing one's ideas, knowledge, opinions

(Continued)

Table A.1   (Continued)

5. Chooses and organizes material well	6. Encourages students to think critically during the class	7. Encourages students to relate their experience to class content	8. Encourages students to offer their own knowledge, ideas or opinions
Provides the right amount of material for the time allowed	Challenges assumptions		

Developing interpersonal skills			
9. Leaves students feeling stimulated to think and learn more about subject	10. Encourages students to respond to one another	11. Introduces activities in which students interact with one another	12. Encourages students to engage/challenge one another
Selects engaging material, examples, cases, problems, etc. Encourages students to do further reading/research Encourages students to follow up their own ideas and lines of thinking Encourages students to see the session as part of an ongoing open learning process	Devizes ways to get students to address and respond to one another Is positive with respect to student contributions and interactions Provides opportunities for students to play different roles in a group (leader, reporter, etc.)	Provides opportunities for teamwork, leadership, group communication Arranges the students within the room or space to allow for group interaction Uses activities and technology (games, simulations, role play, etc.) which motivate students to interact	Encourages students to challenge or question respectfully one another's ideas and opinions Provides opportunities (debate, role play) for student interaction Provides opportunities for student presentations Provides opportunities for students to critique and evaluate one another

STRUCTURED OBSERVATION OF TEACHING: FORMS

Part I: pre-observation session

Teacher	Session
Course	Session length
Topic	

Specific learning objectives planned for the session
For example, knowledge and understanding; key/core skills; cognitive skills; subject-specific (including practical and professional) skills; interpersonal skills

Part II: observation activity

Teacher		Session	
Course		Session length	
Topic			

Time	Observed activity	Description/comment

Part III: structured observation of teaching: follow-up form

Teacher		Session	
Course		Session length	
Topic			

Dimension of critical matrix	Area of observation	S D	D	A	S A	Observations	Suggestions
Providing support	1. Maintains students' curiosity and interest to end of the session						
	2. Makes material and content clear and accessible to students						
	3. Acknowledges and clarifies students' role(s) during session						
	4. Communicates effectively						
	5. Chooses and organizes material well						
Encouraging independence	6. Encourages students to think critically during the class						
	7. Encourages students to relate their experience to class content						
	8. Encourages students to offer their own knowledge, ideas or opinions						
	9. Leaves students feeling stimulated to think and learn more about subject						
Developing the interpersonal	10. Encourages students to respond to one another						
	11. Introduces activities in which students interact with one another						
	12. Encourages students to engage/challenge one another						

references

Abercrombie, M.L.J. (1966) 'Small group', in B. Foss (ed.), *New Horizons in Psychology*. Harmondsworth: Penguin Books.

Akerlind, G. (2005) 'Academic growth and development – how do university academics experience it?', *Higher Education*, 50: 1–32.

Akerlind, G. (2007) 'Constraints on academics' potential for developing as a teacher', *Studies in Higher Education*, 32: 21–37.

Akerlind, G. (2008) 'A phenomenographic approach to developing academics' understanding of the nature of teaching and learning', *Teaching in Higher Education* (in press).

Alderman, G. and Brown, R. (2005) 'Can quality assurance survive the market? Accreditation and audit at the crossroads', *Higher Education Quarterly*, 59: 313–28.

Aleamoni, L.M. (1999) 'Student rating myths versus research facts from 1924 to 1998', *Journal of Personnel Evaluation in Education*, 13: 153–66.

Altbach, P.G., Berdahl, R.O. and Gumport, P.J. (eds) (2005) *American Higher Education in the Twenty-first Century: Social, Political, and Economic Challenges*. Baltimore, MD: Johns Hopkins University Press.

Altbach, P.G., Gumport, P.J. and Berdahl, R.O. (eds) (2001) *In Defense of American Higher Education*. Baltimore, MD: Johns Hopkins University Press.

Anderson, C., Day, K. and McLaughlin, P. (2006) 'Mastering the dissertation: lecturers' representations of the purposes and processes of master's level dissertation supervision', *Studies in Higher Education*, 31: 149–68.

Anderson, L.W., Krathwohl, D.R., Airasian, P.W., Cruickshank, K.A., Mayer, R.E., Pintrich, P.R., Raths, J. and Wittrock, M.C. (2000) *A Taxonomy for Learning, Teaching, and Assessing: A Revision of Bloom's Taxonomy of Educational Objectives*. Boston, MA: Allyn & Bacon.

Anderson, N. and King, N. (1995) *Innovation and Change in Organization*. London: International Thomson Business Press.

Angelo, T. and Cross, K.P. (1993) *Classroom Assessment Techniques: A Handbook for College Teachers* (2nd edn). San Francisco, CA: Jossey-Bass.

Aravamudan, N., Calkins, S., Schuller, M. and Rubel, D. (2008) 'Integrating teaching and technology: facilitating student-centered teaching for graduate students at a research university', *Journal of Graduate and Professional Student Development*.

Argyris, C. and Schon, D. (1978) *Organizational Learning: A Theory of Action Perspective*. Reading, MA: Addison-Wesley.

Aronson, J., Lustina, M.J., Good, C., Keough, K., Steele, C.M. and Brown, J. (1999) 'When white men can't do math: necessary and sufficient factors in stereotype threat', *Journal of Experimental Social Psychology*, 35: 29–46.

Ashcroft, K. and Palacio, D. (1996) *Researching into Assessment and Evaluation*. London: Kogan Page.

Bain, K. (2004) *What the Best College Teachers Do*. Cambridge, MA: Harvard University Press.

Baker, P. and Copp, M. (1997) 'Gender matters most: the interaction of gendered expectations, feminist course content, and pregnancy in student course evaluations', *Teaching Sociology*, 25: 29–43.

Bakhtar, M. and Brown, G. (1988) 'Styles of lecturing: a study and its implications', *Research Papers in Education*, 3: 131–53.

Bakhtin, M. (1986) *Speech Genres and Other Late Essays*. Austin, TX: University of Texas Press.

Bales, R.F. (1970) *Personality and Interpersonal Behaviour*. New York: Holt, Rinehart & Winston.

Barnett, R. (1994) *The Limits of Competence: Knowledge, Higher Education and Society*. London: Open University Press.

Barnett, R. (1997a) 'Beyond competence', in F. Coffield and B. Williamson (eds), *Repositioning Higher Education*. London: SRHE/Open University Press.

Barnett, R. (1997b) *Higher Education: A Critical Business*. London: SRHE/Open University Press.

Barnett, R. (2000) *Realising the University*. Buckingham: SRHE/Open University Press.

Barnett, R. (2003) *Beyond All Reason: Living with Ideology in the University*. London: SRHE/Open University Press.

Barnett, R. and Hallam, S. (1999) 'Teaching for supercomplexity: a pedagogy for higher education', in P. Mortimore (ed.), *Understanding Pedagogy and its Impact on Learning*. London: Paul Chapman.

Barrett, M.S., Bornsen, S.E., Erickson, S.L., Markey, V. and Spiering, K. (2005) 'The personal response system as a teaching aid', *Communication Teacher*, 19: 89–92.

Bass, R.J. (2000) 'Technology, evaluation, and the visibility of teaching and learning', *New Directions for Teaching and Learning*, 83: 35–50.

Baxter Magolda, M. (1992) *Knowing and Reasoning in College: Gender-related Patterns in Students' Intellectual Development*. San Francisco, CA: Jossey-Bass.

Baxter Magolda, M. (2000) 'Teaching to promote holistic learning and development', *New Directions for Teaching and Learning*, 82: 88–98.

Becher, T., Henkel, M. and Kogan, M. (1994) *Graduate Education in Britain*. London: Jessica Kingsley.

Becher, T. and Trowler, P. (2001) *Academic Tribes and Territories: Intellectual Enquiry and the Culture of Disciplines* (2nd edn). Philadelphia, PA: Open University Press.

Becker, H. (1986) *Writing for Social Scientists*. London: University of Chicago Press.

Belenky, M.F., Clinchy, B.M., Goldberger, N.R. and Tarule, J.M. (1986/1997) *Women's Ways of Knowing: The Development of Self, Voice, and Mind*. New York: Basic Books.

Bennett, J.B. (1998) *Collegial Professionalism: The Academy, Individualism, and the Common Good*. Phoenix, AZ: Oryx Press.

Bennett, J.B. (2003) *Academic Life: Hospitality, Ethics, and Spirituality*. Bolton, MA: Anker.

Bhattarai, M.D. (2007) 'ABCDEFG IS – the principle of constructive feedback', *Medical Education*, 46: 151–6.

Biggs, J.B. (2003) *Teaching for Quality Learning at University*. London: Open University Press.

Biggs, J.B. and Collis, K. (1982) *Evaluating the Quality of Learning: The SOLO Taxonomy*. New York: Academic Press.

Biggs, J., Tang, C. and Tang, C.S.-K. (2007) *Teaching for Quality Learning at University*. London: Open University Press.

Bligh, D. (2000a) *What's the Point in Discussion?* Exeter: Intellect Press.

Bligh, D. (2000b) *What's the Use of Lectures?* Exeter: Intellect Press.

Bloom, B.S. (1956) *Taxonomy of Educational Objectives* (2 vols). New York: Longmans Green.

Bode, M., Drane, D., Ben-David Kolikant, Y. and Schuller, M. (2009) 'A clicker approach to teaching calculus', *Notices of the American Mathematical Society*, 56(2): 253–6.

Bogaard, A., Carey, S.C., Dodd, G., Repath, I.D. and Whitaker, R. (2005) 'Doing politics: small group teaching: perceptions and problems', *Politics*, 25: 116–25.

Bok, D.C. (2003) *Universities in the Marketplace: The Commercialization of Higher Education*. Princeton, NJ: Princeton University Press.

Bongey, C.B. (2005) 'Using a course management system (CMS) to meet the challenges of a large lecture class', *Campus-wide Information Systems*, 22: 252–62.

Booth, S. and Annenberg, E. (2005) 'Academic development for knowledge capabilities, learning, reflecting and developing', *Higher Education Research and Development*, 24: 373–86.

Bosshardt, W. and Watts, M. (2001) 'Comparing student and instructor evaluations of teaching', *Journal of Economic Education*, 32: 3–17.

Boud, D. (1989) 'Some competing traditions in experiential learning', in S. Weil and I. McGill (eds), *Making Sense of Experiential Learning: Diversity in Theory and Practice*. Buckingham: SRHE/Open University Press.

Boud, D. (1995) *Enhancing Learning through Self-assessment*. London: Kogan Page.

Boud, D., Cohen, R. and Sampson, J. (2001) *Peer Learning in Higher Education: Learning from and with Each Other*. Sterling, VA: Stylus.

Boud, D. and Feletti, G. (eds) (1997/2001) *The Challenge of Problem-based Learning* (2nd edn). London: Kogan Page.

Boud, D. and Walker, D. (1998) 'Promoting reflection in professional courses: the challenge of context', *Studies in Higher Education*, 23: 191–206.

Boyer, E.L. (1990) *Scholarship Reconsidered: Priorities of the Professoriate.* San Francisco, CA: Carnegie Foundation for the Advancement of Teaching/Jossey-Bass.

Boyer, E.L. (1998) *Reinventing Undergraduate Education: A Blueprint for America's Research Universities: The Boyer Commission on Educating Undergraduates.* Washington, DC: Carnegie Foundation for the Advancement of Teaching.

Bransford, J., Brown, A.L. and Cocking, R.R. (2000) *How People Learn: Brain, Mind, Experience, and School* (expanded edn). Washington, DC: National Academy Press.

Brew, A. (1999) 'Research and teaching: changing relationship in a changing context', *Studies in Higher Education*, 24: 291–301.

Brew, A. (2003) 'Teaching and research: new relationships and their implications for inquiry-based teaching and learning in higher education', *Higher Education Research and Development*, 22: 3–18.

Brew, A. (2006) *Research and Teaching: Beyond the Divide.* Basingstoke: Palgrave Macmillan.

Brew, A. and Boud, D. (1995) 'Teaching and research: establishing the vital link with learning', *Higher Education*, 29: 261–73.

Brew, A. and Peseta, T. (2004) 'Changing postgraduate supervision practice: a programme to encourage learning through reflection and feedback', *Innovations in Education and Teaching International*, 41: 15–22.

Brockbank, A. and McGill, I. (1998) *Facilitating Reflective Learning in Higher Education.* Buckingham: SRHE/Open University Press.

Brookfield, S. (1986) *Understanding and Facilitating Adult Learning.* San Francisco, CA: Jossey-Bass.

Brookhart, S.M. (2004) 'Assessment theory for college classrooms', *New Directions for Teaching and Learning*, 100: 5–14.

Brown, G. and Atkins, M. (1988) *Effective Teaching in Higher Education.* London: Methuen.

Brown, G., Bull, J. and Pendlebury, M. (1997) *Assessing Student Learning in Higher Education.* London: Routledge.

Brown, J.S. and Duguid, P. (2000) *The Social Life of Information.* Boston, MA: Harvard Business School Press.

Brown, S. and Knight, P. (1994) *Assessing Learners in Higher Education.* London: Kogan Page.

Brown, S. and Race, P. (1995) *Assess Your Own Teaching Quality.* London: Kogan Page.

Bruner, J. (1966) *Towards a Theory of Instruction.* London: Oxford University Press.

Bruner, J. (1990) *Acts of Meaning.* Cambridge, MA: Harvard University Press.

Bruner, J. (1996) *The Culture of Education.* London: Harvard University Press.

Burgan, M. (2006) 'In defense of lecturing', *Change*, 30–4.

Calkins, S. and Kelley, M.R. (2005) 'Mentoring and the faculty–TA relationship: faculty perceptions and practices', *Mentoring and Tutoring*, 13: 259–80.

Calkins, S. and Kelley, M.R. (in press) 'Who writes the past? Student perceptions of Wikipedia knowledge and credibility in a world history classroom', *Journal on Excellence in College Teaching*.

Calkins, S. and Light, G. (2007) 'Conceptions of mentoring among senior faculty at a research intensive university.' Paper presented at the annual meeting of the American Educational Research Association (AERA), Chicago, April.

Calkins, S. and Light, G. (2008) 'Promoting student-centered teaching through a project-based faculty development program', *To Improve the Academy*, 26: 217–29.

Calkins, S. and Micari, M. (2008) 'Students grading teachers: fifty years of discourse on the value of teaching evaluations in higher education.' Paper presented to the Midwest History of Education Society annual meeting, Chicago, October.

Campbell, D. and Campbell, M. (1995) *The Student's Guide to Doing Research on the Internet*. Reading, MA: Addison-Wesley.

Carbonne, E. (1998) *Teaching Large Classes: Tools and Strategies*. London: Sage.

Carr, W. and Kemmis, S. (1983) *Becoming Critical: Knowing through Action Research*. Victoria: Deakin University Press.

Carr, W. and Kemmis, S. (1986) *Becoming Critical: Education, Knowledge and Action Research*. London: Falmer Press.

Carraccio, C. and Englander, R. (2000) 'The objective structured clinical examination: a step in the direction of competency-based evaluation', *Archives of Pediatrics and Adolescent Medicine*, 154: 736–41.

Carrington, G. (2004) 'Supervision as a reciprocal learning process', *Educational Psychology in Practice*, 20: 31–42.

Case, S.M. and Swanson, D.B. (2001) *Constructing Written Test Questions for the Basic and Clinical Sciences* (3rd edn). Philadelphia, PA: National Board of Medical Examiners.

Cassidy, S. (2007) 'Assessing "inexperienced" students' ability to self-assess: exploring links with learning style and academic personal control', *Assessment and Evaluation in Higher Education*, 32: 313–30.

CHEA (2001) *Accreditation and Student Learning Outcomes: A Proposed Point of Departure* (available online at http://www.chea.org/Research/index.asp#other).

CHEA (2008) *US Accreditation and the Future of Quality Assurance* (available online at http://www.chea.org/store/index.asp).

Chidambaram, L. and Bostrom, R.P. (1996) 'Group development (I): a review and synthesis of development models', *Group Decision and Negotiation*, 6: 159–87.

Chomsky, N. (1998) 'Chomsky warns of corporate secrecy threat', *The Times Higher Education Supplement*, 20 November: 60.

Chopra, A.J. (1999) *Managing the People Side of Innovation: Eight Rules for Engaging Minds and Hearts*. West Hartford, CT: Kumerian Press.

Clark, B.R. (1997) 'The modern integration of research activities with teaching and learning', *Journal of Higher Education*, 21: 31–42.

Coffey, M. and Gibbs, G. (2001) 'The strategic goals of the training of university teachers', in C. Rust (ed.), *Improving Student Learning Strategically*. Oxford: Oxford Centre for Staff and Learning Development.

Coffield, F. and Williamson, B. (eds) (1997) *Repositioning Higher Education*. London: SRHE/Open University Press.

Cohen, L., Manion, L. and Morrison, K. (2000) *Research Methods in Education*. London: Falmer Press.

Colbeck, C.L. (1998) 'Merging in a seamless blend: how faculty integrate teaching and research', *Journal of Higher Education*, 69: 647–71.

Colbeck, C.L. (2002) 'Assessing institutionalization of curricular and pedagogical reforms', *Research in Higher Education*, 43: 397–421.

Colbeck, C.L. and Michael, P.W. (2006) 'The public scholarship: reintegrating Boyer's four domains', *New Directions for Institutional Research*, 129: 7–19.

Colby, A., Ehrlich, T., Beaumont, E. and Stephens, J. (2003) *Educating Citizens: Preparing America's Undergraduates for Lives of Moral and Civic Responsibility*. San Francisco, CA: Carnegie Foundation for the Advancement of Teaching/ Jossey-Bass.

Committee on Science, Engineering and Public Policy (COSEPUP) (2007) *Rising above the Gathering Storm: Energizing and Employing America for a Brighter Economic Future*. Washington, DC: National Academies Press.

Conceição, S.C.O. (2007) 'Understanding the environment for online teaching', *New Directions for Adult and Continuing Education*, 113: 5–11.

Contractor, N.S., Wasserman, S. and Faust, K. (2006) 'Special topic forum on building effective networks – testing multitheoretical, multilevel hypotheses about organizational networks: an analytic framework and empirical example', *Academy of Management Review*, 31: 681–704.

Cooper, J.L., MacGregor, J., Smith, K.A. and Robinson, P. (2000) 'Implementing small-group instruction: insights from successful practitioners', *New Directions for Teaching and Learning*, 81: 63–76.

Cooper, J.L. and Robinson, P. (2000a) 'The argument for making large classes seem small', *New Directions for Teaching and Learning*, 81: 5–16.

Cooper, J.L. and Robinson, P. (2000b) 'Getting started: informal small-group strategies in large classes', *New Directions for Teaching and Learning*, 81: 17–24.

Cox, R. (1973) 'Traditional examinations in a changing society', *Universities Quarterly*, 27: 200–16.

Cox, R. (1975) 'Students and student assessment: a study of different perceptions and patterns of response to varied forms of assessment in the University of Essex.' Unpublished PhD thesis, University of Essex.

Cox, R. (1976) *Improving Teaching in Higher Education*. London: University Teaching Methods Unit (UTMU), Institute of Education.

Cox, R. (1985) 'Higher education: assessment of students', in T. Husen and T. Postlethwaite (eds), *International Encyclopedia of Education*. Oxford: Pergamon.

Cox, R. (1987) *Study of Students' Responses to the First Year of an Engineering Course*. London: Centre for Higher Education Studies (Institute of Education, University of London).

Cox, R. (1992) 'Learning theory and professional life', *Media and Technology for Human Development*, 4: 217–32.

Cox, R. (1996) 'Teaching, learning and assessment in higher education', *Anthropology in Action*, 3: 2.

Cox, R. (2007) 'The impact of student feedback and assessment', in D. Good et al. (eds), *University Collaboration for Innovation: Lessons from the Cambridge-MIT Institute. Global Perspectives on Higher Education* 4. Rotterdam: Sense Publishers.

Cox, R., Kontianien, S., Rea, N. and Robinson, S. (1981) *Learning Teaching: An Evaluation of a Course for Teachers in General Practice*. London: University Teaching Methods Unit (UTMU), Institute of Education.

Craig, R. and Amernic, J. (2006) 'PowerPoint presentation technology and the dynamics of teaching', *Innovative Higher Education*, 31: 147–60.

Cryer, P. (1996) *The Research Student's Guide to Success*. Buckingham: Open University Press.

Curzan, A. and Damour, L. (2006) *First Day to Final Grade: A Graduate Student's Guide to Teaching*. Ann Arbor, MI: University of Michigan Press.

Dahlgren, L.-O. (2005) 'Learning conceptions and outcomes', in F. Marton et al. (eds), *The Experience of Learning*. Edinburgh: Scottish Academic Press.

Dall'Alba, G. (2005) 'Improving teaching: enhancing ways of being university teachers', *Higher Education Research and Development*, 24: 361–72.

Davis, B.G. (2001) *Tools for Teaching*. San Francisco, CA: Jossey-Bass.

DeBard, R. (2004) 'Millennials coming to college', *New Directions in Student Services*, 106: 33–45.

De Bono, E. (1994) *Parallel Thinking*. London: Penguin Books.

Delamont, S., Atkinson, P. and Parry, O. (2000) *The Doctoral Experience: Success and Failure in Graduate School*. London: Falmer Press.

Dewey, J. (1938) *Experience and Education*. New York, NY: Collier Books.

deWinstanley, P.A., Robert, A. and Bjork, R.A. (2002) 'Successful lecturing: presenting information in ways that engage effective processing', *New Directions for Teaching and Learning*, 89: 19–31.

DfES (2003) *The Future of Higher Education*. London: Department for Education and Skills.

Diamond, N. (2002) 'Small group instructional diagnosis: tapping student perceptions of teaching', in K.H. Gillespie (ed.), *A Guide to Faculty Development*. Bolton, MA: Anker.

D'Inverno, R., Davis, H. and White, S. (2003) 'Using a personal response system for promoting student interaction', *Teaching Mathematics and its Implications*, 22: 163–9.

Dornan, T., Carroll, C. and Parboosingh, J. (2002) 'An electronic learning portfolio for reflective continuing professional development', *Medical Education*, 36: 767–9.

Drane, D., Smith, H.D., Light, G., Pinto, L. and Swarat, S. (2005) 'The Gateway Science Workshop Program: enhancing student performance and retention in the sciences through peer-facilitated discussion', *Journal of Science Education and Technology*, 14: 337–52.

Dressel, P. (1976) *Improving Degree Programmes*. London: Jossey-Bass.

Duke, C. (1997) 'Towards a lifelong curriculum', in F. Coffield and B. Williamson (eds), *Repositioning Higher Education*. London: SRHE/Open University Press.

Dunkin, M. and Biddle, B. (1974) *The Study of Teaching*. New York, NY: Holt, Rinehart & Winston.

Eaton, J. (2006) *An Overview of Higher Education*. Washington, DC: CHEA.

Ehrenberg, R.G. (2000) *Tuition Rising: Why College Costs so Much*. Cambridge, MA: Harvard University Press.

Ehrenberg, R.G. and Zhang, L. (2004) 'The changing nature of faculty employment.' Paper prepared for the TIAA-CREF Institute conference 'Retirement, retention and recruitment: the three R's of higher education in the 21st century', New York City, 1–2 April.

Eisner, E. (1994) *The Educational Imagination: On the Design and Evaluation of School Programs*. New York, NY: Macmillan.

Eliot, T.S. (1961) 'The hollow men', in T.S. Eliot, *Selected Poems*. London: Faber & Faber.

Ellis, R.A., Hughes, J., Weyers, M. and Riding, P. (2009) 'University teacher approaches to design and teaching and concepts of learning technologies', *Teaching and Teacher Education*, 25(1): 109–17.

Elton, L. (2008) 'Recognition and acceptance of the scholarship of teaching and learning', *International Journal for the Scholarship of Teaching and Learning*, 2: 1–5.

Entwistle, N. (1988) *Styles of Learning and Teaching*. London: David Fulton.

Entwistle, N. (1998) 'Conceptions of teaching for academic staff development: the role of research.' Conference paper on 'Development training for academic staff', Goldsmiths College, London, 26 March.

Entwistle, N. (2005) 'Contrasting perspectives on learning', in F. Marton et al. (eds), *The Experience of Learning*. Originally published Edinburgh: Scottish Academic Press, republished Edinburgh: Centre for Teaching, Learning, and Assessment.

Entwistle, N. and Entwistle, A. (1992) 'Experience of understanding in revising for degree examinations', *Learning and Instruction*, 2: 1–22.

Entwistle, N. and Tait, H. (1990) 'Approaches to learning, evaluations of teaching and preferences for contrasting academic environments', *Higher Education*, 19: 169–94.

Entwistle, N., Tait, H. and McCune, V. (2000) 'Patterns of response to an approach to studying inventory across contrasting groups and contexts', *European Journal of Psychology of Education*, 15: 33–48.

Entwistle, N., Thompson, S. and Tait, H. (1992) *Guidelines for Promoting Effective Learning in Higher Education*. Edinburgh: Centre for Research on Learning and Instruction, University of Edinburgh.

Erhmann, S. (1996) *Adult Learning in a New Technological Era*. Paris: OECD.

Fagen, A.P., Crouch, C.H. and Mazur, E. (2002) 'Peer instruction: results from a range of classrooms', *The Physics Teacher*, 40: 206–9.

Feather, S.R. (1999) 'The impact of group support systems on collaborative learning groups' stages of development', *Information Technology, Learning, and Performance Journal*, 17: 23–34.

Feldman, K.A. (1987) 'Research productivity and scholarly accomplishment of college teachers as related to their instructional effectiveness: a review and exploration', *Research in Higher Education*, 26: 227–98.

Fleming, N.D. (1995) 'I'm different; not dumb. Modes of presentation (VARK) in the tertiary classroom', in A. Zelmer (ed.), *Research and Development in Higher Education: Proceedings of the 1995 Annual Conference of the Higher Education and Research Development Society of Australasia (HERDSA)*, 18: 308–13.

Francis, H. (1997) 'The research process', in N. Graves, and V. Varma (eds), *Working for a Doctorate: A Guide for the Humanities and Social Sciences*. London: Routledge.

Freire, P. (2000) *The Pedagogy of the Oppressed* (30th anniversary edn). New York: Continuum International.

Gandolfo, A. (1998) 'Brave new world? The challenge of technology to time-honored pedagogies and traditional structures', *New Directions for Teaching and Learning*, 76: 23–38.

Gardiner, D. (1989) *The Anatomy of Supervision*. Milton Keynes: SRHE/Open University Press.

Gardner, H. (1993) *Frames of Mind: The Theory of Multiple Intelligences*. New York: Basic Books.

Gardner, H. (1999) *Intelligence Reframed: Multiple Intelligences for the 21st Century*. New York: Basic Books.

Geiger, R.L. (2005) 'Autonomy and accountability: who controls academe?', in P.G. Altbach et al. (eds), *American Higher Education in the Twenty-first Century: Social, Political, and Economic Challenges*. Baltimore, MD: Johns Hopkins University Press.

Gibbons, M., Limoges, C., Nowotny, H., Scott, P. and Trow, M. (1994) *The New Production of Knowledge: The Dynamics of Science and Research in Contemporary Societies*. London: Sage.

Gibbs, G. (1981) *Teaching Students to Learn*. Milton Keynes: Open University Press.

Gibbs, G. (1995) 'Changing conceptions of teaching and learning through action research', in A. Brew (ed.), *New Directions in Staff Development*. Milton Keynes: SRHE/Open University Press.

Gibbs, G. and Coffey, G. (2004) 'The impact of training of university teachers on their teaching skills, their approach to teaching and the approach to learning of their students', *Active Learning in Higher Education*, 5: 87–101.

Gibbs, G., Habeshaw, S. and Habeshaw, T. (1993a) *53 Interesting Ways to Assess your Students*. Bristol: Technical and Educational Services.

Gibbs, G., Habeshaw, S. and Habeshaw, T. (1993b) *53 Interesting Ways to Appraise your Teaching*. Bristol: Technical and Educational Services.

Gibbs, G. and Jenkins, A. (eds) (1992) *Teaching Large Classes in Higher Education*. London: Kogan Page.

Gilbert, A. and Gibbs, G. (1999) 'A proposal for an international collaborative research program to identify the impact of initial training on university teachers', *Research and Development in Higher Education*, 21: 131–43.

Good, D., Greewald, S. and Cox, R. (2007) *University Collaboration for Innovation: Lessons from the Cambridge-MIT Institute. Global Perspectives on Higher Education. Vol. 4*. Rotterdam: Sense Publishers.

Gough, H. and Woodworth, D. (1960) 'Stylistic variations among professional research scientists', *Journal of Psychology*, 49: 87–98.

Grant, B. (2003) 'Mapping the pleasures and risks of supervision', *Discourse: Studies in the Cultural Politics of Education*, 24: 175–90.

Graves, N. and Varma, V. (eds) (1997) *Working for a Doctorate: A Guide for the Humanities and Social Sciences*. London: Routledge.

Gray, D.E. (2004) *Doing Research in the Real World: Qualitative and Quantitative Approaches*. London: Sage.

Gray, K., Chang, R. and Radloff, A. (2007) 'Enhancing the scholarship of teaching and learning: evaluation of a scheme to improve teaching and learning through action research', *International Journal of Teaching and Learning in Higher Education*, 19: 21–32.

Greenwood, D. (2007) 'Teaching/learning action research requires fundamental reforms in public higher education', *Action Research*, 5: 249–64.

Griffin, P., Coates, H., McInnis, C. and James, R. (2003) 'The development of an extended course experience questionnaire', *Quality in Higher Education*, 9: 259–66.

Gu, Q. and Brooks, J. (2008) 'Beyond the accusation of plagiarism', *System*, 36: 337–52.

Habeshaw, S., Habeshaw, T. and Gibbs, G. (1984) *53 Interesting Things to Do in your Seminars and Tutorials*. Bristol: Technical and Educational Services.

Hafer, G.H., Ballard, K., Montgomery, D., Thanavaro, J. and Wessely, A. (2002) 'Teaching squares: improving teaching through observation and reflection.' Paper presented at the 22nd annual Lilly Conference on College Teaching, Oxford, OH.

Hale, E. (1964) *Report of the Committee on Teaching Methods*. London: HMSO.

Hall, R. (2002) 'Aligning learning, teaching and assessment using the web: an evaluation of pedagogic approaches', *British Journal of Educational Technology*, 33: 149–58.

Hannan, A. (2005) 'Innovating in higher education: contexts for change in learning technology', *British Journal of Educational Technology*, 36: 975–85.

Hanson, A. (1993) 'A separate theory of adult learning', in P. Edwards et al. (eds), *Boundaries of Adult Learning*. London: Routledge/Open University Press.

Harry, K. (ed.) (1999) *Higher Education through Open and Distance Learning*. London: Routledge.

Harry, K. and Perraton, H. (1999) 'Open and distance learning for the new society', in K. Harry (ed.), *Higher Education through Open and Distance Learning*. London: Routledge.

Harvey, D. (1998) 'University, Inc.', *The Atlantic Monthly*, 282: 112–16.

Hattie, J. and Timperley, H. (2007) 'The power of feedback', *Review of Educational Research*, 77: 81–112.

HEA (2007) *The Higher Education Academy's Approach to the Accreditation of Institutional Professional Development Activity* (available online at http://www.heacademy. ac.uk/ourwork/institutions/accreditation).

Hensley, R.B. (2003) 'Technology as environment: from collections to connections', *New Directions for Teaching and Learning*, 94: 23–30.

HEQC (1996) *Graduate Standards Programme: Draft Report*. London: Higher Education Quality Council.

Heron, J. (2001) *Helping the Client: A Creative Practical Guide* (5th edn). London: Sage.

Higgins, J.S., Maitland, G., Perkins, J., Richardson, S. and Warren Piper, D. (1989) 'Identifying and solving problems in engineering design,' *Studies in Higher Education*, 1: 169–81.

HLC (2007) *Institutional Accreditation: An Overview*. Chicago, IL: Higher Learning Commission (available online at http://www.ncahlc.org/).

Ho, A., Watkins, D. and Kelly, M. (2001) 'The conceptual change approach to improving teaching and learning: an evaluation of a Hong Kong staff development programme', *Higher Education*, 42: 143–69.

Hodgson, V. (2005) 'Lectures and the experience of relevance', in F. Marton et al. (eds), *The Experience of Learning: Implications for Teaching and Studying in Higher Education*. Edinburgh: Scottish Academic Press.

Holquist, M. (1990) *Dialogism: Bakhtin and his World*. London and New York, NY: Routledge.

Holub, T. (2002) *College Rankings. ERIC Clearinghouse on Higher Education*. Washington, DC: ERIC (identifier: ED468728).

Hounsell, D. (2005) 'Contrasting conceptions of essay-writing', in F. Marton et al. (eds), *The Experience of Learning: Implications for Teaching and Studying in Higher Education* (3rd (Internet) edn). Edinburgh: University of Edinburgh, Centre for Teaching, Learning and Assessment.

Hounsell, D. and Hounsell, J. (2007) 'Teaching-learning environments in contemporary mass higher education', in N.J. Entwistle et al. (eds), *Student Learning and University Teaching. British Journal of Educational Psychology Monograph Series II*. Leicester: BPS.

Hounsell, D. et al. (2007) *Learning and Teaching at University: The Influences of Subjects and Settings. Teaching and Research Briefings 31*. London: Economic and

Social Research Council, Teaching and Learning Research Programme (available online at http://www.tlrp.org).

Howe, N. and Strauss, W. (2003) *Millennials Rising: The Next Great Generation.* New York: Vintage.

Hu, S. (2005) 'Grading problems in higher education: beyond grade inflation', *ASHE Higher Education Report*, 30: 1-7.

Hubball, H.T. and Burt, H. (2006) 'The scholarship of teaching and learning: theory-practice integration in a faculty certificate program', *Innovative Higher Education*, 30: 327–44.

Huber, M.T. and Morreale, S. (2002) *Disciplinary Styles in the Scholarship of Teaching and Learning: Exploring Common Ground.* Washington, DC: American Association for Higher Education and the Carnegie Foundation for the Advancement of Teaching.

Hutchings, P. and Shulman, L. (1999) 'The scholarship of teaching: new elaborations, new developments', *Change*, 31: 10-15.

ILT (1999a) *ILT Consultation: The National Framework for Higher Education Teaching.* York: Institute for Learning and Teaching.

ILT (1999b) *The National Framework for Higher Education Teaching.* York: Institute for Learning and Teaching.

Ingrams, R. (1997) 'If Richard Branson wants to be a future president of this country, he really must try to get his trains to run on time', *Observer Review*, 9 November.

Jaques, D. (2000) *Learning in Groups.* London: Kogan Page.

Jaques, D. and Salmon, G. (2007) *Learning in Groups: A Handbook for Face-to-face and Online Environments.* London: Taylor & Francis.

Jarvis, P. (1987) *Adult Learning in the Social Context.* London: Croom Helm.

Jarvis, P. (1992) *Paradoxes of Learning: On Becoming an Individual in Society.* London: Jossey-Bass.

Jarvis, P., Holford, J. and Griffin, C. (1998) *The Theory and Practice of Learning.* London: Kogan Page.

Jenkins, A., Breen, R., Lindsay, L. and Brew, A. (2003) *Reshaping Teaching in Higher Education: Linking Teaching with Research.* London: Kogan Page.

Johnson, M.C. and Guth, P.L. (2002) 'Using GPS to teach more than accurate positions', *Journal of Geoscience Education*, 50: 241-6.

Johnson, M.H. and Cooper, S.L. (1994) 'Developing a system for assessing written art criticism', *Art Education*, 47: 21-6.

Johnson, R. (2000) 'The authority of the Student Evaluation Questionnaire', *Teaching in Higher Education*, 5: 419-34.

Johnston, S. (1997) 'Examining the examiners: an analysis of examiners' reports on doctoral theses', *Studies in Higher Education*, 22: 333-47.

Jones, C., Mackintosh, M. and McPherson, A. (1973) *Questions of Uncertainty: Non-cognitive Predictors of Achievement.* Edinburgh: Centre for Educational Sociology, University of Edinburgh.

Jones, M.G. and Harmon, S.W. (2002) 'What professors need to know about technology to assess on-line student learning', *New Directions for Teaching and Learning*, 91: 19–30.

Karabenick, S.A. and Sharma, R. (1994) 'Seeking academic assistance as a strategic learning resource', in P.R. Pintrich et al. (eds), *Student Motivation, Cognition, and Learning: Essays in Honor of Wilbert J. McKeachie*. Hillsdale, NJ: Lawrence Erlbaum Associates.

Kember, D. (1997) 'A reconceptualisation of the research into university academics' conceptions of teaching', *Learning and Instruction*, 7: 255–75.

Kember, D. (2000) *Action Learning, Action Research: Improving the Quality of Teaching and Learning*. London: Kogan Page.

Kember, D. (2007a) *Action Learning and Action Research: Improving the Quality of Teaching and Learning*. London: Routledge.

Kember, D. (2007b) *Reconsidering Open and Distance Learning in the Developing World: Meeting Students' Learning Needs*. London: Routledge.

Kemmis, S. and McTaggart, R. (1988) *The Action Research Planner*. Victoria: Deakin University Press.

Kennedy, D. (1997) *Academic Duty*. Cambridge, MA: Harvard University Press.

Khan, B.H. (2006) 'Flexible learning in an open and distributed environment', in Badrul H. Khan and Badrul Huda Khan (eds), *Flexible Learning in an Information Society*. Arlington, VA: Information Resources Press.

Kirp, D.L. (2003) *Shakespeare, Einstein, and the Bottom Line: The Marketing of Higher Education*. Cambridge, MA and London: Harvard University Press.

Kivinen, O. and Ristelä, P. (2003) 'From constructivism to a pragmatist conception of learning', *Oxford Review of Education*, 29: 363–75.

Knowles, M. (1978) *The Adult Learner: A Neglected Species*. Houston, TX: Gulf.

Knowles, M. (1984) *Andragogy in Action*. London: Jossey-Bass.

Knowles, M.S., Holton, E.F. and Swanson, R.A. (2005) *The Adult Learner: The Definitive Classic in Adult Education and Human Resource Development by PhD* (6th edn). San Francisco, CA: Elsevier.

Ko, S. and Rossen, S. (2004) *Teaching Online: A Practical Guide* (2nd edn). Boston, MA: Houghton Mifflin.

Kolb, D. (1984) *Experiential Learning*. Englewood Cliffs, NJ: Prentice Hall.

Kolb, D., Osland, J. and Rubin, I. (1994) *Organizational Behavior: An Experiential Approach*. New York, NY: Prentice Hall.

Kreber, C. (2002) 'Controversy and consensus on the scholarship of teaching', *Studies in Higher Education*, 27: 151–7.

Kuh, G. (1994) *Student Learning Outside the Classroom: Transcending Artificial Boundaries. ASHE-ERIC Higher Education Report 8*. Washington, DC: ERIC.

Kuhn, T. (1970) *The Structure of Scientific Revolutions*. London: University of Chicago Press.

Kuncel, N.R., Hezlett, S.A. and Ones, D.S. (2001) 'A comprehensive meta-analysis of the predictive validity of the graduate record examinations: implications for graduate student selection and performance', *Psychological Bulletin*, 127: 162–81.

Lasry, N. (2008) 'Clickers or flashcards: is there really a difference?', *The Physics Teacher*, 46: 242–4.

Laurillard, D. (1993) *Rethinking University Teaching*. London: Routledge.

Lave, J. and Wenger, E. (2000a) 'Legitimate peripheral participation in communities of practice', in R. Cross and S. Israilit (eds), *Strategic Learning in a Knowledge Economy*. London: Butterworth-Heinemann.

Lave, J. and Wenger, E. (2000b) *Situated Practice: Legitimate Peripheral Participation*. Cambridge: Cambridge University Press.

Lee, V.S. (2004) *Teaching and Learning through Inquiry: A Guidebook for Institutions and Instructors*. Sterling, VA: Stylus.

Lejk, M. and Wyvill, M. (2002) 'Peer assessment of contributions to a group project: student attitudes to holistic and category-based approaches', *Assessment and Evaluation in Higher Education*, 27: 569–77.

Levy, B.D., Katz, J.T., Wolf, M., Sillman, J., Handin, R. and Dzau, V. (2004) 'An initiative in mentoring to promote residents' and faculty members' careers', *Academic Medicine*, 79: 845–50.

Lewin, K. (1951) *Field Theory in Social Sciences*. New York: Harper & Row.

Lewis, H.R. (2006) *Excellence Without a Soul*. New York: Public Affairs.

Lewis, K.G. (2001) 'Making sense of student written comments', *New Directions for Teaching and Learning*, 87: 25–32.

Lewis, K.G. (2002) 'The process of individual consultation', in K.H. Gillespie (ed.), *A Guide to Faculty Development*. Bolton, MA: Anker.

Lieberg, C. (2008) *Teaching your First College Class: A Practical Guide for New Faculty and Graduate Student Instructors*. Sterling, VA: Stylus.

Light, G. (1995) 'The literature of the unpublished: student conceptions of creative writing in higher education.' PhD thesis, Institute of Education, University of London.

Light, G. (1996) 'The limits of literature: creative writing in the university classroom', *Writers in Education*, 9: 13–18.

Light, G. (2000) 'Lifelong learning: challenging learning and teaching in higher education', in A. Hodgson (ed.), *Policies, Politics and the Future of Lifelong Learning*. London: Kogan Page.

Light, G. (2003) 'Realizing academic development: embedding teaching practice in the practice of research', in R. Macdonald and H. Eggins (eds), *The Scholarship of Academic Development*. London: Open University Press.

Light, G. (2008) 'The puzzle of teaching in higher education: implications for the structure of academic practice', in *Ideas on Teaching, Volume 6: Selected Papers from TLHE 2006 – Quality in Higher Education*. Singapore: Centre for the Development of Teaching and Learning, National University of Singapore.

Light, G. and Calkins, S. (2006) 'Faculty conceptions of academic practice.' Paper presented at the EARLI biennial workshop: 'Phenomenography and Variation Theory: The Ways Forward', University of Hong Kong.

Light, G. and Calkins, S. (2007) 'Academic learning: integrating faculty conceptions of research and teaching.' Paper presented at the American Educational Research Association (AERA) annual meeting, Chicago, April.

Light, G. and Calkins, S. (2008) 'The experience of faculty development: patterns of variation in conceptions of teaching', *International Journal for Academic Development*, 13: 27–40.

Light, G., Calkins, S., Luna, M. and Drane, D. (2008) 'Assessing the impact of faculty development programs on faculty approaches to teaching', *International Journal of Teaching and Learning in Higher Education*.

Light, R.J. (2001) *Making the Most of College: Students Speak their Minds*. Cambridge, MA: Harvard University Press.

Lippett, R. and White, R.K. (1961) 'An experimental study of leadership and group style', in E. Maccoby et al. (eds), *Readings in Social Psychology*. London: Methuen.

Liu, N.C. and Cheng, Y. (2005) 'The academic ranking of world universities', *Higher Education in Europe*, 30: 127–36.

Loomer, B. (1976) 'Two kinds of power', *Process Studies*, 6: 5–32.

Lubinescu, E.S., Ratcliff, J.L. and Gaffney, M.A. (2001) 'Special issue: how accreditation influences assessment', *New Directions for Higher Education*, 113: 5–21.

Luft, J. (1984) *Group Processes: An Introduction to Group Dynamics*. Palo Alto, CA: Mayfield.

Lyotard, J.-F. (1984) *The Postmodern Condition: A Report on Knowledge*. Minneapolis, MN: University of Minnesota Press.

MacGregor, J. (2000) 'Restructuring large classes to create communities of learners', *New Directions for Teaching and Learning*, 81: 47–61.

Malcolm, N. (1967) *Ludwig Wittgenstein: A Memoir*. London: Oxford University Press.

Marsh, H.W. and Hattie, J. (2002) 'The relation between research productivity and teaching effectiveness: complementary, antagonistic or independent constructs?', *Journal of Higher Education*, 73: 603–14.

Marsh, H.W. and Roche, L.A. (1997) 'Making students' evaluations of teaching effectiveness effective', *American Psychologist*, 52: 1187–97.

Martin, D.F. (2005) 'Plagiarism and technology: a tool for coping with plagiarism', *Journal of Education for Business*, 80: 149–52.

Martin, E. (1984) 'Power and authority in the classroom: sexist stereotypes in teaching evaluations', *Signs*, 9: 482–92.

Marton, F. (1988a) 'Describing and improving learning', in R. Schmeck (ed.), *Learning Strategies and Learning Styles*. New York and London: Plenum Press.

Marton, F. (1988b) 'Phenomenography: a research approach to investigating different understandings of reality', in R. Sherman and R. Webb (eds), *Qualitative Research in Education: Focus and Methods*. London: Falmer Press.

Marton, F., Beatty, E. and Dall'Alba, G. (1993) 'Conceptions of learning', *International Journal of Educational Research*, 19: 277–300.

Marton, F. and Booth, S. (1997) *Learning and Awareness*. Mahwah, NJ: Lawrence Erlbaum Associates.

Marton, F., Hounsell, D. and Entwistle, N. (eds) (2005) *The Experience of Learning*. Edinburgh: University of Edinburgh, Centre for Teaching, Learning and Assessment.

Marton, F. and Saljo, R. (2005) 'Approaches to learning', in F. Marton et al. (eds), *The Experience of Learning*. Edinburgh: University of Edinburgh, Centre for Teaching, Learning and Assessment.

Marton, F. and Tsui, A.B.M. (2004) *Classroom Discourse and the Space of Learning*. Mahwah, NJ: Lawrence Erlbaum Associates.

Martyn, M. (2007) 'Clickers in the classroom: an active learning approach', *Educause*, 2: 71–4.

Mason, R. (1994) *Using Communications Media in Open and Flexible Learning*. London: Kogan Page.

Mason, R. (1998) *Globalising Education: Trends and Applications*. London: Routledge.

Mazur, E. (1997) *Peer Instruction: A User's Manual. Series in Educational Innovation*. Upper Saddle River, NJ: Prentice Hall.

McCoubrie, P. (2004) 'Improving the fairness of multiple-choice questions: a literature review', *Medical Teacher*, 26: 709–12.

McGaghie, W.C., Issenberg, S.B., Petrusa, E.R. and Scalese, R.J. (2006) 'Effect of practice on standardised learning outcomes in simulation-based medical education', *Medical Education*, 40: 792–7.

McGee, P. and Leffel, A. (2005) 'Ethics and decision-making in a course management system: instructor and learner development education', *Communication and Information*, 5: 265–84.

McKeachie, W.J. (1990) 'Research on college teaching: the historical background', *Journal of Educational Psychology*, 82: 189–200.

McKeachie, W.J. (2006) *Teaching Tips: Strategies, Research, and Theory for College and University Teachers* (12th edn). Boston, MA: Houghton Mifflin.

McKeachie, W.J., Pintrich, P., Lin, Y.-G. and Smith, D. (1986) *Teaching and Learning in the College Classroom*. Ann Arbor, MI: University of Michigan, Office of Educational Research and Improvement.

McKenzie, J. (2003) 'Variation and change in university teachers' ways of experiencing teaching.' Doctoral thesis, University of Technology, Sydney.

Meredith, M. (2004) 'Why do universities compete in the ratings game? An empirical analysis of the effects of the US News and World Report College Rankings', *Research in Higher Education*, 45: 443–61.

Merriam, S.B. (ed.) (1993) *An Update on Adult Learning Theory: New Directions for Adult and Continuing Education*. San Francisco, CA: Jossey-Bass.

Meyer, J.H.F., Land, R. and Davies, P. (2007) 'Threshold concepts and troublesome knowledge. 4. Issues of variation and variability', in R. Land et al. (eds), *Threshold Concepts within the Disciplines*. Rotterdam: Sense.

Mezirow, J. (1983) 'A critical theory of adult learning and education', in M. Tight (ed.), *Adult Learning and Education*. London: Croom Helm.

Micari, M., Streitwieser, B. and Light, G. (2005) 'Undergraduates leading undergraduates: peer facilitation in a science workshop program', *Innovative Higher Education*, 30: 269–88.

Middlehurst, R. (1997) 'Enhancing quality', in F. Coffield and B. Williamson (eds), *Repositioning Higher Education*. London: SRHE/Open University Press.

Miller, J. and Chamberlain, M. (2000) 'Women are teachers, men are professors: a study of student perceptions', *Teaching Sociology*, 28: 283–98.

Miller, L. (2007) 'Issues in lecturing in a second language: lecturer's behaviour and students' perceptions', *Studies in Higher Education*, 32: 747–60.

Montero, J.M., San-Segunda, R., Macias-Guarasa, J., Cordoba, R. de and Ferreiros, J. (2006) 'Methodology for the analysis of instructors' grading discrepancies in a laboratory course. Part II. Contributions in: engineering education research, engineering design, simulation and games, pre-college education, logistics, engineering systems, sports engineering', *International Journal of Engineering Education*, 22: 1053–62.

Moran, L. and Myringer, B. (1999) 'Flexible learning and university change', in K. Harry (ed.), *Higher Education through Open and Distance Learning*. London: Routledge.

Morgan, G. (2003) *Faculty Use of Course Management Systems*. Boulder, CO: EDUCAUSE Center for Applied Research (ECAR).

Morling, B., McAuliffe, M., Cohen, L. and DiLorenzo, T.M. (2008) 'Efficacy of personal response systems ("clickers") in large, introductory psychology classes', *Teaching of Psychology*, 35: 45–50.

Moro, B. (1997) 'A pedagogy of the hypermedia', in A.-K. Korsvold and B. Ruschoff (eds), *New Technologies in Language Learning and Teaching*. Strasbourg: Council of Europe Publishing.

Morse, J.A. and Santiago, G. (2000) 'Accreditation (institutions): college faculty; college outcomes assessment; faculty college relationship; higher education; standards', *Academe*, 86: 30–4.

Mullen, C.A. and Forbes, S.A. (2000) 'Untenured faculty: issues of transition, adjustment and mentorship', *Mentoring and Tutoring*, 8: 31–45.

National Leadership Council for Liberal Education and America's Promise (2007) *College Learning for the New Global Century*. Washington, DC: Association of American Colleges and Universities.

NCIHE (1997) *Higher Education in the Learning Society (the Dearing Report)*. London: National Committee of Inquiry into Higher Education.

Newble, D. and Cannon, R. (1989) *A Handbook for Teachers in Universities and Colleges: A Guide to Improving Teaching Methods*. London: Kogan Page.

Noss, R. and Pachler, N. (1999) 'The challenge of new technologies: doing old things in a new way, or doing new things?', in P. Mortimore (ed.), *Understanding Pedagogy and its Impact on Learning*. London: Paul Chapman.

Oblinger, D. (2003) 'Boomers, gen-xers, and the millennials: understanding the new students', *Educause*, July/August: 37–47 (available online at http://net.educause.edu/ir/library/pdf/erm0342.pdf).

O'Donovan, B., Price, M. and Rust, C. (2004) 'Know what I mean? Enhancing student understanding of assessment standards and criteria', *Teaching in Higher Education*, 9: 325–35.

Okri, B. (1995) *Astonishing the Gods*. London: Phoenix.

Ong, W. (1982) *Orality and Literacy*. London and New York: Methuen.

Oppenheim, A.N. (2000) *Questionnaire Design, Interviewing and Attitude Measurement*. London: Continuum International.

Oppenheimer, M. (2008) 'Judgment day', NYTimes.com (available online at http://www.nytimes.com/2008/09/21/magazine/21wwln-evaluations-t.html?_r=1andoref=slo...10/8/2008).

Ory, J.C. (2000) 'Teaching evaluation: past, present, and future new directions for teaching and learning', *NEW*, 83: 13–18.

Parlett, M. and Hamilton, D. (1977) 'Evaluation as illumination', in M. Parlett and G. Deardon (eds), *Introduction to Illuminative Evaluation: Studies in Higher Education*. Cardiff-by-Sea, CA: Pacific Soundings Press.

Pask, G. (1976) 'Styles and strategies of learning', *British Journal of Educational Psychology*, 46: 128–48.

Pearson, M. and Brew, A. (2002) 'Research training and supervision development', *Studies in Higher Education*, 27: 135–50.

Penrose, R. (1989) *The Emperor's New Mind*. London: Vintage.

Perry, W. (1970) *Forms of Intellectual and Ethical Development in the College Years*. New York: Holt, Reinhart & Winston.

Perry, W.G. (1998) *Forms of Ethical and Intellectual Development in the College Years: A Scheme*. San Francisco, CA: Jossey-Bass.

Peterson, M. (1997) 'Language teaching and networking', *System*, 25: 29–37.

Phillips, D.C. (1995/2000) 'An opinionated account of the constructivist landscape', in D.C. Phillips (ed.), *Constructivism in Education: Opinions and Second Opinions on Controversial Issues*. Chicago, IL: University of Chicago Press.

Phillips, D.C. (2007) 'The good, the bad, and the ugly: the many faces of constructivism', reprinted in R.R. Curren (ed.), *Philosophy of Education: An Anthology*. Malden, MA: Blackwell.

Phillips, E. and Pugh, D. (2005) *How to Get a PhD: A Handbook for Students and their Supervisors*. Buckingham: Open University Press.

Piaget, J. (1950) *The Psychology of Intelligence*. London: Routledge & Kogan Paul.

Pieron, H. (1963) *Examens et Docimologie*. Paris: PUF.

Pincas, A. (1999) 'Problems and principles in the use of computer networks for course delivery.' Certificate in Online Education and Training, Institute of Education, University of London.

Press, E. and Washburn, J. (2000) 'The kept university', *The Atlantic Monthly*, 285: 39–54.

Pring, R.A. (1995) *Closing the Gap: Liberal Education and Vocational Preparation*. London: Hodder & Stoughton.

Prosser, M. and Trigwell, K. (1999) *Understanding Learning and Teaching: The Experience in Higher Education*. London: SRHE/Open University Press.

Purdy, J.P. (2005) 'Calling off the hounds: technology and the visibility of plagiarism', *Pedagogy: Critical Approaches to Teaching Literature, Language, Composition, and Culture*, 5: 275–95.

QAA (1999) *Code of Practice for the Assurance of Academic Quality and Standards in Higher Education, Postgraduate Research Programmes*. Cheltenham: Quality Assurance Agency (http://www.qaa.ac.uk/).

Ramsden, P. (1992/2003) *Learning to Teach in Higher Education*. London: Routledge.

Ramsden, P. (2005) 'The context of learning in academic departments', in F. Marton et al. (eds), *The Experience of Learning*. Edinburgh: University of Edinburgh, Centre for Teaching, Learning and Assessment.

Ramsden, P. and Moses, I. (1992) 'Associations between research and teaching in Australian higher education', *Higher Education*, 23: 273–95.

Raubenheimer, C.D. and Myka, J.L. (2005) 'Using action research to improve teaching and student learning in college', *Journal of College Science Teaching*, 34: 12–16.

Readings, B. (1996) *The University in Ruins*. Cambridge, MA: Harvard University Press.

Reason, P. and Bradbury, H. (2001) *Handbook of Action Research: Participative Inquiry and Practice*. London: Sage.

Research Assessment Exercise (RAE) (n.d.) Available online at http://www.rae.ac.uk/.

Richardson, J.T.E. (2005) 'Students' perceptions of academic quality and approaches to studying in distance education', *British Educational Research Journal*, 31: 7–27.

Roberts, F.D., Kelley, C.L. and Medlin, B.D. (2007) 'Factors influencing accounting faculty members' decision to adopt technology in the classroom', *College Student Journal*, 41: 423–35.

Roberts, M. (2008) 'Adventures in podcasting', *PSOnline* (www.apsanet.org), 585–93.

Robertson, D. (1997) 'Social justice in a learning market', in F. Coffield and B. Williamson (eds), *Repositioning Higher Education*. London: SRHE/Open University Press.

Rocco, S. (2007) 'Online assessment and evaluation', *New Directions for Adult and Continuing Education*, 113: 75–86.

Rogers, C. (1969) *Freedom to Learn*. Columbus, OH: Merrill.

Rommetveit, R. and Blakar, R.M. (1979) *Studies of Language, Thought and Communication*. London: Academic Press.

Rorty, R. (1989) *Contingency, Irony and Solidarity*. Cambridge: Cambridge University Press.

Rosenberg, J.L., Lorenzo, M. and Mazur, E. (2006) 'Peer instruction: making science engaging', in J.J. Mintzes and W.H. Leonard (eds), *Handbook of College Science Teaching*. Arlington, VA: NSTA Press.

Rowley, J. and Slack, F. (2004) 'What is the future for undergraduate dissertations?', *Education and Training*, 46: 176–81.

Rowntree, D. (1987) *Assessing Students: How Shall We Know Them?* London: Harper & Row.

Rowntree, D. (1994) *Preparing Materials for Open, Distance and Flexible Learning*. London: Harper & Row.

Rudd, E. (1985) *A New Look at Postgraduate Failure*. Guildford: SRHE/NFER Nelson.

Rudd, E. (1986) 'The drop-outs and the dilatory on the road to the doctorate', *Higher Education in Europe*, 11: 31–6.

Russell, J., Greenhalgh, T., Boynton, P. and Rigby, M. (2004) 'Soft networks for bridging the gap between research and practice: illuminative evaluation of CHAIN', *British Medical Journal*, 328: 1174.

Ryan, A.M. and Pintrich, P.R. (1997) 'Should I ask for help? The role of motivation and attitudes in adolescents' help seeking in math class', *Journal of Educational Psychology*, 89: 329–41.

Ryan, A.M., Pintrich, P.R. and Midgley, C. (2001) 'Avoiding seeking help in the classroom: who and why?', *Educational Psychology Review*, 13: 93–114.

Ryan, R.M. and Deci, E.L. (2000) 'Self-determination theory and the facilitation of intrinsic motivation, social development, and well-being', *American Psychologist*, 55: 68–78.

Sadlo, G. and Richardson, J.T. (2003) 'Approaches to studying and perceptions of the academic environment in students following problem-based and subject-based curricula', *Higher Education Research and Development*, 22: 253–74.

Salmon, P. (1992) *Achieving a PhD*. Stoke-on-Trent: Trentham.

Samulelowicz, K. and Bain, J. (2001) 'Revising academics' beliefs about teaching and learning', *Higher Education*, 41: 299–325.

Saussure, F. de (1966) *Course in General Linguistics*. New York, NY: McGraw-Hill.

Scanlon, P.M. (2003) 'Student online plagiarism: how do we respond?', *College Teaching*, 51: 161–5.

Schon, D. (1983) *The Reflective Practitioner*. New York: Basic Books.

Schon, D. (1987) *Educating the Reflective Practitioner*. London: Jossey-Bass.

Shapiro, H.T. (2005) *A Larger Sense of Purpose: Higher Education and Society*. Princeton, NJ and Oxford: Princeton University Press.

Shevlin, M., Banyard, P., Davies, M. and Griffiths, M. (2000) 'The validity of student evaluation of teaching in higher education: love me, love my lectures?', *Assessment and Evaluation in Higher Education*, 25: 397–405.

Shulman, L. (1998) 'Course anatomy: the dissection and analysis of knowledge through teaching', in P. Hutchings (ed.), *The Course Portfolio: How Faculty can Examine their Teaching to Advance Practice and Student Learning*. Washington, DC: American Association for Higher Education.

Silvestone, J.M. (2004) 'Performance-based assessment: improving the value of laboratory and skills examinations', *New Directions for Teaching and Learning*, 100: 65–71.

Sloboda, J. and Newstead, S. (eds) (1995) *Guidelines for the Assessment of the PhD in Psychology and Related Disciplines*. London: BPS/UCOSDA.

Smith, K.A. (2000) 'Going deeper: formal small-group learning in large classes', *New Directions for Teaching and Learning*, 81: 25–46.

Smith, K.A. and MacGregor, J. (2000) 'Making small-group learning and learning communities a widespread reality', *New Directions for Teaching and Learning*, 81: 77–88.

Snooks, M.K. (2004) 'Using practice tests on a regular basis to improve student learning', *New Directions for Teaching and Learning*, 100: 109–13.

Sorcinelli, M.D. (2006) *Creating the Future of Faculty Development: Learning from the Past, Understanding the Present*. Bolton, MA: Anker.

Sowden, C. (2005) 'Plagiarism and the culture of multilingual students in higher education abroad', *ELT Journal*, 59: 226–33.

Sprague, J. and Massoni, K. (2005) 'Student evaluations and gendered expectations: what we can't count can hurt us', *Sex Roles*, 53: 11–12, 779–93.

Spring, J. (2008) 'Research on globalization and education', *Review of Educational Research*, 78: 330–63.

Stanley, M., Brooker, R. and Gilbert, R. (2001) 'Examiner perceptions of using criteria in music performance assessment', *Research Studies in Music Education*, 18: 46–56.

Steele, C.M. (1997) 'A threat in the air: how stereotypes shape intellectual identity and performance', *American Psychologist*, 52: 613–29.

Stenhouse, L. (1975) *An Introduction to Curriculum Research and Development*. Oxford: Heinemann.

Stephens, B.R. (2005) 'Laptops in psychology: conducting flexible in-class research and writing laboratories', *New Directions for Teaching and Learning*, 101: 15–26.

Stevens, D.D. and Sterling, A.J.L. (2004) *Introduction to Rubrics: An Assessment Tool to Save Grading Time, Convey Effective Feedback and Promote Student Learning*. Sterling, VA: Stylus.

Styles, I. and Radloff, A. (2001) 'The synergistic thesis: student and supervisor perspectives', *Journal of Further and Higher Education*, 25: 97–106.

Surry, D.W. and Land, S.M. (2000) 'Strategies for motivating higher education faculty to use technology', *Innovations in Education and Training International*, 37: 145–53.

Svinicki, M.D. (2004) 'Authentic assessment: testing in reality', *New Directions for Teaching and Learning*, 100: 23–9.

Swarat, S., Drane, D., Smith, H.D., Light, G. and Pinto, L. (2004) 'Opening the gateway: increasing minority student retention in introductory science courses', *Journal of College Science Teaching*, 34: 18–23.

Tang, C. (1998) 'Effects of collaborative learning on the quality of assessments', in B. Dart and G. Boulton-Lewis (eds), *Teaching and Learning in Higher Education*. Camberwell: Australian Council for Educational Research.

Taniguchi, M.I. (2003) 'Internet metaphors matter', *New Directions for Teaching and Learning*, 94: 13–21.

Taylor, J. and Swannell, P. (1997) 'From outback to Internet: crackling radio to virtual campus', in *Proceedings of InterAct: International Telecommunications Union*. Geneva: ITU (CD-ROM).

Teller, E., Teller, W. and Talley, W. (1991) *Conversations on the Dark Secrets of Physics*. London: Pitman.

Tessmer, M. (1993) *Planning and Conducting Formative Evaluations*. London: Kogan Page.

Thelin, J.R. (2004) *A History of American Higher Education*. Baltimore, MD: Johns Hopkins University Press.

Thomson, K. and Falchikov, N. (1998) '"Full on until the sun comes out": the effects of assessment on student approaches to studying', *Assessment and Evaluation in Higher Education*, 23: 379–91.

Tisani, N. (2008) 'Challenges in producing a portfolio for assessment: in search of underpinning educational theories', *Teaching in Higher Education*, 13: 549–57.

Todd, M.J., Smith, K. and Bannister, P. (2006) 'Supervising a social science undergraduate dissertation: staff experiences and perceptions', *Teaching in Higher Education*, 11: 161–73.

Toohey, S. (1999) *Designing Courses for Higher Education*. Buckingham: Open University Press/SRHE.

Trigwell, K. (2003) 'A relational approach model for academic development', in H. Eggins and R. Macdonald (eds), *The Scholarship of Academic Development*. Buckingham: Society for Research into Higher Education.

Trigwell, K. and Shale, S. (2004) 'Student learning and the scholarship of university teaching', *Studies in Higher Education*, 29: 523–36.

Trow, M. (2001) 'From mass education to universal access: the American advantage', in P.G. Altbach et al. (eds), *In Defense of American Higher Education*. Baltimore, MD: Johns Hopkins University Press.

Tuckman, B.W. (1965) 'Developmental sequence in small groups', *Psychological Bulletin*, 63: 384–99 (reprinted 2001 in *Group Facilitation: A Research and Applications Journal*, 3: 66–81).

US Department of Education (2006) *A Test of Leadership: Charting the Future of US Higher Education: A Report of the Commission Appointed by Secretary of Education*

Margaret Spellings (the Spellings Report). Washington, DC: US Department of Education.

Usher, A. and Savino, M. (2006) *A World of Difference: A Global Survey of University League Tables*. Toronto: Educational Policy Institute.

Usher, R., Bryant, I. and Johnson, R. (1997) *Adult Education and the Postmodern Challenge: Learning Beyond the Limits*. London: Routledge.

UTMU (1976) *Improving Teaching in Higher Education*. London: UTMU, Institute of Education.

Van de Ven, A. and Poole, M. (2005) 'Alternative approaches for studying organizational change', *Organization Studies*, 26: 1377–404.

Van Rossum, E.J. and Schenk, S.M. (1984) 'The relationship between learning conception, study strategy and learning outcome', *British Journal of Educational Psychology*, 54: 73–83.

Vygotsky, L.S. (1986) *Thought and Language*. Cambridge, MA: MIT Press.

Warren Piper, D. (1975) 'Organisational points to bear in mind when designing a course: some analytic models', in D. Bligh et al. (eds), *Teaching Students*. Exeter: Exeter University Teaching Services.

Warren Piper, D. (1976) 'Educational objectives', in *Improving Teaching in Higher Education*. London: UTMU, Institute of Education.

Watkins, C. and Mortimore, P. (1999) 'Pedagogy: what do we know?', in P. Mortimore (ed.), *Understanding Pedagogy and its Impact on Learning*. London: Paul Chapman.

Watkins, D., Dahlin, B. and Ekholm, M. (2005) 'Awareness of the backwash effect of assessment: a phenomenographic study of the views of Hong Kong and Swedish lecturers', *Instructional Science*, 33: 283–309.

Watts, M.M. (2003a) 'Technology as catalyst', *New Directions for Teaching and Learning*, 94: 3–12.

Watts, M.M. (2003b) 'Taking the distance out of education', *New Directions for Teaching and Learning*, 94: 97–103.

Webb, N.M. and Mastergeorge, A.M. (2003) 'Promoting effective helping behavior in peer-directed groups', *International Journal of Educational Research*, 39: 73–97.

Webster, D.S. (1985) 'Does research productivity enhance teaching?', *Educational Record*, 66: 60–3.

Weinstein, C.E. (2003) 'Teaching students how to learn', in *McKeachie's Teaching Tips: Strategies, Research, and Theory for College and University Teachers*. Boston, MA: Houghton Mifflin.

Wenger, E. (1998) *Communities of Practice*. New York, NY: Cambridge University Press.

Wenger, E., McDermott, R. and Snyder, W. (2002) *Cultivating Communities of Practice*. Cambridge, MA: Harvard Business School Press.

White, C.P. (2004) 'Student portfolios: an alternative way of encouraging and evaluating student learning', *New Directions for Teaching and Learning*, 100: 37–42.

Wininger, S.R. (2005) 'Using your tests to teach: formative summative assessment', *Teaching of Psychology*, 32: 164–6.

Winter, R. (1996) 'Some principles and procedures for the conduct of action research', in O. Zuber-Skerrit (ed.), *New Directions in Action Research*. London: Falmer Press.

Wittgenstein, L. (1968) *Philosophical Investigations*. Oxford: Blackwell.

Wolfer, T.A. and Johnson, M.M. (2003) 'Reevaluating student evaluation of teaching: the teaching evaluation form', *Journal of Social Work Education*, 39: 111–21.

Wolverton, M. (1998) 'Treading the tenure-track tightrope: finding balance between research excellence and quality teaching', *Innovative Higher Education*, 23: 61–79.

Woolhouse, M. (2002) 'Supervising dissertation projects: expectations of supervisors and students', *Innovations in Education and Teaching International*, 39: 137–44.

Yazedjian, A. and Kolkhorst, B.B. (2007) 'Implementing small group activities in large lecture classes', *College Teaching*, 55: 164–9.

Young, M. (1998) *The Curriculum of the Future: From the New Sociology of Education to a Critical Theory of Learning*. London: Falmer Press.

Zuber-Skerrit, O. (1992a) *Professional Development in Higher Education: A Theoretical Framework for Action Research*. London: Kogan Page.

Zuber-Skerrit, O. (1992b) *Action Research in Higher Education: Examples and Reflections*. London: Kogan Page.

Zuber-Skerrit, O. (1997) *New Directions in Action Research*. London: Falmer Press.

authors' index

subject index